Praise for *Cooperating with the Holy Spirit*

"For years, we'll be discovering the thousands upon thousands of ways God moved through this outpouring. Having this journal of how it unfolded at 'ground zero,' told by voices who were there serving the cause, is such a gift to the church. Their stories will help all of us connect and process our own experiences even as we continue to carry this fire out into the world."

—**Carolyn Moore**, bishop, Global Methodist Church, and author of *Supernatural: Experiencing the Power of God's Kingdom*

"As a student and employee, I've seen firsthand the work of the Holy Spirit at Asbury in Hughes Auditorium. This book is a great reminder of the humility of the Asbury team and community. Gen Z students are hungry for Jesus. I was so encouraged to see how the community of Wilmore embraced this movement of the Holy Spirit. Thank you, Asburians, for your example to all of us."

—**David A. Hoag**, president, Council for Christian Colleges & Universities

"What a beautiful book! Its words leap off the page, telling stories of the 2023 Outpouring at Asbury from the people who were there, helping to steward those divinely appointed weeks in Wilmore. The reader can't help but be riveted, inspired, and wrapped up in a divine hug. Reading it makes one thankful and hungry for God's presence in equal measure."

—**Tammie Grimm**, associate professor of Congregational Formation, Wesley Seminary

"Suzanne Nicholson has assembled an outstanding array of writers who provide both firsthand experience of the revival and scholarly interpretation of its significance. As the history of revival in the United States is written, this will be an invaluable resource for historical and theological reflection. We can learn a great deal from these essays on the Asbury Outpouring, including how to respond when the next such move of God takes place."

—**David F. Watson**, academic dean, United Theological Seminary

"The Holy Spirit often uses testimony as a generative force that, in some measure, recreates the world being described. This book of remembrance on the Asbury Outpouring is such a testimony. It beckons us to enter a sacred space where temporal time gives way to the joys of eternity. It invites us to taste and see the wonders and depths of holy love that flowed from the divine life into the lives of the thousands of people who made the pilgrimage to Hughes Auditorium in February 2023."

—**Cheryl Bridges Johns**, distinguished visiting professor and director of Pentecostal House of Study, United Theological Seminary

"Thank you for the backstage pass to witness the Holy Spirit's outpouring on the campus of Asbury University in February 2023. Learning how God used you during this time is a powerful demonstration that the Spirit works through his people as they humbly bow and follow his leading. Thank you for reminding us of the incredible joy and responsibility of being the hands and feet of Christ, especially to serve and prepare the next generation—I am convinced God has specially called them for such a time as this!"

—**Ross Allen**, president, Bethel University

COOPERATING WITH THE HOLY SPIRIT

COOPERATING WITH THE HOLY SPIRIT

THEOLOGICAL AND PRACTICAL REFLECTIONS ON THE ASBURY OUTPOURING

WRITTEN BY MEMBERS OF THE
ASBURY COMMUNITY

SUZANNE NICHOLSON
EDITOR

COOPERATING WITH THE HOLY SPIRIT
Theological and Practical Reflections on the Asbury Outpouring

ISBN 978-1-68426-232-8

Printed in the United States of America

Library of Congress Cataloging-in-Publication Data
Names: Nicholson, Suzanne, editor.
Title: Cooperating with the Holy Spirit : theological and practical reflections on the Asbury outpouring / written by members of the Asbury community ; Suzanne Nicholson, editor.
Description: Abilene, Texas : Abilene Christian University Press, [2025] | Includes bibliographical references.
Identifiers: LCCN 2024034679 (print) | LCCN 2024034680 (ebook) | ISBN 9781684262328 (paperback) | ISBN 9781684268146 (ebook)
Subjects: LCSH: Revivals—Kentucky—Wilmore—21st century. | Asbury University—History—21st century. | Wilmore (Ky.)—Church history—21st century.
Classification: LCC BV3775.W5 C66 2025 (print) | LCC BV3775.W5 (ebook) | DDC 269/.2409769483—dc23/eng/20240814
LC record available at https://lccn.loc.gov/2024034679
LC ebook record available at https://lccn.loc.gov/2024034680

Cover design by Bruce Gore | Gore Studio Inc.
Interior text design by Scribe Inc

For information contact:
Abilene Christian University Press
ACU Box 29138
Abilene, Texas 79699
1-877-816-4455
www.acupressbooks.com

25 26 27 28 29 30 31 / 7 6 5 4 3 2 1

"My mouth will tell of your righteous deeds,
  of your saving acts all day long—
  though I know not how to relate them all."

—Psalm 71:15

Contents

Acknowledgments 11

Introduction 13

PART ONE
THE ASBURY OUTPOURING

1 Beginnings: The Rattling of the Bones 23
Jeannie Banter

2 The Early Days of the Outpouring 35
Greg Haseloff

3 When the World Comes to Wilmore 49
Sarah Thomas Baldwin, Christine Endicott, and Madeline Black

4 The Multicultural, Multiethnic, and Multinational Aspects of the Asbury Outpouring 63
Juan A. Gonzalez

5 Divine Timing 75
Carol Anderson and Barbara Hamilton

6 Overflowing Grace at Asbury Theological Seminary 87
Jessica LaGrone

PART TWO
BIBLICAL, HISTORICAL, AND THEOLOGICAL FOUNDATIONS

7 God's Presence and Empowerment in Scripture and Beyond 99
Julianne Burnett, Joy Vaughan, and Sam Kim

8 The Asbury Outpouring and the History of Evangelical Revivals 117
Kevin L. Anderson

9 Hughes Auditorium and a Theology of Sacred Space 139
W. Brian Shelton

10 Seeking the Kingdom of God through Prayer:
A Theological Reflection on the Asbury Outpouring 153
Craig D. Saunders

11 Viewing the Asbury Outpouring through a Wesleyan Lens 167
Suzanne Nicholson

PART THREE
PRACTICAL CONSIDERATIONS

12 Uncertainty, Mission, and Holy Imagination:
Order and Orchestration in the Outpouring 183
Kevin Brown

13 "Then Let Us His Praise Sing On": Lessons in Humility
and Musical Worship from the Asbury Outpouring 193
Dan Pinkston

14 Surprise: Stewarding Unprecedented Media Coverage
during the Outpouring 207
Abby Laub

15 No Place to Park: Problem-Solving with City Officials 219
Harold L. Rainwater

16 Sharing the Outpouring through Witnessing Teams 231
Bridgette Campbell

17 The Asbury Outpouring: Implications for the Marketplace 245
Robin Lim

18 The Tension of Spiritual Outpourings *and* Ordinary Life 259
Maria Brown

About the Contributors 269

Acknowledgments

We would like to thank the administration of Asbury University for its gracious support of this project, including the award of an Outpouring minigrant to fund two writing retreats during the fall semester of 2023 for chapter authors to work on this book and a course release in the spring of 2024 for the editor to refine the chapter submissions.

We are grateful for the support of our colleagues, friends, families, and students who have encouraged us, read drafts of chapters, and recounted their memories of the events of the Outpouring. In addition, we would like to thank Jason Fikes and Abilene Christian University Press for believing in this project and supporting its publication.

Finally, we are ever so grateful to the students who responded to the Holy Spirit on February 8, 2023, by lingering in Hughes Auditorium after chapel had ended. Their faithfulness led the rest of us to experience a powerful movement of God, the stories of which we tell here.

To God be the glory!

Introduction

Suzanne Nicholson, editor

God has a habit of showing up in unexpected places. When Moses was going about his daily business, tending to his sheep, the angel of the Lord appeared to him in a flaming bush. When Jacob was concerned about his dysfunctional relationship and impending reunion with his brother Esau, an angel appeared and wrestled with him through the night. When Saul the Pharisee zealously headed to Damascus to arrest those with allegedly blasphemous beliefs, the resurrected Jesus suddenly appeared in his path.

When students at Asbury University, a small Christian liberal arts university in central Kentucky, gathered for a regularly scheduled chapel service on February 8, 2023, the Holy Spirit unexpectedly urged students to linger in Hughes Auditorium after the official service ended. Overwhelmed by the goodness of God, many of those in attendance repented of their sins, offered or rededicated their lives to Christ, interceded in prayer for the world, or simply sat and received a deep peace. The worship service that normally runs forty-five minutes continued for two and a half weeks in response to the gentle, sweet Spirit of the Lord. More than fifty thousand people from across the world flocked to the town of six thousand so they, too, could experience the powerful presence of God that flooded Hughes Auditorium and beyond.

News of this movement of God spread like wildfire on social media as those in Hughes posted video clips and testimonies of powerful worship experiences. By the time official services had ended, posts about the Outpouring had received more than 285 million hits across various social media platforms. The world was watching. Even today, long after the services have ended, visitors still come to Asbury University hoping to set foot inside Hughes Auditorium and experience the place where God powerfully visited his people. More than one of these visitors described their desire "to touch the hem of Jesus's garment"—likening the experience to the bleeding woman who sneaked through the crowd to touch Jesus and receive healing (Mark 5:25–34).

What does one do in the aftermath of an intense experience of the presence of God? In the Old Testament, the people of God set up monument stones as a testimony to what God had done and as a physical reminder of the power and presence of God. In Genesis 28:10–22, Jacob had a dream in the middle of the night in which Yahweh renewed his promise to Abraham. When Jacob awoke, he declared, "Surely the Lord was in this place, and I did not know it!" (v. 16). Jacob took the stone upon which he had rested his head and made it into a monument, setting it up as a pillar and pouring oil over it. Similarly, in Joshua 4:1–8, after the Israelites miraculously crossed through the Jordan River to enter the Promised Land, the Lord commanded Joshua to take twelve stones from the middle of the Jordan as a memorial. So too, Samuel erected a stone monument to God—an Ebenezer, or "stone of help"—after God delivered the Israelites from the hands of the Philistines (1 Sam. 7:7–12).

In a modern collegiate setting, memorial stones look a bit different. Academics give testimony through the books they write. This book, written by nearly two dozen faculty and staff who witnessed the events firsthand, serves as our remembrance of what God has done among us. It is intentionally collaborative—with many diverse voices, stories, and writing styles—because this reflects the Outpouring itself. As a community, we worked together to steward this movement of God, regardless of our status or positions. We met needs as they arose—whether mopping the floor of Hughes Auditorium, providing food, serving on the prayer team, or simply directing visitors to parking spaces and available restrooms. The community served together, and now it bears witness together.

In many ways we feel like John, who wrote at the end of his Gospel, "Jesus did many other things as well. If every one of them were written down, I suppose that even the whole world would not have room for the books that would be written" (21:25). We simply cannot tell all the stories. We have tried to cover important themes and paint with broad brushstrokes the events that happened during these two and a half weeks and beyond. Yet this book is more than a recounting of stories. The three sections address the experience of the Outpouring, the biblical and theological foundations of revivals, and practical wisdom for those who find themselves wondering how to navigate such events.

The first section begins by explaining the narrative arc of the Outpouring. In Chapter One, Jeannie Banter takes up Ezekiel's narrative of the valley of dry bones to describe the first "rattlings" of revival. Although we commonly refer to February 8 as the beginning of the Outpouring, she discusses the varied ways in which the Holy Spirit stirred prior to that chapel service. Asbury University has a history of spontaneous revivals, and those who have experienced these moves of God in previous decades have continued to pray for recurrences. Small groups and various Christian organizations with connections to the university experienced powerful spiritual awakenings in the days and months leading up to the revival. The Spirit was preparing us for what lay ahead.

Greg Haseloff describes in Chapter Two the early days of the Outpouring, when Hughes Auditorium was filled mostly with students and Wilmore residents. He discusses some of the pressing needs of Generation Z—the anxiety, depression, and suicidal ideation that led many students to throw themselves at the feet of Jesus, hungering for release and renewal.

As word spread beyond Wilmore, however, the shape of the Outpouring shifted to a position of welcoming outsiders. Sarah Baldwin, Christine Endicott, and Madeline Black detail in Chapter Three some of the decision-making logistics that leaders navigated. They discuss the sacrificial service, Christ-centered worship, consecrated stewardship, and radical humility that marked these later days of the Outpouring.

The diverse nature of participants in the Outpouring is addressed in Chapter Four by Juan Gonzalez, who describes the ethos of diversity on campus and the multinational impact of the Outpouring as part of God's design for his Kingdom. He explains the powerful impact of the Witnessing Circle that took place the night before the Outpouring, in which attendees repented of the history of slavery and prejudice in the central Kentucky area. The performance of the multiethnic Gospel Choir during the February 8 chapel service further prepared hearts to receive God's grace. As the Outpouring grew, people from around the world showed up in Wilmore, providing a foretaste of the heavenly, multiethnic worship described in Revelation 7:9–10.

In addition to repentance and healing, many of those in attendance experienced remarkable instances of divine timing. Carol Anderson and Barbara Hamilton describe in Chapter Five the varied ways that God brought together people at serendipitous moments, matching those in great need with those prepared to pray and provide. In some instances, lessons learned decades earlier came to the forefront during the Outpouring.

As the Outpouring grew, the university ran out of space in Hughes Auditorium to seat everyone who wanted to attend. The Wilmore community rallied to meet the needs of the spiritually hungry who flowed into town. Both Asbury Theological Seminary (located across the street from the university) and several local churches provided overflow space for worship. In Chapter Six, Jessica LaGrone addresses the ways in which the seminary opened its doors to respond to the overflowing grace of a "good crisis." She reflects on the need for both mountaintop moments and daily church life that band disciples together in the body of Christ.

Whereas the first section of the book describes *what* happened, the second section of the book asks *why* the Holy Spirit sometimes appears among the people of God in extraordinary ways. Julianne Burnett, Joy Vaughan, and Sam Kim explore in Chapter Seven the scriptural witness to God's sudden appearances among his people, as well as the call to spread the gospel to all nations.

Kevin Anderson then takes a historical look at revivals in Chapter Eight in order to detect patterns in the way God regularly has worked to call sinners to salvation and awaken believers to a fresh commitment to discipleship in modern times. From pre-Reformation times through the Reformation and First and Second Great Awakenings to the mid-century prayer revival and twentieth-century revivals, he compares the characteristics of these movements of the Holy Spirit with what we experienced at the Outpouring.

When these kinds of revivals occur, people are drawn to particular sites where the Spirit is powerfully present. Brian Shelton investigates in Chapter Nine a theology of sacred space—that is, the difference between a mere location and a place of encounter with God, where despair meets hope and anguish meets resolution. After considering various theologies of sacred space, he describes the experiences of some of those who discovered sacred space in Hughes Auditorium.

A key activity in Hughes was prayer. In Chapter Ten, Craig Saunders explores a theology of prayer by focusing on how Jesus instructed his disciples to pray in the Gospel of Matthew. Saunders then considers examples of those in Scripture who thirsted for living water, finding similarities with his experiences serving on the prayer team during the Outpouring.

In Chapter Eleven, I examine how key components of John Wesley's theology provide a lens through which to make sense of spiritual outpourings. Concepts including sin, prevenient grace, repentance, justification, assurance, the new birth, means of grace, sanctification, and Christian perfection provide foundations for this discussion. I then explore the question of the "fruits test" for evaluating revivals and our need to continually cooperate with the Holy Spirit long after revivals have ended.

After discussing *what* happened at the Outpouring and *why* God moves in these ways, the third section of the book points to practical application.

Because we believe that God will continue to move among his people—and we have seen this already at other universities—we have included this section to give practical insights into *how* to address the various challenges that arise during outpourings of the Spirit. We hope this provides wisdom for others. Asbury University President Kevin Brown kicks off this section in Chapter Twelve with a discussion of the consideration of mission, the need for "holy imagination" in the midst of uncertainty, and the call to "strive upward." Although leaders like to cite policies and management principles, he suggests that a mission focus and willingness to be flexible as the Spirit leads are key to navigating the changing dynamics of an outpouring like the one we experienced.

Dan Pinkston then addresses in Chapter Thirteen the complexities of leading worship for unplanned movements of God. The primarily student-led worship did not include the projection of lyrics on screens or the use of hymnals. Rather, the use of familiar or easily learned worship songs allowed those present in Hughes to join together in praise. He discusses how the design of these hymns facilitates the unity of worship, as well as the importance of humility in leading.

As word of the Outpouring spread, managing the media became an important responsibility. Abby Laub discusses the global media frenzy in Chapter Fourteen. She provides wisdom for navigating media requests, protecting students who are called upon to share their testimonies, and shaping the story of God's profound presence on campus.

The desperate hunger of those who flocked to town was not without its problems. In Chapter Fifteen, Wilmore Mayor Harold Rainwater tackles the infrastructure challenges that occur when a town of six thousand suddenly hosts tens of thousands of unplanned guests. His discussion gives insight into adaptable management for city officials who must navigate caring for their taxpaying citizens while offering hospitality to visitors.

In Chapter Sixteen we begin to turn to the questions of what happens after the initial movement of the Holy Spirit. Although the Outpouring services officially ended after two and a half weeks, the testimonies about the profound work of God have continued. Bridgette Campbell describes the ways in which students have traveled to various churches, conferences, and nations to share their experiences of the living God. She demonstrates the importance of telling the story of the movement of God so that others can share in the hope of a loving and present Savior.

The Outpouring affected not only college students but also men and women from all walks of life whom the Holy Spirit challenged to manifest radical humility, selfless relationships, and holiness. In Chapter Seventeen, Rob Lim discusses the experiences of marketplace leaders who attended the Outpouring and how they brought the lessons they learned into the secular arena after they left Hughes Auditorium.

In the final chapter, Maria Brown discusses the complexities of the work of the Holy Spirit in students' lives as they process their experiences of the Outpouring. She chronicles their challenge to walk in step with the Spirit, learning to live in new ways even as they face old patterns of behavior. Looking to the Incarnation of Jesus, she considers the complexity of human experience and encourages believers to embrace the hope that arises out of the messiness of the Christian walk.

Before turning to Chapter One, a few explanations are in order. When it became clear that God was moving in a powerful way on Asbury's campus in February of 2023, many people asked what we should call this movement. Was it a revival? A spiritual outpouring? An awakening?[1] As worship grew on campus, *outpouring* came to be used more frequently than other terms. President Kevin Brown explains that using *revival* might have invited comparisons with the 1970 revival that occurred on campus, and leaders wanted to avoid that distraction. *Outpouring* is more general, but it forestalled any premature defining of this experience of the Holy Spirit. Brown recalls leaders discussing the question and comparing the situation to the story of Jesus healing the blind beggar in John 9. When the man was questioned by Jewish leaders who accused Jesus of being a sinner, the healed man responded, "I do not know whether he is a sinner. One thing I do know, that though I was blind, now I see" (v. 25). Asbury's leaders suggested a parallel version for those who questioned whether a "revival" was occurring on campus: "Whether this is a revival, renewal, awakening, or something else . . . I do not know. Here is what I do know: thousands of hungry-hearted visitors are seeking the Lord and being met."

The concept of an "outpouring" also picks up language from Scripture about God "pouring out" his Spirit on all people, as the prophet Joel

1. J. Edwin Orr proposed the following distinctions between the terms: "Outpourings of the Spirit are exclusively the work of God; but revivals are the work of God with the response of believers; awakenings are the work of God with the response of the people." See *The Outpouring of the Spirit in Revival and Awakening and Its Issue in Church Growth* (Bedford, UK: British Church Growth Association, 2000), 5. Asbury's use of *outpouring* is not meant to imply that no response of believers occurred; rather, the focus is on the significant experience of the Holy Spirit, without further defining the response to this experience.

declared in 2:28–29 and the apostle Peter affirmed at Pentecost in Acts 2:16–21. In another speech soon thereafter, Peter called upon his fellow Jews in Jerusalem to repent so "that times of refreshing may come from the presence of the Lord" (Acts 3:20 ESV).[2] It is this kind of refreshing to which the term *outpouring* points. Similarly, theologians Jason Vickers and Thomas McCall define a spiritual outpouring as "the idea that, *from time to time and in ways that are unscripted and beyond human control, God makes God's presence and power manifest in a manner that is readily discernible, that leads to repentance and deep joy, and that conveys life-changing forgiveness and grace.*"[3] This describes well the experience of the Asbury Outpouring.

The title of this book—*Cooperating with the Holy Spirit*—arises from our conviction that this outpouring was initiated by God. Those who lingered after chapel that Wednesday simply responded to what God was already doing. It is true that prayer precipitated the event: Many people had prayed for years for an outpouring of the Spirit on campus because they had heard of—or experienced themselves—earlier movements of the Holy Spirit. What God had initiated they asked to be repeated. And so the pattern continues: God moves, and the people respond. We merely cooperated with what God was already doing among us. This book is a testimony to that movement of God.

2. Another moment of divine timing occurred with this passage. Spring semester 2023, I was teaching a class on Acts of the Apostles, and the day before the Outpouring began, I discussed this very verse with my students!

3. Jason E. Vickers and Thomas H. McCall, *Outpouring: A Theological Witness* (Eugene, OR: Cascade, 2023), 7, emphasis in original.

PART ONE

THE ASBURY OUTPOURING

CHAPTER ONE

BEGINNINGS

The Rattling of the Bones

Jeannie Banter
Director of the Christian Life Project, Asbury University

To tell the story of the 2023 Asbury Outpouring is to tell the story of God's love, faithfulness, and relentless pursuit of his children throughout all generations. One of the most frequently asked questions about the Outpouring relates to its beginning: "How did it start?" This simple question seems impossible to answer. How do you start something that God has orchestrated? The answer is we cannot and did not. However, before February 8, we heard sounds of life, similar to those in Ezekiel 37:7: "There was a noise, a rattling sound."

Ezekiel 37 is the powerful account of God raising up a "vast army" of Spirit-filled people from "dry bones." During the Outpouring, we witnessed firsthand God do this again; the Spirit of God breathed on the dry bones of Generation Z.[1] While the Outpouring that occurred on February 8 was not planned, what is clear is that in the days, weeks, and months leading up to the eighth, many of us heard the "rattling sounds" of dry bones coming back to life.

I heard an early rattling of the bones on Saturday, October 15, 2022, while I sat among forty-eight Asbury students on Asbury's Set Apart Retreat, a weekend retreat that helps students cultivate a Christian worldview. As I sat watching students respond to the love and grace of Jesus in confession and repentance, I heard the Lord ask me the same question he asked Ezekiel: "Can these bones live?" (Ezek. 37:3). I knew in that moment

1. Generation Z is defined as the "generation born between the late 1990s and about 2010." "Gen Z," Dictionary.com, accessed August 29, 2024, https://www.dictionary.com/browse/gen-z.

God was asking me to think beyond the fifty students I was leading on that retreat; God was asking for their generation. "Jeannie, do you believe the dry bones of Generation Z can live?" Thinking about the "dry bones" of Generation Z, I reflected on the headlines of news stories I had seen over the years and what our own students were experiencing—significant mental health struggles; addictions to pornography, alcohol, illicit drugs, and various forms of media; mistrust in institutions of education, religion, government, and the family because of the significant abuse by and moral failures of their leaders; a generation more connected to the world and yet lonely, isolated, anxious, afraid, depressed, and left to navigate it on their own. Could these dry bones live?

I found myself not fully knowing how to answer the question, but I found solace in Ezekiel's answer: "Sovereign Lord, you alone know" (Ezek. 37:3). In my simple answer, hope as I have never experienced before began to spring forth like mighty rushing water in my heart for what God wanted to do in this generation. As the service ended that night, I stood in front of those forty-eight college students, shared Ezekiel 37, and proclaimed that I was beginning to see a "vast army" come to life right before my eyes. I knew without a doubt I was hearing the rattling sounds of the dry bones of Generation Z coming to life.

Rattling Sound: Prayer

Why did the Outpouring occur at Asbury? I honestly have no idea; but if I had one guess, it would be because of the prayers of the people in our community for an outpouring of God's Spirit and love. When I say the Asbury community, I include Asbury University students, faculty, staff, alumni, friends, donors, Asbury Theological Seminary, the Wilmore faith community, and people around the world who have been touched by one of the numerous revivals throughout the university's history. The Asbury community has a holy imagination for what God can do because as a collective we have borne witness to the mighty move of God in a generation, a community, and throughout the world again and again.

As one who has experienced firsthand two of the mighty moves of God at Asbury (2006 and 2023), I must confess: I honestly cannot stop asking God for more of himself. I ask for more of God, not out of a place of greed, but out of a place of utter dependence. These outpourings have shown me the need to be utterly dependent on God to step in and bring to life all the dead places both in my own life and in the lives of all those around the world.

Much of my life has changed since February 2023, but especially my prayer life. Long before February, I met weekly with a friend to pray for revival on our campus and throughout the world. This practice continues now, months later. However, what has changed is that now when I pray, I offer up prayers that will outlive me. I am confident that what occurred at Asbury and then throughout the world that February was the result of the cumulative prayers of generations of people interceding for God to move in the next generation. I want to offer intercessions that increase the spiritual temperature for generations to come.

The "rattling sounds" of increased prayer can be traced throughout each of the previous revivals at Asbury University. In the days, months, and years leading up to February 8, prayer groups and gatherings for revival and awakening were springing up across both campuses (Asbury University and Asbury Theological Seminary) and throughout the Wilmore community. A month before COVID-19 shut down the world in March 2020, Asbury celebrated the fiftieth anniversary of the 1970 Asbury Revival. The 1970 revival lasted for 144 unbroken hours as God poured himself out during a regularly scheduled chapel service at which the speaker felt God leading him to open the podium for student testimonies.[2] The days following were full of confession, repentance, testimony, and God pouring out his love and Spirit not only on Asbury's campus but wherever the story was told.

The 2020 remembrance of what God did fifty years prior was a catalyst for a renewed call to prayer for God to do it again. Even when groups could not physically meet in person, groups gathered over Zoom to pray for an outpouring of the Holy Spirit. Students at the university formed prayer groups, conducted prayer walks on campus, and individually felt called to intercede for revival on campus and in this generation. World Gospel Mission Student Center—under the direction of James Ballard, Elle Crossman, and student leaders, in the months before February 2023—started the "Prayer Furnace" to pray for revival, the campus, and the world.

Members of the Asbury University staff and faculty met in small groups and individually to contend for revival. In 2021, Dr. Kevin J. Brown, president of Asbury University, wrote prayer prompts that were handed out to members of the Asbury University alumni community. The first prompt was dedicated to praying for an "Outpouring of the Holy Spirit—Pray for

2. Matt Kinnell, "Asbury Revival," Asbury University, accessed August 29, 2024, https://www.asbury.edu/academics/resources/library/archives/history/asbury-revival/.

Asbury University to experience a powerful moving of the Holy Spirit that would set our students on fire and turn our campus, community, and world upside down."[3] The Asbury University alumni, under the leadership of Lisa Harper, were pivotal in praying for an outpouring. Alumni have met every month since April 2020 via Zoom to pray for Asbury University and for God to move in the hearts and lives of students. Various prayer groups led by retired seminary faculty and lay leaders brought seminary students together weekly to pray for revival and awakening. Titus Women's Fellowship felt a burden to pray daily for revival on campus months before February. God was bringing his people to their knees to intercede for a fresh outpouring of his Spirit, specifically among Generation Z.

One of the "rattling sounds" of prayer that has challenged me the most came from the prayer life of Rev. HongToo Leow. While Rev. Leow was serving as a visiting professor from Malaysia Bible Seminary at Asbury Theological Seminary, he received a dream about revival and felt God leading him to contend in prayer for this dream to become a reality.[4] After receiving confirmation in another word from the Lord, Rev. Leow moved his family from Malaysia to Wilmore, Kentucky, to pray for revival.[5] Rev. Leow faithfully prayer-walked Wilmore contending for revival. His presence in the community could not be missed; rain or shine, hot or cold, Rev. Leow walked and prayed for God to pour himself out again in a fresh way.

As Rev. Leow walked, he wore cardboard signs saying, "Holy Spirit, you are welcome here," or "Repent, believe in Jesus, for the Kingdom of God is near."[6] These placards were signposts to point to Jesus and for us to know these walks were on mission to what God has called him to do. On February 8, he was one of the first people that came to my mind, and when he did, my heart overflowed with deep gratitude for his faithfulness. Rev. Leow did more than pray for our community; his life has modeled for all of us what it means to live on mission wherever God sends you—even

3. Kevin Brown, President Kevin J. Brown's Prayer Prompts, Asbury University Office of the President, Summer 2021.
4. HongToo Leow, message to author, December 20, 2023.
5. Salt&Light, "God Is Faithful and Almighty. He Promised He Would Do It and *He Did It*: Malaysian Pastor in Asbury," Salt&Light, accessed December 20, 2023, https://saltandlight.sg/news/god-is-faithful-and-almighty-he-promised-he-would-do-it-and-he-did-it-malaysian-pastor-in-asbury/?fbclid=IwAR0yHijpimGI5lls0nRTDaoKBkWUOQ0pf0LJIr6Z4VHTEmqoLMv8NJZPiTQ.
6. As an example, see "HongToo Leow Is Feeling Blessed," Facebook, February 16, 2023, https://www.facebook.com/hongtoo.leow.

when God's "sending" involves moving your family from Malaysia to a tiny town in central Kentucky to pray for a mighty move of God.

Each prayer lifted in the hours, days, months, and years leading up to February 8—those that were written and those that were prayed in the secret places—is evidence of the "rattling sounds" of dry bones coming back to life.

Rattling Sound: Hunger

Over the months leading to February, we began to see an increase in the hunger of our students for God. The "rattling sound" of hunger pangs arose in a generation waking up to the reality that there must be something more than the unsatisfied life they were living. One of the definitions for *hunger* is to "strongly desire."[7] Our students began to "taste and see that the Lord is good" (Ps. 34:8); as they tasted his goodness, they strongly desired more of God, and their appetites were being changed in the process. Our students were beginning to awaken to the reality that they were filling their lives with "junk food" (pride, jealousy, addiction, comparison, perfectionism, celebrity Christianity) that kept them spiritually malnourished. Junk food does not taste as good when you begin to realize you have been invited to sit at the "banqueting table" of the Lord, full of his love (Song of Sol. 2:4). With this realization, our students were becoming increasingly dissatisfied with the things of this world that promised fulfillment and satisfaction but never delivered on their promises.

One of the places we began to hear the "rattling sounds" of hunger leading people to God's banqueting table was in chapel. Throughout the decades, Asbury University chapels have hosted renowned preachers, theologians, and the brightest minds from around the world. As a community we gather three times a week—Monday, Wednesday, and Friday—to worship through prayer, song, testimony, and the Word. While chapel is required at Asbury, most students show up expectant for God to meet with them. As part of our culture of expectancy and responsiveness in chapel, it is not uncommon to have students linger after chapel, praying both in their seats and at the altar to make right their relationship with God and one another. This is true every year, but in the fall and early spring (2022–23), there were several chapels where the altar was full of students in prayer, confession, and repentance.

7. "Hunger," Dictionary.com, accessed August 29, 2024, https://dictionary.com/browse/hunger.

One chapel sermon that left a resounding "rattling sound" in my ears in the fall of 2022 was preached by Rev. Steve DeNeff, pastor of College Wesleyan Church in Marion, Indiana. Pastor Steve has been a frequent and fan-favorite chapel speaker at Asbury over the last two decades. That October morning, Pastor Steve preached from Ezekiel 36:25–27 on God turning our hearts of stone into hearts of flesh. He shared that God's heart transformation in each of us gives us a "new operating system."[8] During the altar call, he invited students to ask God to give them a new operating system, one not of behavioral modification as the world has taught them but of the Holy Spirit, which leads to complete transformation from the inside out. As Pastor Steve gave the altar call, with my eyes closed, I began to hear the loud "rattling sounds" of hunger. From all around the room I began to hear the squeaking sound of the old wooden chairs as students stood up and put their seats up. Soon after came the sound of shuffling feet across the room and on the balcony. Then came the distinct creaking sound of the altar as students knelt in prayer. When I opened my eyes seconds later, not only was the altar full, but students were three deep behind the altar, and the areas to the side of thc altar were packed.

The first words that came to mind as I saw the students all over the front of Hughes were "Thank you, Jesus." It had been a hard couple of weeks on campus for students with various frustrations and anxieties. The weeks before this chapel felt weighty. Many of us on staff had been praying for a move of God. Moreover, it was the beginning of midterms, when campus always seems to hit a slump. This morning, however, in the middle of the frustration, anxieties, and slumps, God showed up, and the "rattling sounds" of life were undeniable. This call to a "new operating system"—this call to holiness—was so personal, but it was also communal. As individuals were getting up from the altar, transformed, our community was being transformed. Dry bones were coming back to life.

The momentum from that chapel continued as a little over a week later forty-eight students went on Asbury University's Set Apart Retreat, discussed previously. The "rattling sounds" of hunger on the retreat were undeniable as students stepped into places of surrender, healing, freedom, and living out their identity as beloved sons and daughters of the King. The Holy Spirit moved powerfully, drawing students closer to God, kindly

8. Steve DeNeff, "You Are What You Love," Asbury University, October 5, 2022, https://www.asbury.edu/podcasts/102511/.

revealing areas of sin that were keeping us from living in the fullness of life that God offers, and showing each one who God is and who we are to God.

With each session, the "rattling sounds" were getting louder as students were leaning into all that God had for them on this retreat. You could physically feel the closeness of the presence of God, and we began to wonder what else was in store for us on the retreat. On the second night, Zach Meerkreebs preached on areas that keep us from living into our full identity as beloved sons and daughters. The main session was set to last an hour; however, it lasted over three hours as the Holy Spirit spoke a better word over the identities of the students in the room. Students began to drop to their knees in confession and repentance for the ways in which they had misplaced their identity. Others began to intercede for one another, for family members and friends, and for the lost to know the truth of their identity. The hours were full of worship through song, personal prayer, communal intercession, confession, repentance, and praise. Tears drenched the floor, and hallelujahs filled the air. Students were set free! As we left the session, I walked beside several students back to our rooms. During the walk, I commented to the students that the session lasted over three hours. One of the students looked at me in complete awe and said, "Are you serious? I thought it was only thirty minutes!" When God shows up, time stands still, and there is no place you would rather be than in his presence.

When I close my eyes, I can still hear the echo of the "rattling sounds" of a vast army coming to life that night. During the sixteen days of the Outpouring in February 2023, multiple students from the October Set Apart Retreat came up to me, all saying the same thing: "Jeannie, we have already tasted this before on retreat," or "Doesn't this remind you of retreat?" Yes, it did! Those students were right; those of us on that retreat had already tasted an outpouring of God's Spirit and love. Those three hours in Classroom #1 at Laguna Beach Christian Retreat Center were only a foretaste of the sixteen days in February, and those sixteen days are only a foretaste of eternity.

Rattling Sound: Desperation

Desperation is not often thought of as a sign of new life coming, but in the spiritual world, desperation is often the exact place where God does some of his best work bringing dead things back to life. Desperation can be described as "the feeling that you have when you are in such a bad situation that you will do anything to change it."[9] The "rattling sounds" of desperation are audible. They are heard in the cries of the brokenhearted, the groans of those who have no words left for the grief and anguish they have experienced, and the shouts of anger and frustration over the brokenness of a fallen world.

The "rattling sound" of desperation rising from the people of God in the months and years leading up to February 8 was deafening. I am not sure anyone would look over the years 2020–23 and say those were the best years we experienced as a body of believers, as a country, or in the world. The word that encompasses those years for me is *division*. The divisiveness we experienced permeated the very fabric of our beings. From opinions about masks to political-party affiliation to the color of our skin, we were told to draw lines in the sand, pick sides, and believe that the "other" was the enemy personified. Countries went to war, cities burned, and brother revolted against brother as the world cried out in desperation. The ripple effects of division were felt in our communities, in the workplace, in the pews of our churches, around dinner tables, and around the world. We were a people in desperate need of a savior.

We in the Asbury community were not immune from the effects of the divisiveness happening in the country, and tensions were felt within the body. Instead of trust, skepticism reared its ugly head. Where peace and belonging once reigned, fear and isolation began to take up residence on our campus. Students tried to navigate the complexities of becoming adults amid the local, national, and global crises we were facing. If we as middle-aged adults were having a difficult time navigating the challenges of these years, how could we expect eighteen- to twenty-two-year-olds to know how to navigate these realities?

Generation Z came of age in years marked by divisiveness, tension, and deep unsettledness that were shaking the foundation of much of what they had known. The cost of what we witnessed in the world was an unprecedented rise in the anxiety, depression, and suicidal ideation of Generation Z. Articles and news stories captivated the attention of a nation, describing the mental health crisis facing this generation. A 2023 study conducted by the American Psychological Association, for example, found that "about two-thirds of 18- to 34-year-olds [Gen Z and young millennials] said stress makes it hard for them to focus (67 percent) and feel as though no

9. "Desperation," Collins English Dictionary, accessed August 29, 2024, https://www.collinsdictionary.com/us/dictionary/english/desperation.

one understands how stressed they are (66 percent). That age group was also the most likely to say that most days, their stress is 'completely overwhelming' (58 percent), that it renders them numb (50 percent), and that most days they are so stressed they can't function."[10] Asbury students were not immune to the mental health struggle facing their generation. As a community, we walked alongside students who lived with daily anxiety and depression. Some students battled with thoughts of suicide throughout the year. University personnel offered support and help for students living in these realities. These students bravely fought every day to attend class, finish assignments, and partake in basic life necessities. Many of these precious students were in desperate situations, wondering if there was any hope.

The "rattling sounds" of their desperate tears and cries pierced the hearts of our administration, faculty, and staff. Conversations happened throughout the university in board rooms, around copiers, and at the tables in the cafeteria: "How can we best come around our students right now? What are we going to do to help the mental health crisis our students are facing?" The reality of the brokenness our students were experiencing was palpable.

Desperation: I saw it in my eyes as I looked in the mirror, and I saw it in the eyes of my colleagues around the table. We were taking action to meet the growing needs of our students, and we also knew that even with all the right action steps, we still desperately needed God to break through for this generation. This desperation brought us to our knees. In the months leading up to February 2023, I would describe the posture of our community as "on our knees," desperately crying out for God to come and push back the darkness from our students, our nation, and the world.

It's not lost on me that in the history of Asbury University, most of the outpourings on our campus have occurred during the month of February. For some, that would seem coincidental, while others may speculate it must be planned, since it's always in the same month. To me, however, it shows the kindness of God coming for his children. February is one of the most difficult months for mental health on college campuses. The "winter blues" sets in during February, as many days—especially in Kentucky—are gray, gloomy, and overcast. Counseling center numbers typically increase in the month of February as people battle depression and suicidal ideation. It makes sense that God, our Good Father, would choose February—a month

10. Anna Medaris, "Gen Z Adults and Younger Millennials Are 'Completely Overwhelmed' by Stress," American Psychological Association, November 1, 2023, https://www.apa.org/topics/stress/generation-z-millennials-young-adults-worries.

known for darkness and despair—to pour himself out and allow his light and love to push back the darkness.

Two days before the Outpouring—Monday night, February 6—I was on the phone with a colleague. We both shared our desperation for God to move in the lives of our students. We could sense an increase in anxiety and depression as we settled into the gloomy February weather. We wondered aloud how students would be able to make it to the end of the semester with all that they were experiencing. We both said to each other, "If God doesn't show up, I don't know if they can make it to the end." We cried and we prayed that night for God to push back the darkness, to reveal himself during the mental health crisis of our students and Generation Z, and to step into the midst of our brokenness. While we prayed in desperation, neither one of us had any idea that two days later God would answer those desperate cries.

Rattling Sounds: The Seventy-Two Hours Leading up to February 8

While we did not realize all that was in store for us in the coming days, it was evident that God was moving in a new way. The "rattling sounds" of dry bones coming to life were frequent and loud. I'm reminded of the words found in the book of Isaiah, "See, I am doing a new thing! Now it springs up; do you not perceive it?" (Isa. 43:19). We knew God was doing a new thing; we could perceive it. However, we did not yet have eyes to see the fullness of all God was doing.

On Sunday, February 5, the World Gospel Mission (WGM) Student Center hosted Global Café, a weekly Sunday night worship service focused on learning, praying, and going to the world for the sake of Christ. The speaker that evening was Matthew Luce, founder and missionary of Beehive Global Collective. Instead of preaching a typical missions sermon, Mat felt led to change direction and share his testimony with the students. I watched as the students visibly began to lean forward as he shared of the grace and freedom offered to them in Jesus Christ. As Mat closed the evening, he invited students to pray with the various leaders in the room for grace, healing, and the freedom found in Jesus Christ. Over the next hour, students poured their hearts out to several of us leaders, asking Jesus to meet them in the middle of their sin, brokenness, and trauma. Students were being set free on a cold, dark Sunday night in the basement of the WGM Student Center.

On February 7, as part of regularly scheduled programming for Black History Month, Asbury hosted a Witnessing Circle. This event was designed to honor, dignify, and lament Black men, women, and children who were enslaved in the central Kentucky region during the antebellum period of American history. During the Witnessing Circle, leaders read aloud archived deeds from central Kentucky counties, pausing to remember and honor the men, women, and children listed in the deeds as property, not people.

Many in attendance have described the Witnessing Circle as a "sacred space." To those in the room, it was evident that God was present. After the reading of the deeds, Benjamin Black, leader of the Asbury Gospel Choir, and choir member Georges Dumaine sang "Lift Every Voice and Sing," the Black National Anthem.

As Georges sang the lyrics, the Holy Spirit began to minister to his heart. Georges recounts that the second and the third stanzas of the hymn provoked him to marvel at the wisdom of God to inspire the author to intertwine God's Word and promises into the song. He was moved that the lyrics also provided keys for the Black community to experience breakthroughs as well as encouragement to keep God front and center. Georges began to weep as he felt the presence of Jesus fill the room. Georges recounts that the tears were flowing not only because of the injustice suffered by Black men, women, and children but also because Jesus was present amid the reading of these deeds honoring these men, women, and children who had borne the brunt of much injustice. It is no surprise that our God, the God of justice, would stand right amid that space. Georges and others have testified that for them, the Outpouring began on February 7 as Jesus revealed himself in the middle of the Witnessing Circle, standing up for the injustice of Black men, women, and children.

On the evening of February 7, the Gospel Choir—which would lead worship during chapel on the eighth—met to practice. The "rattling sounds" from standing in the presence of God during the Witnessing Circle reverberated during practice. The Gospel Choir, under the leadership of Benjamin Black, sensed God wanted to move in a powerful way during chapel the next morning. Benjamin, a Spirit-filled man of God, sensed that the movement of God was not unopposed; there was significant darkness opposing the work of God. He led the Gospel Choir in a time of intercession for the campus, praying against spiritual attack and leading the students in the choir to pray for every person who would sit in one of the seats in Hughes Auditorium the next day. Their intercession and prayerful covering of Hughes and the students pushed back the darkness and held open space for the Spirit of God to flow freely in those coming days.

That same night, a woman from the Wilmore community, Maria Walker, continued the same practice she had done every night for one and a half years: She faithfully prayer-walked Asbury's campus with her dog, asking God to "do it again." Maria stated, "I love Wilmore and Asbury, but was not satisfied with the nice peaceful life that was like a little brook running over pebbles in the sunshine. I prayed for this brook to turn into a roaring river, for a spiritual awakening."[11] Between midnight and 1:00 a.m. on February 8, she walked our campus again, praying for our students, faculty/staff, and administration. She stated that as she passed by Hughes that night, instead of walking by as she prayed, she sat on the front steps, asking God when he was going to answer her prayers. She cried out, "Fill this place with your glory!"[12] Nine hours later, God indeed filled the whole campus and the community with his glory!

On Wednesday morning, February 8, World Gospel Mission Student Center held its weekly prayer meeting, referred to as the Prayer Furnace. Students gathered in the early hours of February 8 to intercede for campus and to cry out for revival on our campus. A few brief hours later they witnessed a direct answer to prayer.

We will never know all the "rattling sounds" that were present in the years, months, and days leading up to February 8. None of these actions alone started the Outpouring, but each one served to prepare the way for us to receive an outpouring of his Spirit and love. These stories are but a glimpse of the lavish love of the Good Father, preparing his people for an outpouring of his Spirit and love. The "rattling sounds" were only the beginning of what we would witness over the coming days, months, and into eternity. God was raising up a "vast army" in Generation Z, beyond what we could "ask or imagine" (Eph. 3:20).

11. Maria Walker, message to author, December 22, 2023.
12. Walker, message.

CHAPTER TWO

THE EARLY DAYS OF THE OUTPOURING

Greg Haseloff
Associate dean of Spiritual Life and University Pastor, Asbury University

> [The Outpouring was] unplanned and unexpected . . . the absolute absence of human leadership. . . . [It] occupies everybody and all our wakeful hours. . . . Unusual profound conviction pervades the assembly. The entire chapel is an altar. . . . [The story] cannot be told in human words. I wish I could portray its grandeur. Its glory, and its graciousness.
>
> —Asbury College President B. F. Haynes, 1905[1]

Though Dr. Haynes's reflections are from 1905, we both agree that our Outpouring stories "cannot be told in human words"—so we proceed with this limitation. The desire of students at Asbury to live in sync with the Holy Spirit postured them to have hearts open to the Holy Spirit's movement. The story began with February 8 being an ordinary chapel day. Zach Meerkreebs preached that morning what he described as a mediocre sermon continuing a themed chapel series titled "Love in Action." On a Wednesday morning in the fifth week of the semester, the Gospel Choir led our worship. Students who help lead musically often show up with a long list of daily commitments, running into chapel for their responsibilities and running out to get to their next class. On this unique morning, however,

1. Robert Canary, *Spontaneous Revivals: Asbury College 1905–2006, Firsthand Accounts of Lives Transformed* (Lexington, KY: CreateSpace, 2017), i.

several in the Gospel Choir led with a heightened spiritual sensitivity—as they had been uniquely impacted by two events the day prior. They were entering chapel worship with a different kind of expectancy, more attuned to the Holy Spirit's presence. Choir members had an extended prayer time at the close of their practice the night before, and several students had been deeply impacted by a "Witnessing Circle" they experienced prior to choir practice.[2] Therefore, on February 8, their sense that the Spirit was stirring broke several of them out of their routine entrance and exit of chapel.

The movement of God on February 8 was preceded by prayer—intercession that cried out for Holy Spirit–inspired repentance, confession, and spiritual hunger. From the onset, testimonies of healing from depression and anxiety, along with other stories of powerful transformation, began to infuse the atmosphere with love, joy, and peace. This chapter on the early days of the Asbury Outpouring explores student experiences of prayer and worship that exponentially increased into a movement of salvations and healings, with thousands of Gen Zers and thousands in older generations becoming "living transformations" compelled to share the good news of Jesus.

Prayer That Preceded and Prayer That Ignited

Students leading and participating in a growing prayer movement ripened our campus for cooperating with the Holy Spirit. Knowing the existence of the prayer movement is essential in understanding the atmosphere of campus on February 8. Chapel ended that Wednesday morning close to 10:50 a.m., which is a time almost indelibly marked in the mind of any Asburian. That is the time to start moving to the next class, the time to grab your backpack, the time for chapel to end. An Asbury student had likely landed in their chapel seat that day already mentally prepared for where they were heading at 10:50 a.m.: going to their next class, to their next friend conversation, or to lunch! At 10:50 a.m., after Zach Meerkreeb's message, student leader Zeke Atha came to the mic to release the student body for their 11:00 a.m. class and invite those who could stay to remain and continue in a posture of worship. The Gospel Choir sang a closing song they had prepared. Some students left, and others continued to sense the Lord keeping them in Hughes. About thirty-five students stayed after

2. More specific details of these stories are shared in Jeannie Banter's and Juan Gonzalez's chapters in this volume.

chapel that day, and they lingered in a posture of patience, worship, and longing for God to come near.

Both singing and instrumental worship continued over the next ten to fifteen minutes. Along with the students spread across Hughes were five or six staff, including me. During those first few minutes after chapel ended, a move happened that almost looked synchronized. A dozen students came from different seats scattered in different sections of the auditorium to kneel at the altar. The altar had been virtually empty, and suddenly, about thirty minutes after the dismissal of chapel, much of the altar rail was full. I was filled with holy awe, and I suspect others sensed the same. As I assess my sensitivities from serving in Hughes as a college pastor, that moment was likely a turning point. In that moment the manifest presence of God became thicker than anything I had experienced in previous years in Hughes Auditorium. Jesus was distinctly present in the quietness, waiting, desperation, and seeking that was unfolding in that space and time. While a dozen students prayed at the altar and four or five students provided a musical backdrop, others were in their seats, and several conversations continued in an atmosphere of prayer and worship. The Holy Spirit was present and moving in a beautiful way.

One student approached me asking for prayer for her father, who doctors feared had cancer. Lauren thought the oncologist would be running tests the following day. I stood with her and prayed for her father. Lauren left Hughes to head to lunch. Two minutes later she came rushing back into the auditorium in a swift walk, exuberantly pointing to her cell phone. Her dad had just texted her, and he didn't have cancer! Though the timing of the tests was different than she had thought, the Lord provided a quick answer! The immediacy of prayers being answered became a commonplace occurrence—on the very first day, the next day, and every single hour of those sixteen days of the intensified, accelerated work of God.

The Inauguration of Testimonies

A dozen of the students who stayed after chapel remained in prayer at the altar. Students were praying for friends, other students, and their families. An atmosphere of both peace and the loving presence of God filled the room. Somewhere close to 11:45 a.m., Charlie approached me and asked if he could share a testimony. The room was shifting from singing to quiet prayer, and Charlie—like others—was trying to discern what God was doing and how he was calling them to respond. I knew Charlie well as a respected student leader. With pastoral prudence for the situation unfolding, I asked him what he would like to share. As a middle schooler he had lost a brother to suicide, which created a sense of hopelessness and despair in him. Since there was a small number of people in Hughes, I made the quick decision that Charlie could share—and do so very simply from the floor—standing in front of the altar where everyone could hear him with ease. He gave testimony to God's faithfulness during his middle school years and how Jesus was gracious to restore hope in him, bringing him through the grief of such a heavy loss. His testimony elevated the atmosphere, speaking hope to the other students present. This story immediately became grafted into the foundation of this extraordinary movement of God, as if Jesus were bringing generational healing, healing that would magnify in the hours and days ahead. Testimonies like this one, extolling that hope and healing were available to all believers, would become distinctive of the Outpouring. The Lord was healing brokenness and pain and bringing hope to the captive and weary.

Throughout the afternoon and evening, we heard more testimonies. Along with singing, we also had periods of silence. Word spread about something special happening in Hughes, and the thirty-five or so present before lunch began to double. We likely had more than two hundred people in Hughes by 2:00 p.m. As worship leaders guided beautiful and joyful singing, the lyrics were distinctly vertical—so clearly exalting Jesus. When singing morphed into quietness, the silence provided a holy awe, highlighting that we were on holy ground. Throughout the sixteen days, this reverent sensitivity to the Lord's presence with his people permeated Hughes and extended outside, across the semicircle front drive of the university, to the venues of Asbury Theological Seminary and even local church venues! As more and more students encountered the transformative work of the Holy Spirit across these early hours, we began hearing their readiness to share testimonies of how God was meeting them. It became apparent that we needed to provide a space for students to share what God was doing. We asked students who were encountering God to come forward if they had a word to share. A line quickly formed, and we celebrated for anywhere from thirty minutes to an hour as fifteen to twenty students shared beautiful and amazing stories of being saved, delivered, and healed!

During those early days, two of us would each hold a microphone, stand at the front of the two aisles in Hughes Auditorium, and let students line up to share a story of God's work, guided by the ABCs of testimony: A = **A**ll about Jesus; B = **B**e brief; C = **C**urrent, not old news; and D = **D**on't preach!

On the second day I stood at the front, serving as a shepherd in one of the two lines. One of the testimonies was from Zoe. She and I knew each other well because she had been serving as a Spiritual Life Assistant (floor chaplain) for the last two years. She was a mature spiritual leader. She shared about her own battle with anxiety and depression and how Jesus was unfolding a new degree of healing for her. She was overflowing with joy as she shared! I sensed the Lord reminding me how many others might be listening to Zoe's testimony while living with anxiety or their own stories of depression. I invited people to stand if they were desperate for God to move in their own life like he did in Zoe's. Dozens stood up. Zoe then prayed over them: for healing and wholeness, for a breaking of the enemy's lies, for a restoration of hope, for freedom from the debilitating effects of anxiety and depression, and for a growing certainty that they were known and loved by God. Faith that God could bring healing in these areas of mental health began to elevate. We heard more stories of Jesus bringing hope into a student's mental health battle every time we heard testimonies! Zoe shared more of her own testimony on the last night of the Outpouring, known as the Collegiate Day of Prayer, on February 23. To place an exclamation point on her story, she declared, "Generation Z will no longer be a generation defined by anxiety and depression!"

Tarrying Prayer and Waves of Liquid Love

The Gospel Choir had led the early hours of the Outpouring with an expression of "tarrying prayer"—singing that was filled with deliberate waiting, patience, and longing to be with God. Singing of this nature paralleled a great amount of the lingering across the sixteen days of outpouring and also reflected a style of deliberate waiting that has been present in African American worship for centuries. Testimonies like Charlie's and Zoe's began giving evidence of the transformational presence and work of the Holy Spirit. The movement from joy-filled singing to peaceful silence flowed across the gathering of hungry people, who were seeking unity with God in the midst of a tumultuous world. Over and over, people described the room as being filled with the love of God. The palpability of this loving presence was reminiscent of Charles Finney's description of God as "liquid love." Finney had been a lawyer, and after his conversion to Christianity, he became one of the most well-known preacher-evangelists of the nineteenth century. After reading Scripture, he came to faith in his home and wrote these words describing his encounter with God:

> Without any expectation of it, without ever having the thought in my mind that there was any such thing for me, without any recollection that I had ever heard the thing mentioned by any person in the world, the Holy Spirit descended upon me in a manner that seemed to go through me, body and soul. I could feel the impression, like a wave of electricity, going through and through me. Indeed, it seemed to come in waves and waves of liquid love; for I could not express it in any other way. It seemed like the very breath of God.[3]

From the very beginning hours of the Outpouring to the final day, worshipers drank deeply of the "liquid love" of God! At the very core of our repeating the term *outpouring* was this essential characteristic: God himself was pouring out his love and pouring out his Holy Spirit, because to experience the Holy Spirit of God is to encounter love (Gal. 5:22–23). The very breath of God filled thousands and thousands with a love that infused hope, inspired healing, compelled joyful worship, and instilled peace!

By the second or third day, the gathering included more than college students; it included dozens of Asbury alumni, close friends of the university who were always investing in and praying for our students, and members of many local churches that are relationally connected to the university and pray for our campus. Asbury alumni are highly invested in their alma mater and would quickly drive hours to join in a movement of God on campus. Dr. John Musick was one of those friends, and he shared an image with me, a vision of what he saw God doing. The vision involved a vase, which was being held by God. Prayers were going into this vase—prayers that people had been placing into the vase for years and years, prayers that represented cries to God. The Lord was holding this vase over Hughes Auditorium, over this gathering of worshipers, and the hand of God was pouring out the vase over the gathering. Others shared visions almost identical to this description. The emptying vase over Hughes represented decades of prayers being answered: God was responding to the cries of his people. While many of us go days and weeks without recognizing the work of God answering a prayer, the Outpouring was infused with accelerated answers to prayer, an intensification of God responding to his people.

3. K. Alan Snyder, "Waves and Waves of Liquid Love: Charles Finney's Conversion Experience," *Pondering Principles . . .* (blog), April 28, 2013, https://ponderingprinciples.com/2013/04/28/waves-waves-of-liquid-love-charles-finneys-conversion-experience/.

While the tabernacled presence of God created a sense of immediate answers to prayer, the vision of the emptying vase also signified the Lord's response to prayers that were months and years old. The goodness of God overflowed. Many came to Hughes to taste of this goodness, as though they had been waiting for years and years for God to reveal himself in this manner. Others came as if their hope was being restored, as if they had reached the end of tarrying and waiting, and the sweetness of Jesus's timing recaptured their affections. The nature of renewal, awakening, and revival provides something greater than a "reset" for his people. The move of his Spirit restores hope, deepens faith, and expands believers' experience with the love of God—"waves and waves of liquid love" refreshing the body of Christ for worship and mission. As God poured out a vase of answered prayers during those days in February, it was as if he were declaring his name like he once did to Moses: "The Lord, the Lord, the compassionate and gracious God, slow to anger, abounding in love and faithfulness, maintaining love to thousands, and forgiving wickedness, rebellion and sin" (Exod. 34:6–7a).

Immediate Fruit of Outpouring: Salvation, Confession, Repentance, and Reconciliation

In our rhythm of worship through song, Scripture, testimonies, prayer, and preaching/teaching, multiple invitations were interwoven in each movement. The second night etched a vivid image in my mind as Zach invited any students who did not know Jesus to give their hearts to him. The eight or ten who responded then came to the front to kneel at the altar. I had a very clear vantage point, looking down from the altar at the students who responded, and I witnessed a huddle of praying students around every single new believer! First, I moved closer to join one circle of students around Seth as he knelt to recommit his life to Jesus. The group of students around Seth had become his friends over the last six months of school. They did life with him—living in the residence hall, going to class, eating together in the dining hall, immersed in the college journey. I still weep remembering the ecstatic joy as they knelt beside their friend, praying for him, exemplifying the most holy huddle I could witness. Caleb and Emma Grace were next to Seth, and it's hard to know anyone who could be more thrilled about a friend's spiritual transformation than Caleb. Together they exemplified what every new believer hopefully experiences—an intense community of fellow believers passionately devoted to one another for the journey of discipleship. About ten of these huddles of love existed from one side of the altar to the other. An outpouring of salvation and rededication was beginning. As soon as the new believers and recommitments had concluded a corporate prayer committing themselves to the lordship of Jesus, they were asked to stand. The roar of celebration in the auditorium was a sound that pushed against the gates of hell. The Lion of Judah was exalted as King!

Alongside the salvations occurring in the first three days was a strong movement of confession. In the plethora of confessions taking place, we began to see dozens and dozens experiencing freedom from addictions. As a campus pastor, I pray with many students confessing addictions to pornography across the course of a school year, but each day of the Outpouring held more confessions than a year of college ministry. The enthroned presence of Jesus compelled worshipers to be clean, removing anything between them and the manifest presence of God. Young people came forward with authentic honesty and contrite hearts, confessing to the trappings of pornography, alcohol, and other addictions. They came repentant and had an immediate hunger for purity, to be set free, to be filled with the Spirit's power, and to no longer fall to temptation. Men and women coming to the altar were longing for consecration, longing to be filled with holy love for a sustained journey of discipleship and allegiance to Jesus as King!

Confessions also centered around reconciliation. The same compelling draw for seekers to have nothing between them and the Spirit of Jesus brought deep contrition for any discord in relationships. A longing to be right with one another saturated the Outpouring. In the afternoon of the first day, a staff member came and asked for prayer. After praying together, they had a clear direction of who they needed to go see to begin reconciling a relationship. As they walked away, my heart sensed a nudge from the Holy Spirit, drawing my attention to a relationship where I was holding bitterness and envy. Within moments I was standing with the person to whom I needed to confess. The gentle presence of Jesus had both of us longing for reconciliation, making horizontal relationships with one another right so that Jesus would continue having his way that day. The Holy Spirit was unifying his body by restoring relationships, and this was a beautiful gift to our campus, to families attending the Outpouring, to marriages, to friendships, and to churches that found themselves drawn into reconciliation.

Everything that happened in the first three days increased exponentially across the next two weeks. What began as a lingering of students and a hungering within Generation Z mushroomed into a lingering of thousands—a transdenominational gathering of tens of thousands of women and men from around the country and around the world collectively worshiping with a "hunger and thirst for righteousness." The words of 2 Chronicles 16:9 resonated over and over across the Outpouring: "The eyes of the Lord search the whole earth in order to strengthen those whose hearts are fully committed to Him."

Healing after a Pandemic

If the "waves of this liquid love" flowed across periods of time, the first wave of outpouring most distinctly covered the last three years for Generation Z. March 2020 is forever ingrained in our minds as the beginning of the global pandemic of our era. On March 13, 2020, Asbury students departed for a two-week spring break—and later learned that they would be unable to return for the rest of the semester as the pandemic quickly altered school, work, family life, and social life for every sector of the population around the world. Asbury's freshman class that year—the Surrendered Class—were seniors in February 2023 when the Outpouring occurred. All four classes on campus lived through the pandemic as teenagers and experienced loss on various levels because of the COVID-19 crisis.

The sociological and psychological impact of COVID-19 was arguably the hardest on Generation Z, creating intense challenges during their formative years. The Outpouring fruit of healing from anxiety, depression, and suicidal ideation felt like healing from the pandemic. Over and over, we cited the promise of God in Joel 2: "Be glad, people of Zion, rejoice in the Lord your God, for he has given you the autumn rains because he is faithful. . . . I will repay you for the years the locusts have eaten" (Joel 2:23a, 25a). From early in the pandemic, I often heard faculty say, "We are going to see the detrimental effects of this isolation for years to come." The gracious, gracious outpouring of the Spirit of God in February 2023 accelerated the healing and brought redemption to hundreds and literally thousands in Generation Z who suffered through the social isolation of the three years prior. The anxiety and depression that manifested through the pandemic were, in the blink of an eye, countered by overwhelming peace and joy overflowing from the heart of God to a gathering of desperate and hungry worshipers. Because God is faithful, we witnessed him bringing redemption from the months and years the "locusts had stolen"!

Singing Infused with Peace and Joy

Stripped-down, simple music filled with joy dominated the atmosphere across the sixteen days of outpouring. The band often included no more than a guitar, a song leader, and a simple acoustic setup on stage right of Hughes. No flashing lights. Rarely was there electronic amplification, and we did not project lyrics during those sixteen days. Simple worship was Generation Z's new expression of radical humility. The voices of worship leaders were more vulnerable, more authentic, with less production. All the honor and all the praise went to Jesus! Songs like "Waymaker," "Gratitude," "New Wine," "I Speak Jesus," and "Break Every Chain" flooded the atmosphere with celebration.[4] Praise felt like it was going to lift the roof off the auditorium. Joy so distinctly covered the faces of the people in that room that observers described them as heavenly countenances. Most often, we walk through crowds of strangers with a stoic face, and we are cautious where we look. The atmosphere during the Outpouring, however, led people to walk the aisles with joy and engage one another with their eyes, the love of God inhabiting the gathering. Peace, joy, and freedom permeated the room and enveloped every worshiper. Songs like "Yeshua" covered the gathering with holy awe as people sang in gentle whispers, and songs like "Worthy of It All" fixed participants' attention on Jesus as both the conductor and recipient of all the praise. The distinction between earth and heaven was minuscule—seemingly gone. The veil had thinned, and we experienced Jesus enthroned. Healing was taking place, and the anxiety and depression complicated by the pandemic were being swallowed up by peace and joy! The fruit of the Holy Spirit named in Galatians 5:22–23 was palpable and available for the young and old alike, bringing deep soul restoration for thousands of worshipers!

Compelled to Share This Outpouring of the Holy Spirit

Within forty-eight hours, this sudden outpouring of the love of God began manifesting signs of moving outward. This generous presence of his Spirit was not only for the Asbury community. During the first two days, our students laid their hands on the walls of Hughes and prayed: "Lord, send

4. For a discussion of the song choices and their impact on the Outpouring, see Dan Pinkston's chapter in this volume.

this generous outpouring of your love to the world. Send the small flame you have lit in Wilmore to all those in need of light!" The first two expressions of this outward movement involved the collegiate nature of the Outpouring.

First, we started to hear stories of one or two other schools that experienced prolonged chapel services and lingering worship. Second, we began hearing the hearts of college students who were flocking to Hughes on the first and second day—students coming from schools like the University of Kentucky and University of the Cumberlands, as well as schools further away, like Mount Vernon Nazarene (Ohio) and Indiana Wesleyan. Initially, we met small groups of students from various campuses; by the end of the second day, the size of the groups increased, and the number of campuses multiplied. Thursday night as we interacted with visiting university students, they asked for prayer as they prepared to leave. With palpable excitement and zeal, they asked us to pray over them, that God would use them as sparks of revival in their own collegiate ministries and across their campuses. We asked those who were preparing to travel back to their campuses to come to the front to receive prayer from leaders and the entire body. Students left with new passion, deeply burdened for their campuses. Paul's words from 2 Corinthians 5:20 began shaping another element of this outpouring, the multiplication and spreading of the Good News: "So we are Christ's ambassadors; God is making his appeal through us." During the first week, these "commissioning prayers" over visiting university students were a beautiful and exciting element of the late-night worship. In the end, students from more than 280 different colleges and universities traveled to Wilmore to participate in the Outpouring and went back home with a fresh touch of the Holy Spirit.

A third sign of this outward movement began emerging on Saturday, the fourth day. I stood next to a worship pastor from the nearby community of Versailles. He asked if a student could come and share about the Outpouring during their Sunday worship the next day. I looked up and saw Asher, who had already given his testimony a day or two prior. He was a second-year student, already involved on campus as a student leader, and he was clearly having a transforming encounter with Jesus during the early days of the Outpouring. Asher immediately connected with the worship pastor and went to share the next morning. The following day, I had a conversation with Friederich about sharing a testimony with a group of college students at the University of the Cumberlands. Friederich was a business major who was volunteering as a Spiritual Life Assistant during the 2022–23 school year. He began recruiting friends, and on day six of the Outpouring they traveled the two hours to give witness to another campus of how the Holy Spirit was at work at Asbury. Before the Outpouring was even a week old, we were receiving numerous appeals from schools and churches from around the country requesting witness teams. By the end of February, we received seventy-five invitations for students to share their Outpouring experiences. We were blessed by these requests and wanted to honor what God was doing. Unwilling to keep this experience to themselves, students were ready to go with enthusiasm—to jump in a car or board a plane to go and give witness to the mighty move of God they had encountered.[5]

Peace, Humility, and Heaven

Believers searching for an authentic expression of peace and humility migrated to "the outpouring town," increasing the number of people in Wilmore to two and half times its size on day eleven of the Outpouring. Seekers were desperate for an authentic encounter with the peaceful presence of God in the midst of a divided society and a violent world. On a macro level, the Outpouring was a "burning bush moment," with thousands enraptured by the bush burning like a bonfire, and they were drawn to step close and hear what the Lord was saying. Unbelievers were saying yes to Jesus by the hundreds. Believers were kneeling for fresh consecration—to be filled with the Holy Spirit, to live as people of peace and humility in a world ripe for the Church of Jesus Christ to animate a fresh message of hope. A hungry world is looking for the antidote to violence and division instead of people claiming to be "Christians" while delivering messages of division and hatred. Joan Puls (Sisters of St. Francis) affirms how much peace and humility are needed in a self-indulgent world: "The ability to let go, to abandon oneself in faith and obedience, creates a heart that is docile and humble. . . . Both virtues are fairly absent in our assertive, self-confident, self-indulgent circles. But uncovering their meaning and their message [to twenty-first-century Christians] is crucial for a spirituality of our times."[6] The students who abandoned themselves at the altar of worship in those opening hours—and the fifty thousand plus who let go of daily routines,

5. For more on the witnessing teams sent to tell the story of the Outpouring, see Bridgette Campbell's chapter in this volume.
6. Joan Puls, *Every Bush Is Burning: A Spirituality for Our Times* (Mystic, CT: Twenty-Third Publications, 1985).

commitments, and demands to travel in faith to the Outpouring—were part of a sixteen-day movement that overflowed with peace and humility.

Despite being a university pastor, I cannot claim a deeply developed theology of revival prior to February 8. However, my understanding of heaven is captured by and centered on the redemptive work of Jesus making all things new: "He will wipe every tear from their eyes. There will be no more death or mourning or crying or pain, for the old order of things has passed away. He who was seated on the throne said, 'I am making everything new!'" (Rev. 21:4–5a). As heaven descended into the Outpouring worship, thousands experienced Jesus "making everything new"! This new work was desperately needed—on our campus, in Generation Z, in our culture, in our churches, in our country, and in our world. David Benner's words on prayer might provide another aspect of the nature of God in the special days of February 2023:

> God's presence is grounded not simply in the promises of Scripture but in creation. Creation was not simply an event at a discrete moment in time. When God called the world into being, God established a reality that was absolutely dependent on continuous, sustaining, divine presence. This is why Thomas Aquinas argued that we should never think of creation as an event with a before and after. Creation is ongoing. It is now. It is the unremitting outpouring of the life of God—an outpouring that is essential to sustain all that is.[7]

Both Aquinas and Benner highlight that creation is continuing; it is unfolding because of divine presence. The early days of the Outpouring provided laser focus that God the Creator, Jesus the Redeemer, and the Spirit who refreshes were mightily at work—providing an "unremitting outpouring" that would not leave any generation of humanity without a witness to the love of Jesus Christ. His continuous, divine presence is highlighted in Revelation, when a loud voice from the throne of God declares to John: "It is done. I am the Alpha and the Omega, the Beginning and the End. To the thirsty I will give water without cost from the spring of the water of life" (Rev. 21:6). Here at Asbury University in February 2023, the hungry lingered. The thirsty came. The spring with the water of life flowed. Thanks be to God for "the unremitting outpouring" of his presence flowing to make *all* things new!

7. David Benner, *Opening to God: Lectio Divina and Life as Prayer* (Downers Grove, IL: InterVarsity, 2010), 66.

CHAPTER THREE

WHEN THE WORLD COMES TO WILMORE

Sarah Thomas Baldwin
Vice president of Student Life, Asbury University

Christine Endicott
Director of Conference Services, Asbury University

Madeline Black
Assistant director, World Gospel Mission Student Center at Asbury University[1]

The whole town gathered at the door.

—Mark 1:33

Heaven continued to cram into Hughes Auditorium after February 8, 2023. That Saturday, people filled every seat, and others stood two or three deep in the aisles. Across the front of the auditorium, young adults sat cross-legged in rows while they worshiped and prayed, hands uplifted, faces open in praise. Worship had continued nonstop since Wednesday, first with our students and professors, then with students from Asbury Seminary and the surrounding region.

That night, people spilled out the entrances and squeezed into lobbies to experience the presence of Jesus. As the crowd worshiped, prayed,

1. At the time of the Outpouring, Madeline Black served as the coordinator of chapel at Asbury University.

took Communion, and responded to Jesus, the singing seemed to connect heaven and earth with the presence of Jesus. Waves of worship washed over us, carrying us, immersing us in the love of God. I stood by the piano with Madeline Black, the coordinator of University Chapel, and watched Christine Endicott, the director of Conference Services, dodge in and out of doorways trying to keep the exits clear, without much success. At that moment, I thought the numbers had crested. What we didn't know was that this beautiful expression of holy worship would scale rapidly, changing our lives and our hearts, and those of thousands of others as well. By the final day of the Outpouring, more than fifty thousand people had descended upon Wilmore, many willing to stand in line in the cold for more than nine hours. They worshiped on the lawn and in other sanctuaries in Wilmore, all desiring to experience the power and the presence of Jesus. Over sixteen days, one holy *yes* after another, God poured out love on Gen Z and beyond, reaching around the world and back, with the wooden altar of Hughes serving as the focal point for surrender to Jesus Christ. Madeline, Christine, and I, among many others, provided scaffolding to equip the uninvited-but-welcome guests to experience the overwhelming flood of the love of God.

Three waves of the Outpouring developed. The first wave included our own students and then other college students. The second wave developed as the Outpouring became a national and then international event. The third wave restored the priority of Gen Z in the services and moved to a livestream format. Finally, after much discernment and prayer—and the reality of depleting city, community, and university resources—we released the Outpouring into the world by the power of God on February 23, 2023, with the Collegiate Day of Prayer as the benediction.

Two questions arose again and again in our hearts in those days. First, "What is God asking of us?" and then, "Are we willing to give it?" Sixteen days may be just over two weeks on a calendar, but the spiritual examen from these days had eternal spiritual significance for participants, volunteers, and worship stewards alike. Daily, even minute by minute, we had the profound gift and challenge to discern what God asked and then determine how to respond. Both questions prompted deep spiritual awakening, holy awareness, and transformative growth. We continue to wrestle with what God asked, what we had and did not have to give, and how the Holy Spirit empowered us to say yes as individuals and as a community.

Over the days, several themes emerged as the movement of God grew: step-by-step obedience, generous giving, sacrificial service, Christ-centered worship, consecrated stewardship, and radical humility. These principles provided important scaffolding to help us steward this spontaneous and extravagant gift of God.

Step-by-Step Obedience

> If you keep my commands, you will remain in my love, just as I have kept my Father's commands and remain in his love.
>
> —John 15:10

The very first evening, a few members of the president's cabinet and others stood in a circle in the basement of Hughes Auditorium, listening to the music wafting down from above. The composite photographs of the graduated classes of the university graced the walls of the hallways and the lobby area where we stood, silently reminding us of how God had moved in Hughes Auditorium in previous years. We pondered how our students responded to the Holy Spirit upstairs with open hearts and faces turned to heaven and one another. Just three years earlier, we had celebrated the fiftieth anniversary of the 1970 Revival, which also stirred spontaneously in Hughes Auditorium. With holy imagination sparked in our minds and hearts for a spontaneous movement of God, we wondered if this was what our students were experiencing upstairs. In these early hours of what would become a 380+ hour marathon of ministry and worship, the Holy Spirit invited us to say the first of thousands of yeses: Yes, we would leave Hughes open overnight, allowing the students to linger in worship. It was not a hard decision to make. It felt like, "Of course." Of course we would leave Hughes open. Of course we would find a way to staff it. Of course we would support our students as they experienced this fresh outpouring of the love of Jesus upon them.

From that point forward, the posture toward the Outpouring was *yes*.

Radical and simple yeses came from every side.

Yes, faculty members would become ushers and altar ministers.

Yes, the facilities team would support the needs of an almost one-hundred-year-old building for sixteen days, plus take care of the wear-and-tear around the campus.

Yes, the alumni team would pass out food and blankets and assist with managing the lengthy lines.

Yes, the institutional technology team would do round-the-clock sound and tech for the services.

Yes, Asbury Seminary would help find space in their chapels for the growing numbers.

Yes, volunteers from the community would come to pray, minister, and usher.

If, in a single moment, Jesus had asked us to steward revival services that would bring fifty-thousand people and round-the-clock work for sixteen days, we most likely would have said no. But instead, step by step, we said yes to the invitation from the Holy Spirit to join in stewarding the love pouring down upon our students and, eventually, visitors from around the world. The simple, hour-by-hour way of responding and leaning into Jesus became a distinctive characteristic of the Outpouring. Each of us experienced the presence of God and then were given an opportunity to respond.

Generous Giving

> You give them something to eat.
>
> —Luke 9:13

As college students flooded Hughes Auditorium from around the United States, community members from Asbury University, Asbury Theological Seminary, and Wilmore rose up instinctively to offer housing and food. College students arrived even the very first night from other universities. Over the course of sixteen days, we counted guests from more than 280 different universities, seminaries, and colleges. Many students stayed in Hughes for the all-night prayer and worship, but some needed housing for multiple nights. Community members assisted with housing immediately. People generously brought food from the very first day, initially and for the most part without request. Although Asbury never asked for financial resources, people gave, handing money to us in the lines, sometimes writing checks and trying to find someone to whom to give the check. Truly, the people of God gave from what they had.

Christine Endicott, one of the core on-the-ground logistics team leaders, shares details of the housing and food situation.

> *On February 9, a student visiting from another school shared their testimony and mentioned, "God spoke to me as I was sleeping in my car last night . . ." As he finished, someone from the crowd connected with University Pastor Greg Haseloff and offered to house him. In discussing this with his wife, Jen, that evening, they pondered how many other people might find themselves in that position.*

They received a phone call from a connection at Spring Arbor University telling them ten students wanted to come to Wilmore but didn't know where they could stay. Greg and Jen quickly decided to open their home to those ten students from Spring Arbor. Jen posted on Facebook, asking friends to message her if they could host other students who needed overnight accommodations. This elicited fifty-two comments and six shares. In her outreach, she realized that Bethanne Mostad, whose husband oversees Asbury Inn and Suites, had started reaching out to people for housing, since the inn and surrounding hotels were full. The two collaborated in their efforts. Jen, having just learned how to create a QR code the previous week, used this skill to print copies of "I can host" and "I need a place to stay" signs around Hughes Auditorium. A neighbor, without Jen's knowledge, noticed her grocery list stuck to the refrigerator and purchased everything on the list, along with many quick snack items to share with the guests they had coming and going from their home. As Jen filled the needs of others, people stepped in to fill her needs. This was the story of the entire hospitality team. We were all able to help because none of us was doing any part of it alone. God's guidance, the prayers of strangers, and an outpouring of generosity oozed from everyone in a simultaneous overflow of the most incredible kindness and grace imaginable.

Unimaginable were the ways in which the Holy Spirit met the exact needs that Jen saw day after day, request after request. Someone would offer a space for five, and a group of five would request housing. When we are all in tune with the Lord, he can do mighty things that an individual cannot accomplish alone. By Jen's estimate, sixty to seventy people opened their homes, and several hundred pilgrims received free housing.

We also received physical sustenance throughout the Outpouring. On the very first night, twenty pizzas arrived anonymously, and someone named Sandy ordered a bunch of Chick-fil-A sandwiches for the worship team and leaders. Jessica Coppedge stepped in to bring food for the staff and worship leaders for the first three to four days and then started a meal train. Those who were not able to cook or bring food often donated money instead. In one day, $2,900 was donated to the meal train. Instacart deliveries, donations from local churches, and food from area restaurants were among the delectables we devoured and appreciated.

A notable rise in energy occurred when homemade feasts were delivered. We all still marvel at the size of one particular pot of ethnic deliciousness. The base of it must have been twelve-to-eighteen inches wide. We all marveled at how you would even get such a pot on a stovetop. The aroma drew the security personnel in quicker than usual, and we all enjoyed the renewal such sustenance provided. Just as the souls in Hughes were being renewed and filled, the bodies were renewed and filled in an adjacent classroom, which became a community gathering space.

In the first couple of days, Barb Boyle, manager of the Windsor Manor Guesthouse, brought tables into the room set aside for the staff food to be served, and then Joe Bruner, assistant vice president of Student Life, set up tables in the back lobby of Hughes to bring in water bottles and packaged snacks for the students who were not leaving. He made many runs to Sam's Club in his red pickup truck. People would walk in with their arms full of boxes of snacks and cases of water. "Where did this come from?" someone inquired. "It was in the red truck." As other obligations took Joe away, and our need for more people to be hands-on increased at Hughes, our snack supply ran low. My radio buzzed: "We are almost out of snacks in the lobby." "Just keep giving them water for now," I replied. By the time I had clipped the radio back on my waistband, two women walked in with boxes of food and stated, "We thought you could use some snacks." A volunteer from Southeast Christian Church in Louisville had heard the conversation and texted his church community to stop at Costco and Sam's Club on their way to Wilmore to bring more food and water. All afternoon the supplies poured in. People packed their cars and vans to the gills with supplies, and someone even brought a U-Haul truck! God continued to provide every need before we could ask. Unexplainable cohesion and continuity.

Sacrificial Service

My command is this: love each other as I have loved you.

—John 15:12

As the uninvited-but-welcome guests continued to arrive, the Outpouring Ground Team developed swiftly. By day seven (February 14, 2023), we began to realize that we may be experiencing a national event as more and more people poured into the tiny two-stoplight town of Wilmore. Working closely with Jessica LaGrone, dean of chapel at Asbury Theological Seminary, we opened worship space in Estes Chapel, the seminary gym, and McKenna Chapel.[2] Next, we worked with Jason Duncan, lead pastor at Great Commission Fellowship, and Nathan Elliott, pastor at Mount Freedom Baptist, to open space at their churches. Each sanctuary had a simulcast from Hughes Auditorium and its own altar ministry team. As the numbers grew, so did the need for volunteers. Incredibly, volunteers showed up, several coming from other states.

2. See Jessica LaGrone's chapter in this volume for more about how the seminary served during the Outpouring.

Other organizations also offered their support. Samaritan's Purse sent us ten security officers to support local law enforcement. The Salvation Army provided portable toilets. A donor provided outdoor propane heaters to warm those waiting in line in the wintry February weather. Local churches sent volunteers to assist with line management and parking. An altar ministry team developed under the capable leadership of Jessica Avery, director of the Awakening Project, and was trained by Bud Simon, a local prayer ministry leader.

Others volunteered countless hours, directing people to open seats, walking the waiting line to offer prayers and encouragement, hauling trash, and most importantly, listening and praying with one another. Professors would show up and say, "I have forty-five minutes between classes. How can I help?" Or, after working a full day or week, staff, faculty, and their families would come in the evenings and weekends to volunteer. The Holy Spirit not only poured out in Hughes. It poured out across the world in goodness, compassion, hope, healing, kindness, and general goodwill for thousands of people who simply offered what they had (time, an open room, musical talent, physical labor, financial assistance) without question. By the end, more than 1,800 people would be counted as part of the volunteer team.

Christine talks about the basics of cleaning the space.

The bathrooms were one of the first areas I began to ponder as I sat in Hughes on that first Saturday. Knowing that our custodial staff typically does not work on the weekend, and having access to the custodial closet, I took it upon myself to check the bathrooms every couple of hours. On one of my trips, I nearly ran into one of our custodians, who then informed me that they already had a plan for continuing to check the bathrooms.

As the crowds increased in the coming days, the hospitality team shared this responsibility with the custodial staff. One group took the even hour, and one group took the odd hour. There was only one time in all the days of checking bathrooms that I found a stall with no toilet paper. This includes the multiple portable toilets we had outside. At the peak of the event, however, Hughes was not the only location where things were pouring out. It was common for me to get a radio shout-out: "The porta-potty is overflowing!" All we could do in response was mark it as closed. The owner came to campus, sucked out all the waste, drove directly to the dump location, and returned. Before he could get back, other toilets had overflowed. He could not keep up. "Pray for the toilets" was said on more than one occasion as we navigated the continuous crowds.

I admit, I ended up doing very little in the cleaning of Hughes. The first night that we closed for overnight hours, I made a plan for cleaning early the next morning—only to arrive and discover that our human resources department and controller's office had already gone through and wiped every seat and mopped all the floors. Another morning, people from Asbury Seminary (across the street) had arrived and were assisting with the cleaning. One of the most precious gifts was from Joanna Coppedge and her five children. They came every morning around 7:00 a.m. to clean the headquarters room. Staff were so busy, it was common to get a plate of food and then be called away never to return. The family cleaned up these plates, dirty desktops, strewn coats, missing gloves, random notebooks and pens, wrappers from stale and unfinished snacks, and terribly messy floors. Every day we walked into a crisp environment with encouraging scripture verses written on our whiteboard. What an incredible gift of time! Once again, the hospitality continued to pour forth, and even the needs we did not know existed were being resolved.

Working on logistics during the Outpouring was like having a giant puzzle in front of me with no picture to guide me. Every time I needed to place the next piece, God handed it to me. As long as I kept looking to him, he provided every piece I needed so that in the end our teams had created a beautiful masterpiece that God had designed and orchestrated! May we all stay in tune with him so that when he needs our piece, it is not missing.

Christ-Centered Worship

> Yet a time is coming and has now come when the true worshipers will worship the Father in the Spirit and in truth, for they are the kind of worshipers the Father seeks. God is spirit, and his worshipers must worship in the Spirit and in truth.
>
> —John 4:23–24

From the very first hours of the Outpouring, the love of God flowed into Hughes—and around the world—through musical worship.[3] The worship centered on Jesus, not on human leadership. The space between the old-fashioned brass-plated lettering of "Holiness Unto the Lord" above the stage and the well-used wooden altar below the stage became a catalyst of praise

3. For more discussion of the structure of worship and the significance of the music used during the Outpouring, see the chapter by Dan Pinkston in this volume.

and prayer. The worship in song, the preaching, and the ministry leadership became the fruit of the interchange between heaven and human expression.

The musicians and worship leaders were almost entirely Generation Z. Emerging and young adults not only led us to the altar first, but they also led us into the heart of Jesus through their testimonies and singing. In addition, a significant feature of the worship was the multiethnic leadership.

Madeline Black and her husband, Ben, stewarded the worship throughout these days. Hour by hour, Madeline and Ben organized worship teams, oriented them to the manner of the Outpouring, prepared them in prayer, and created space for the Holy Spirit to set them apart for God's use.

In her own words, Madeline shares the experience of stewarding the worship teams as the Outpouring grew.

> *On February 8, 2023, I was coordinating Asbury's chapel, and my husband, Benjamin, was directing the Gospel Choir. By God's grace, Ben and I had the privilege of helping coordinate the team of worship leaders. Every person who served with us can attest that we all were both the objects and agents of God's mission. Here are a few lessons God taught us during those days.*
>
> *First, we didn't have a grand strategic plan. The worship stewards team shifted over the course of the Outpouring. Leaders came and went as they felt led, and God always provided in his timing. The Spirit built the structure. At first, I gathered together with Benjamin and a student to listen to the Spirit to see who God was highlighting to lead worship next. The process grew from there. We watched, prayed, listened, and did what God said. The scaffolding that supported God's work started quite organically and then built up over time. The clarity of the voice of the Lord was unparalleled.*
>
> *That might sound strange. Let me try to explain. I grew up playing basketball—practicing layups, free throws, running . . . you get the picture. Then, when it came to the game, you didn't need to think about how to pivot; it was instinctual at that point because practice ingrained it in your muscle memory. For years, we followers of Jesus get to know God by reading his word, praying, and doing life in community. All metaphors fall short, but essentially, following the Lord becomes ingrained in our habits. Then when anxiety rises because of the weightiness of the responsibility, God's Spirit reminds us that God keeps in perfect peace the one whose mind is stayed on him (Isa. 26:3).*
>
> *During this process, we clung to an important value: no independent decisions. Instead, we sought consensus. As we paused for discernment, God brought about unity and blessing. We knew apart from him we could do nothing. When we needed a singer or guitar player, we prayed and asked God for what we needed,*

and soon God would direct members of the worship stewarding team to someone in the room. Nine times out of ten, the person could meet the specific need we'd lifted. We experienced future worship leaders so content in God's presence and in a posture of such great humility that they were happy to serve and unoffended if they didn't. Every couple hours, Jesus brought together multiethnic teams of people who had never met each other to lead worship and give him all the glory. This happened 24/7 for sixteen days. Only Jesus could provide like that.

The worship stewards, like the bands, were from various ethnicities. We had people who were Black, Haitian, White, Latino, and TCKs (people who grew up outside their parents' home country) all leading together. I'm not going to sugarcoat anything—there were challenges! Each ethnic group brings gifts from God, and we had the opportunity to hold those giftings in tandem. One tension arose as we discussed the balance between structure and spontaneity or being "spirit-led." (Some of us noted that the Holy Spirit can also lead by means of structure!) A solution arose when leaders worked together to create a "song template" with music from across a variety of worship streams (gospel, contemporary Christian music, hymns, and other languages) to serve the bands. This helped the bands to better lead songs they might not have been able to come up with spontaneously—and ensured the inclusion of music that was meaningful to a wider variety of people in the room.

Sometimes as a group, we would get too structured. Then a team member—often a Black member—would humbly point this out; the group listened and readjusted to provide a more balanced approach. It takes a lot of security in covenant love to gently say hard things, as well as to receive feedback, not become defensive, and grow from it. I feel so proud of our team for doing this well, by God's grace. Throughout the process of bringing on new members and sending out those who'd served, a culture and system emerged. Our core values were "ethnic unity and radical humility." These values were forged not that February but in the preceding years in beautiful and personal places in the hearts of those privileged to help steward. It's encouraging because the lessons we learn with the Lord in hidden and painful places often become blessings we never would have imagined. God redeems and uses the strangest things for his glory. These were some of the key values of the worship stewards. Because of this, we didn't allow well-known people to lead, not because they wouldn't be wonderful, but on the off chance that celebrity status would distract from God's glory. In all of this, we looked to Jesus and asked him to help us follow.

Consecrated Stewardship

> You are already clean because of the word I have spoken to you. Remain in me, as I also remain in you. No branch can bear fruit by itself; it must remain in the vine. Neither can you bear fruit unless you remain in me.
>
> —John 15:3–4

At Asbury, we hold the movement of "Belong, Become, and Be Set Apart" as the process of building community but also as the journey of sanctification. Our goal is to become more like Jesus and be set apart for God for his purpose. Spiritual growth flourishes in the intersection of simple service and deep adoration of God. In Wesleyan theology and the Holiness tradition, we call the process of being consecrated to God *sanctification*. Sanctification is the journey of becoming more like Jesus both instantly and over time. When we surrender all to Jesus, it is a magnificent exchange—all of Jesus for all of us. It is our heart and soul hidden in God, fully belonging to God. At the moment of surrender, all of Jesus is available to us for all of eternity. As we become more and more filled with Jesus, our whole being becomes immersed in the holiness of God. The more of God in us, the less we sin. Consecration is being sanctified by Jesus for a holy purpose.

During the Outpouring, we established a consecration room so that each worship leader, musician, and steward would be filled, purified, and set apart for service. What happened in the consecration room fueled the whole Outpouring; it became the furnace of God.

Madeline shares about the development of the consecration room.

> *Jesus showed us what consecration means. He regularly separated himself from the crowds to pray (e.g., Luke 6:12). Following this example, we learned to empty ourselves before Jesus and ask him to fill us with his Spirit. We made room to lay down the sin, weight, pride, and fear that so easily entangle us and asked the Spirit to fill us with his life. God ministered to us before we ever ministered to him or the room. We took seriously the verse engraved on the cornerstone of Hughes: "Without holiness no one will see the Lord" (Heb. 12:14). We don't become holy or sanctified by working hard, but just like salvation, holiness is a gift of God. He touches our lips, and we are made clean (Isa. 6:6–7). We are clean because of the word Jesus has spoken. As for myself, there were moments where I experienced God "pull back the curtain" and allow me to get a glimpse of*

his holiness. I couldn't stand; I fell to the ground in love, in reverent fear, in the complete assurance that I was loved.

As we worship stewards sought to listen to and follow Jesus, a dear brother—a freshman student—asked me if we could set aside a room where the lead worshipers could have some tea and pray in a space that wasn't too crowded. Quickly he, a Brazilian friend of mine, my friend's wife, and a South Korean woman began to steward this space. They prayed over the worship leaders whom God's Spirit had highlighted to lead worship next. This space was created on the fourth day.

Radical Humility

From the first day, a core ministry team came together that included a mix of the president's cabinet,[4] the speaker of the day, and a theologian connected to Seedbed—a ministry offshoot of Asbury Theological Seminary. We reacted to two layers of reality: the awareness of the awe and wonder of the presence of God and the reality of the pressure of a rapidly scaling revival. While God moved in Hughes and in the other growing worship venues in Wilmore—including one on the front lawn of Hughes—we navigated the flow of ministry hour by hour.

Our core team committed to stewarding the movement of God as reflected in the practices of those first hours of the Outpouring: simple singing, confession, testimonies, Scripture reading, brief preaching, and teaching on the love of God, salvation, and full surrender. We followed these markers carefully, committed to following the Holy Spirit as our guide. We were also careful not to release leadership to any person or organization that wanted to claim the Outpouring as their own or take the worship in a different direction.

While the majority of our team experienced a high level of trust forged from several years of serving together, we did not all know one another, nor had this team ever served together or discerned anything together as a whole. We called this newly forged team a "lifeboat," thrown together in the river of God over the first few days, with membership drawn from Asbury University leaders, those present in Hughes in the earliest hours,

4. The president's cabinet includes the provost and chief academic officer (Dr. Sherry Powers), the vice president of Enrollment and Marketing (Jennifer McChord), the vice president for Institutional Advancement (Dr. Mark Troyer), vice president for Student Life (Rev. Dr. Sarah Baldwin), vice president for Business Affairs (Glen Hamilton), and vice president for Intercollegiate Athletics and University Strategic Communications (Mark Whitworth).

and those with whom we had prior relationships. The core ministry team started meeting every couple of hours, discerning the movement of God as we went. At first we met in a storage closet behind Hughes, sitting knee to knee in a tight circle with a dry-erase board. Over the next few days, we moved to a larger conference room, and our team grew as more members of Seedbed joined in support.

We set aside university hierarchy as much as we could and sought to truly follow the presence of God without an organizational chart. We shared a raw awareness of the presence of God upon us, leading us and guiding us. When the Israelites left Egypt, God did not give them a map, or in modern language, a GPS. But instead, God gave them his presence. In a similar way, we did not have a map, but we leaned in together to follow Jesus. We did, however, have a blueprint. Paul's words in Philippians 2:2–8 became our pattern for leadership:

> Make my joy complete by being like-minded, having the same love, being one in spirit and of one mind. Do nothing out of selfish ambition or vain conceit. Rather, in humility value others above yourselves, not looking to your own interests but each of you to the interests of the others.
>
> In your relationships with one another, have the same mindset as Christ Jesus:
>
> > Who, being in very nature God, did not consider equality with God something to be used to his own advantage;
> > rather, he made himself nothing
> > by taking the very nature of a servant,
> > being made in human likeness.
> > And being found in appearance as a man,
> > he humbled himself
> > by becoming obedient to death—
> > even death on a cross!

We took seriously the call to put the interest of others above our own and steward this movement in a posture of surrender to God first and then to one another. While this may seem like a lofty spiritual goal that emerged out of much preparation and reflection, it really came forth out of necessity because it was all we had. While we had a holy imagination for how God had worked in the past and could work today, and we knew theologically that the way of surrender and sacrifice is at the core of Christian leadership, what was in front of us was hour-to-hour decision-making with a group of people who had never before served together as a ministry team. We had to listen to God together in real time and under pressure. We could not function any other way. Too much was at stake to lose time or trust.

Themes of sacrificial servanthood, radical humility, and partnership emerged as we strove to be set apart as consecrated ministry stewards. We took on the term *unoffendable* as a way of being in relationship as a team. We worked to listen to God together without a fragile sense of ego or being quick to take offense. Short accounts, in-the-moment forgiveness, and gentle care for one another shaped our identity as a team. We raised hands to be sure that everyone had time to speak and was fully heard. We cofacilitated the group with male and female partnership. We deferred to one another in decision-making. Trust was imperative. Radical humility was required in order to stand under the weight of the outpouring of God.

What Is God Asking of Us?

In those days, the world showed up at our door. People from more than 13 countries, 30 states, and 280 colleges and universities flew, drove, walked, and waited to kneel at the altar, raise hands in worship, pray without ceasing, and experience the profound love of Jesus. God asked us—invited us—to give all we had. I wonder what God is asking of me today. What simple step-by-step obedience am I being invited into with great love?

Are We Willing to Give It?

One of the true miracles of the time was the way that people gave without coercion or arm-twisting. Jesus showed up among us, and the whole community wanted to respond. God pressed us gently, but firmly, to give of our time, energy, and resources; the peace and joy in the obedient "yes" was more than we could have imagined. Certainly, yielding to God was not easy. We grew physically exhausted and spiritually stretched, yet it was the most "of course" thing we could have done. The Spirit of God even today consistently presses us to fulfill his purpose for us, and our peace is found in obedience to his call. Will you give what God is asking? May we continue to say yes to God in the big and small ways.

YES.

CHAPTER FOUR

THE MULTICULTURAL, MULTIETHNIC, AND MULTINATIONAL ASPECTS OF THE ASBURY OUTPOURING

Juan A. Gonzalez
Coordinator of Intercultural Life, Asbury University

In February 2023, Asbury University received a new blessing in the historic visitation from God to our campus. This chapter will highlight the multicultural, multiethnic diversity of the university and the multinational aspects of the Outpouring, including the impact this event had on people from different racial groups in the United States and in many nations of the world. For several years, we have been telling our students "Start here, impact the world"; little did we know how God would impact the world through the outpouring of his Spirit.

An Ethos of Diversity on Campus

Why is it relevant to address diversity in this narrative of the Outpouring? For one, Asbury's Christian identity connects it to the larger church and God's intentions for the community of believers. Scripture exhorts us to become one, as described in one of Jesus's prayers, "that all of them may be one, Father, just as you are in me and I am in you. May they also be in us so that the world may believe that you have sent me" (John 17:21). Jesus's prayer implies diversity in unity. Latasha Morrison describes this multiethnic ethos: "People of all ethnicities are coming together . . . [in] a spirit of multiethnic unity."[1] This is how we experienced the Outpouring!

1. Latasha Morrison, *Be the Bridge: Pursuing God's Heart for Racial Reconciliation* (Colorado Springs, CO: Waterbrook, 2019), 8–9.

It did not matter where people came from or what their color, race, or denomination was. They were here to worship Jesus, in the same manner and with the same heart as the Asbury community.

This chapter cannot address every single aspect of diversity, but it will begin unfolding the importance of the subject, beginning with its simple and "truest definition as the presence of difference."[2] We will view the Outpouring and the presence of diversity through multicultural, multiethnic, and multinational lenses.

Racial/ethnic diversity on campus has been growing in recent years. Such diversity is due to having local and national students from minority groups such as African Americans, Native Americans, Asian Americans, and Hispanic Americans. We are also blessed with international students from five different continents representing almost forty different nations. Asbury is a tapestry of colors, cultures, and ethnicities that continues to grow. It is not random to celebrate the cultures of the world in the activities of our campus. We can hear in our hallways conversations held in different languages, including Spanish, French, Mandarin, and Korean. Our programs intentionally promote not only multicultural activities (i.e., observing distinct cultures) but the intercultural *interaction* of our community. It is a diversity that is organic but also, as it should be in any Christian and academic institution, an intentional diversity in which the greatness of God can be manifested as we experience the inclusion and representation of different ethnicities from within and from outside the country.

How should a Christian community be composed? It is our biblical understanding that God sees beyond race and color, beyond culture and language. It is through this rich diversity of sizes and shapes, textures and features that our God expresses his creativity, since all of humanity has been created in "His own image" (Gen. 1:27). God also delighted in creating humanity as a tapestry that—seen through his eyes—is beautiful and magnificent. It is through this understanding that our multicultural and intercultural efforts are directed. It calls to mind questions such as, "How can we move from being multicultural to become an intercultural community in which every member becomes part of a cohesive reality?" Multiculturalism is good, but we should ask whether multicultural awareness is enough for the Christian church and its Christian academic institutions. Multicultural programming in institutions

2. Michelle R. Loyd-Paige and Michelle D. Williams, *Diversity Playbook: Recommendations and Guidance for Christian Organizations* (Abilene, TX: Abilene Christian University Press, 2021), 29.

often falls short of God's goals for humanity. Interculturalism, on the other hand, promotes interaction between people from different cultures; it seeks unity and sees every individual as part of the group/community. A natural interculturalism, led by the Holy Spirit, can be seen in many of the videos of the recent Asbury Outpouring. Love, grace, and redemption crossing cultural boundaries is what the gospel is about.

Diversity is intentional in universities and academic institutions, especially in institutions with a Christian background. Christian academic institutions are not without fault in lacking diversity or failing to be supportive of their multicultural members; nevertheless, we experience a constant reminder of how God's redeemed community should look on earth and then in heaven. As Loyd-Paige and Williams argue, "Diversity matters to God and if it matters to God, then it should matter to us."[3] We cannot be a good Christian institution if we fail to recognize the value of individuals and the communities those individuals represent.

Multinational Impact

It is not a surprise to us that in a divided and segregated world, God visited a campus that wants to be God's community on earth, welcoming, loving, embracing, and accepting those who come from different ethnic, racial, and cultural backgrounds. Scripture declares that God is God and King of all nations (2 Chron. 20:6; Isa. 52:10; Jer. 10:7) and the God of languages (Isa. 28:11 and 66:18; Acts 2:4, 11). He also made clear that he can bring down the walls of hostility and division (Eph. 2:14; 1 Cor. 1:10) as well as abolish slavery (Exod. 13:14) and injustice (Isa. 30:18) in the nations. His interventions may seem random to us, but God has revealed himself to be a God who acts, who intervenes in human history according to his agenda and not necessarily ours, as revealed in the sending of his Son (Gal. 4:4). Strong reminders of the plans of God for the nations are also found in texts like Genesis 22:18 and Isaiah 52:10, 15 regarding his plan to reach and redeem the nations. Acts 1:8 describes the gospel reaching "to the ends of the earth" through the apostles and the primitive church.

In Revelation 5:9, we find a song that describes the intentional inclusion and diversity of the redeemed church: "You are worthy to take the scroll and to open its seals, because you were slain, and with your blood you purchased for God persons from every tribe and language and people and nation."

3. Loyd-Paige and Williams, 22.

John further emphasizes this diversity in his description of the throne room of God in Revelation 7:9: "After this I looked, and there was a great multitude that no one could count, from every nation, from all tribes and peoples and languages, standing before the throne and before the Lamb, robed in white, with palm branches in their hands." Together they cry out their praise to God. Persons from every tribe, clan, and minority group; those who speak a different language than ours; and those who belong to a people and nation different than ours—those were the ones attracted and invited to gather at Asbury during the Outpouring. By *invitation*, we do not mean a human invitation, a text or a call from our community, but an invitation from God to experience him for the first time or to renew his presence in their lives. And even though manifestations or visitations of God have been present at Asbury in the past, due to the availability of technology, the news of this outpouring spread faster than one could anticipate—not only in this country, but among many nations; not only in English, but in many languages.

God called the attention of our students, staff, and faculty from our daily tasks to make time for him. In the same manner, God called the attention of the nations to Asbury University in order to bring the attention of millions of people to himself.[4] We were surprised by the amount of calls, emails, and visits we received from people of different countries regarding the Outpouring. We received many emails in English but also received emails in different languages such as French, Spanish, and Portuguese. What prompted people from other nations to reach out to an academic institution such as Asbury? Why did people from Europe buy $2,000–3,000 plane tickets, not knowing where they would stay, and pause their life affairs for days just to be at the Outpouring? Why did a family from Latin America sell their car to afford plane tickets to come all the way to Asbury?

By getting to know some of these people and hearing their stories, we were able to see a spiritual hunger and a deep thirst for God. People like them, already in a relationship with God, were willing to come and experience something else—something deeper, greater, needed. They were aware that God is everywhere, but it was as if a sweet voice was calling them to renewal. A couple from Canada shared with us, "We were watching the revival live on our TV back home, and we did not want to leave the living room, because we were afraid we would miss something important.

4. Through the course of the Outpouring, Asbury University had 285 million hits on its various social media platforms.

We needed to come, and that is why we are here now." Testimony after testimony, conversation after conversation, people from around the world decided to come all the way from their countries to Asbury, not because they were seeking something from our institution, but because they were seeking a renewal, a revival, an awakening in their lives.

People from other nations wrote articles and books, made videos and uploaded them to different social platforms, and celebrated the Outpouring in their church services. Asbury's Outpouring became a hopeful event for personal lives and for Christian congregations of different denominations around the world. In the middle of the darkness and the evil humanity faces in every part of the planet, good news is welcomed. What better news to hear than the gospel and the testimonies of God touching people's lives again, healing the sick, forgiving sinners, and restoring the wounded and hurt?

Among the attendees, we had people of all ages singing praises to the Lord Jesus and worshiping God. Young children asked their parents, "Why do we not sing like this at church?" Jesus said of such children, "Let the little children come to me, and do not hinder them, for the kingdom of God belongs to such as these" (Matt. 19:14). Their parents had taken these children to the Master for a blessing. Do we not want the same for our children? Do we not want our churches to be renewed with a new generation of young worshipers?

If we want the best for our children and youth, we should not be surprised when people from other nations want the same. Christian churches from the United States have sent missionaries to other nations and impacted them positively by translating the Bible into different languages and sharing the gospel of Jesus Christ. Still today, Christian churches in other nations look up to American churches as models for worship and for theological and ministerial instruction. Many nations do not have Christian universities, so it caught the attention of believers in other nations when they received news of God touching the lives of our college students.

Outpouring at a University Campus Instead of at a Church

It is curious that God decided to pour out his Spirit on a university campus rather than in a church or at a camp meeting focused on revival. We do not know all the answers, but some aspects of our regular practices offer an invitation for the manifestations of God within our community.

At our Christian university, staff and professors sign contracts with the understanding that moral aspects based on biblical orthodoxy must be followed. The faculty manual, for example, states, "Asbury University is committed to Christian higher education and to its expectation that faculty, administrators and staff will be intentional in growing in Christian maturity and encouraging spiritual development in students through personal example. Faculty should demonstrate by work and example their commitment to Jesus Christ in their personal and professional lives."[5] Christlike behavior is encouraged (such as demonstrating the fruit of the Spirit found in Gal. 5:22–23), and sinful acts (such as idolatry, sexual immorality, drunkenness, pornography, theft, etc.) are prohibited.[6]

The commitment goes beyond signing a job contract, because many of the employees at Asbury see their job as a calling to serve God and his community. We are a community that's not just committed to working during office hours but willing to go the extra mile for the glory of God and to benefit the students and other members of our community. Together we seek the prosperity of the community, transforming lives and impacting young people year after year.

Why might an outpouring be more difficult to manage in a local church? Christian churches have committed staff and members, but most of them do not have a team of more than five hundred employees working over forty hours per week. Even large congregations struggle to find teams of people to organize and sustain an unplanned event such as the one celebrated at Asbury University.

Could it be that the presence of racism in some churches may be another factor in God choosing to pour out his Spirit on a university campus instead? As Martin Luther King Jr. famously said, eleven o'clock on Sunday morning is one of the most segregated hours in Christian America.[7] On our Christian campus, however, we intentionally celebrate the multicultural diversity of our students and staff. We already are a diverse community with leaders who come from different Christian traditions, cultures, countries, socioeconomic statuses, and educational backgrounds. A Christian university such

5. Asbury University Faculty Manual, section 400.3.1.4.
6. See Faculty Manual, section 600.
7. Martin Luther King Jr., "Address Delivered at Albany Movement Mass Meeting at Shiloh Baptist Church," Martin Luther King, Jr. Research and Education Institute, Stanford, August 15, 1962, https://kinginstitute.stanford.edu/king-papers/documents/address-delivered-albany-movement-mass-meeting-shiloh-baptist-church.

as Asbury provides a place where diverse conversations, including those about spirituality, can be held respectfully and regularly. Even though the university was founded in the Wesleyan Holiness tradition, most of the conversation and preaching in our chapel focuses on biblical truths rather than the promotion of a particular denominational or theological view. In academic institutions, we become experts on diversity and have the opportunity to exercise our knowledge on a daily basis. Many of our Christian congregations may not have that challenge or opportunity. The Christian university thus naturally provides a welcoming space for all the members of God's Kingdom who might draw near to experience the movement of the Holy Spirit.

It is interesting to note that several people came to our university campus and were expecting our university staff to structure the Outpouring like a church service. Some visitors expected to see a series of sermons as well as elaborate musical programs and worship. Some of us had to remind our visitors, "We are not a church; we are a Christian academic institution." Although we count among our staff those with ministerial experience (pastors, missionaries, and church leaders), nevertheless, we understood by the guidance of the Lord that we were not going to hold structured services, display our musical abilities, present sermons, collect offerings, or provide baptisms. The Lord Jesus himself through his Holy Spirit was already working in our students, staff, and community. People were reading their Bibles and praying for long periods of time, confessing their sins to God and to one another, crying and sobbing in repentance on their knees, praying for other people at the altar, and staying to worship with little perception of time (some stayed for long hours instead of going home to eat or sleep). God clearly was moving without any need for a structured church service.

Yet the outpouring of God's Spirit spread beyond any single institution. We experienced a time of fellowship with our sister institution across the street, Asbury Theological Seminary, and with many local churches in Wilmore and in the vicinity. Many church leaders and members came to experience the Outpouring and decided to join forces, ministering to groups of people who arrived from all over the country and from different nations around the world. It was the Christian church reaching out to the Lord and serving the masses on a university campus.

The Gospel Choir and the Witnessing Circle

Two events that directly preceded the Outpouring contributed to an inviting atmosphere for the Holy Spirit: the participation in the February 8 chapel of our Gospel Choir and the meeting of the Witnessing Circle the night before the Outpouring. The Gospel Choir was composed of a multicultural (but mostly African American) group of students under the leadership of Benjamin Black. Ben and his wife, Madeline, led our students during the first days of worship at the Outpouring.[8] Their multicultural background helped them to coordinate some of the musical and spiritual aspects of the Outpouring in culturally sensitive ways.[9]

The Witnessing Circle had been on the university's calendar long before any hint of outpouring arose. For the first time, we observed on our campus a ceremony in remembrance of African and African American children, youth, men, and women who sadly were sold as slaves in the vicinity of our campus early in our state's history. Dr. Kevin Brown, president of the university, invited Shea Brown, a friend from our African American community and the director of the Digital Access Project, to come to our campus to remember and mourn the historic circumstances of slavery in this area.[10] Asbury faculty, staff, students, and community members also participated.

The ceremony included a recollection of racial conflict in the area, the reading of historical documents naming those sold into slavery, and the sharing by Witnessing Circle participants about the emotional impact of this history. Conflicting emotions, pain, and words of redemption and freedom were imparted. Music for the event included James Weldon Johnson's "Lift Every Voice and Sing" (the Black National Anthem from 1900). The Witnessing Circle took place on our campus the afternoon before the Outpouring. At the end of the service, some of us were still pondering and asking one another, "What else can we do? How can we share with the rest of the campus about these difficult experiences so we all can be aware of

8. At the time, Ben served as an admissions counselor for Asbury as well as the director of the Gospel Choir. Madeline served as the chapel coordinator.
9. See the chapter by Sarah Thomas Baldwin, Christine Endicott, and Madeline Black in this volume for more insights on culturally sensitive worship.
10. The Digital Access Project expands access to historical records in Fayette County by providing high-quality digital scans of these records. For more information, see "Digital Access Project," University of Kentucky College of Arts and Sciences, The Commonwealth Institute for Black Studies, accessed September 23, 2024, https://cibs.as.uky.edu/digital-access-project.

the freedom we enjoy through Christ?" We left the ceremony with a heavy burden and a contrite heart.

Did empathy, love, repentance, forgiveness, and gratitude in our community help to invite a manifestation of God on our campus? Was God dealing with the social pain—"the experience of pain as a result of interpersonal rejection or loss, such as rejection from a social group, bullying or the loss of a loved one"[11]—of the people of color in our community during this ceremony and during the Outpouring? Was God bringing all this to our attention?

Latasha Morrison notes that "Jesus can make beauty from ashes, but the family of God must first see and acknowledge the ashes."[12] She calls the community of God to a time of repentance and lamenting in order to find hope in God:

> What is the purpose of lament? It allows us to connect with and grieve the reality of our sin and suffering. It draws us to repentant connection with God in that suffering. Lament also serves as an effort to change God's mind, to ask him to turn things around in our favor. Lament seeks God as comforter, healer, restorer and redeemer. Somehow the act of lament reconnects us with God and leads us to hope and redemption.[13]

Before restoration, healing, peace, prosperity, and any other divine blessing come into our lives, God has to deal with the ugliness of sin and address the deepest needs of our souls. As we joined the lament of our African American brothers and sisters, we opened our hearts to the historical pain and suffering that slavery brought to our community. God can do amazing things when his people have contrite hearts and radical humility—these provide an invitation for the presence of God to move among us!

Religious and Doctrinal Diversity

Other interesting aspects arise when we learn about the religious, doctrinal, liturgical, and denominational diversity represented by the people

11. Geoff MacDonald and Lauri A. Jensen-Campbell, eds., *Social Pain: Neuropsychological and Health Implications of Loss and Exclusion* (Washington, DC: American Psychological Association, 2011), 194.
12. Morrison, *Be the Bridge*, 24.
13. Morrison, *Be the Bridge*, 41.

who attended and followed the event. Asbury was founded in the Wesleyan Holiness tradition, with Christian orthopraxy and orthodoxy at the core of its beliefs. John Wesley's insights and doctrinal points of view still echo loudly in our conversations and theological discussions on campus.[14] Nevertheless, it would be a mistake to claim ownership of God and his spiritual manifestations as some people or groups have done in the history of Christianity. In the middle of spiritual cacophony, Jesus, the Good Shepherd, still calls his sheep to him: "I know my sheep and my sheep know me . . . they too will listen to my voice, and there shall be one flock and one shepherd" (John 10:14, 16).

As we revisit the participation of local churches and Christian denominations represented by the attendees and the church leaders who enjoyed the Outpouring, we find a rich diversity of Christians. People attended from Wesleyan-Arminian traditions, such as Methodist, Wesleyan, Church of God, and Anglican churches. Others attended from traditions such as Baptist, Lutheran, and Presbyterian churches. Others came from independent churches. Still others attended from Catholic and Orthodox churches.

Diversity and inclusion are challenges for both academic and religious institutions. Are manifestations of God, such as this outpouring, a way to help and promote diversity, equity, and inclusion among God's people? We are gladly surprised by these opportunities in which people from different nations and ethnic backgrounds come together to worship God, pray for one another, and eagerly interact with other people.

As we continue speaking of diversity in Christian academic institutions—and in churches—we should be reminded that inclusion, love, and intentionality are key terms in the work of those who want to see our society become God's society. This manifestation of God, and the guidance of his Holy Spirit bringing Jesus as the main point of conversation, are clear reminders that God has his own agenda. Any institution, no matter if it is an academic institution, a church, or a government, can be used by God for his glory to impact the people who open their hearts to him as a means to bring change in their surroundings.

As professionals who promote diversity, inclusion, acceptance, and tolerance in our university community, we deal on a regular basis not just with our own preconceived notions and biases but with those dangerous "-isms, divisions, and schisms" that threaten the unity of a multicultural

14. For a Wesleyan interpretation of the events of the Outpouring, see Suzanne Nicholson's chapter in this volume.

community.[15] Historically, the Christian church has been the leader and example of what a spiritual community should look like. Through the Outpouring, God gave the church and our society around the world another opportunity to deal with divisions and walls of separation by calling attention to the life and existence of a small university that at its heart believes that spiritual vitality—a Christian spirituality that embraces diversity—is key to a successful life.

As an academic institution, we wonder about the purposes of God's agenda for the outpouring of his presence among our university community and the attendees of this event. We also wonder about the impact beyond the walls of our institution and how God impacted the nations, not only through social media and technology, but also through the attendance of people who traveled from their own countries to encounter God in our midst. Many Christians around the world claimed this visitation of God to Asbury as their own event.

We had many conversations with our Hispanic/Latino brothers and sisters from around the world regarding the Outpouring. We regularly participate in Jesse Miranda Center's webinars and work in partnership with the NHCLC (National Hispanic Christian Leadership Conference). The Outpouring reached them, as well as other Hispanic/Latino organizations and churches, and they reached out to us. We strengthened our relationship with these groups and met new pastors and organizations around the world through the Outpouring. Phone calls, emails, and online conferences took place because they wanted to hear what the Lord was doing in our midst. Some traveled to campus to participate, arriving from all over the United States and from Latin America. Was God trying to create new bridges between cultures, ethnic groups, and nations through this outpouring? We can attest that he did. We attest that God can use, and did use, the Outpouring as a way to call the attention of his people to "the various dimensions of diversity."[16]

God moves and acts everywhere, in every nation, through the diversity of cultures and languages. God redeems, heals, saves, and sanctifies people. Color, age, gender, nationality, and socioeconomic status are not barriers or detractors for him. Diversity is a facet of God's creativity, greatness, and power. Revivals and outpourings are needed and welcomed at Asbury. We hope and pray to continue living in his holy presence!

15. Morrison, *Be the Bridge*, 43.
16. Morrison, *Be the Bridge*, 48.

CHAPTER FIVE

DIVINE TIMING

Carol Anderson
Adjunct professor of Theatre, Asbury University

Barbara Hamilton
Associate professor of Education, Asbury University

On the afternoon of Wednesday, February 8, Dr. Jim Shores was on his way to teach his theatre history class.[1] As he tells it, "I'm walking down the hall to the classroom, and I see an email on my phone from President Brown: 'As your schedule allows, I invite you to go see what's happening in chapel.' And I thought immediately, 'Revival.'"

That very second, five guys came running down the hall all hyped up, flush in the face, full of the Spirit. They stuck their heads into the computer labs, calling to students working on projects, "Revival! Revival has broken out! You need to head to chapel!" He walked up to them quickly, and they turned—with big goofy grins and so much energy—and exclaimed, "Dr. Shores! Revival has broken out!"

"So it's real?"

"Yes! You need to cancel your class and send your students over there!"

Now, as a professor, when students say you should cancel class, you stiffen a bit. Inside, Jim thought, "Don't tell me to cancel class."

But then he had a sudden flash to twenty years earlier. He used to teach at Montreat College and had been heading up to Asbury to speak in chapel with his wife, Carol. Jim's boss had taught at Asbury years before, so Jim asked if he wanted him to bring back a T-shirt.

1. Carol Anderson is the author of the first portion of this chapter.

Now Jim's boss, a wonderful man, was a little buttoned up, not too emotional, and taught math and physics. Talking to him about when he was at Asbury, Jim suddenly said, "Wait, you were there during the 1970 Revival. What was that like?"

He stiffened and said, "Jim, when that happened, I was going to have nothing to do with it. I thought it was all just emotional hippie stuff. I was angry at all the disruption and didn't cancel any of my classes, and I never went."

Jim looked at him with surprise and probably not very well-disguised horror. "Oh."

But then his boss continued, "It wasn't until later that I realized what I had missed . . ." He teared up. "At that moment, I vowed I would never again stand in the way of the work of the Holy Spirit in my life."

So now, standing in the hall, Jim looked at his students with sudden revelation and said, "Wait! God gave me instructions twenty years ago for this very moment in my life. I'm canceling class and we're all going over!" And that's exactly what they did.

Jim described the atmosphere they experienced:

> When I walked into Hughes at two in the afternoon, with three hundred students worshiping, arms in the air, it was like walking into a cloud that was a hug. I found myself raising my arms, worshiping, with a huge grin on my face, basking in the presence of the Lord, praising him. Within an hour I joined other faculty up at the altar rail praying for students. And that was the beginning of a sixteen-day adventure that has marked all of us forever. I texted my former boss to tell him that—because of his story that came back to me in that moment—I knew what to do.

During the Outpouring, many stories revealed a seeming network of divine timing occurring in our midst, from being at the right place at the right moment to literally hearing "go now" and making amazing God-ordained connections to discovering how one divine-timing moment set in motion several others. Or, as in Jim's case, events that happened years ago provided a long-awaited payoff in the present moment. These events, though remarkable and mysterious, give us a glimpse of how God works in and through time for his purposes.

The Greek word *chronos* means linear time, as in hour after hour. *Kairos* has been defined by philosophers as meaning deep time or by theologians as the right time or the appointed time for the purpose of God.[2] Divine timing has been described as the intersection of *kairos* and *chronos*.[3]

The story about Philip and the Ethiopian in Acts 8:26–40 gives an example of a truly divine-timing experience of grace. An angel of the Lord tells Philip to go to a road that leads from Jerusalem to Gaza, a desert place. There is no explanation of what is supposed to happen on this fifty-mile stretch of road, but Philip obeys. An Ethiopian court official is riding on the same road returning from worship. As he's passing, God tells Philip to "go over and join his chariot." He does so, just as the Ethiopian is trying to interpret a passage in Isaiah about the coming Messiah. Philip calls up to him, "Do you know what you're reading?" The Ethiopian, probably a bit surprised, responds, "How can I, unless someone guides me?" He then asks Philip to hop on board. The Holy Spirit leads the rest of the conversation regarding Jesus, which ends with the man believing and wanting to be baptized.

This was clearly an example of divine timing. Little did we know that moments like this would happen all around us during the Outpouring. What they have in common with the story of Philip is the openness of each person to say yes to the Holy Spirit's leading and the amazing things that happened because of it.

The Spirit's Coordination of Prayer

On day six of the Outpouring, I entered Hughes to begin my evening shift on the prayer team. I was standing off to the side of the platform at the front trying to take stock of where I'd be needed. The altar rail in front of the platform was completely full of prayer-team volunteers already engaged in praying for people young and old.

I was wondering what I should do when I saw a college student crouching on the floor to the side of the speaker platform near me. She was charging her phone in the wall outlet, and I couldn't tell if she was mumbling to herself or praying. Whichever it was, she looked worried. I hesitated, wondering if I should approach her, and heard in my spirit to "just go." So

2. John E. Smith, "Time, Times, and the 'Right Time': *Chronos* and *Kairos*," *The Monist* 53, no. 1 (1969): 1–13.
3. François Hartog, "*Chronos*, *Kairos*, *Krisis*: The Genesis of Western Time," *History & Theory* 60, no. 3 (2021): 425–39.

I walked over, bent down, and asked, "Are you doing OK here, or would you like someone to pray with you?" She looked up at me, surprised, paused a moment, and said, "Yes, prayer would be good."

I crouched down beside her on the floor. I told her my name was Carol and learned her name was Alison. I asked what she would like to pray about.

"Well," she said, "I'm having a media interview in a few minutes and I'm nervous about it."

"Oh, OK. Who is the media interview with?"

"Fox News. It's Tucker Carlson."

"Oh . . . OK." I could tell by the tone of her voice that she was concerned about doing this well.

Even at that moment, I was in wonder at God's timing. With just minutes to spare, God connected Alison with someone to pray for her, even when she had not verbalized her need to the prayer team. I looked at her again and could sense the stress she was carrying.

"Well," I said, "we'll pray in a minute for sure. But I want to say first, what you need to do for this is just forget about Tucker Carlson. He's just a voice speaking to you through your earpiece. He's going to be asking you questions. But you're not talking to him. You're talking to all the girls like you who are watching and want to know if this is real—what it's like here. So look through the lens and imagine you're talking to some friends and tell your story."

She said, "Well that's easy, because I've already told my story like ten times this week."

"Well, then you know what to say."

She smiled.

I said, "I'm amazed that I get to pray with you about this. I teach acting for the camera in the Theatre Department. This is exactly what I tell students when they have to talk into the camera. Just talk like you're talking to a friend."

Alison paused, taking that in.

Then I said, "We need to pray." So I prayed with her, knowing the few minutes we had were moving by swiftly. I asked the Holy Spirit to cover her and give her everything she needed and to help her stay centered in the Lord the whole time. We said "amen," and she was out the door.

I stood there stunned, grateful. I suddenly needed to tell someone about what just happened. I went out the back door of Hughes and into the lobby where I saw my friend Jennifer McChord, head of marketing. I described this remarkable experience with Alison. Jennifer told me she had actually set up this interview. It was only later I learned this was the very first national media interview for the Outpouring.

As we were about to say goodbye, I suddenly felt I should ask if I could pray for her. Jennifer said "YES" with such energy that within moments I felt led to pray for her strength and courage and wisdom. I would not learn until a few months later how the Lord used the timing of those prayers.

Jennifer had been faithfully following the Lord's leading to keep Hughes a place where people could simply come worship and experience Jesus. This included turning down media that wanted to film their stories inside the auditorium. The pressure of the media had intensified, as she was now hearing from major networks and media outlets. She was having to turn down one after another, even though this offered incredible promotion for Asbury—millions of viewers, thousands of readers. But they wanted to film their stories inside Hughes. Jennifer was struggling with keeping this a sacred space, despite the pressure of these opportunities.

I knew none of this. Jennifer told me months later what a hard night it had been. The timing of the prayer and how the Lord answered it were important, as she felt afterward that her perspective significantly changed, and she was able to go back into it all differently. Jennifer added, "And then the fact that you talked with Alison, our student body president, right before she did this. . . ." We both took a moment to marvel again at God's design.

One thing Jennifer didn't know was that I had desired to coach some of the many students having these media interviews to help them be more relaxed on camera. The prayer was never answered, nor did I feel I should pursue it. During the interview for this chapter, Jennifer surprised me by saying, "I was able to coach each of our students in that way, using the advice you gave, and they were able to connect so well. That one statement seemed to always relax them. It was huge."

I took that in, delighted. The Lord had already covered it. In the divine timing of our meeting in the back lobby of Hughes, I'd unknowingly been able to give her what was needed. She didn't need a second person. She just needed the right words to coach students well.

The Full Circle of Divine Timing

Dan Lewis teaches at Asbury University in the Business Department. He's a man of infectious vitality who loves and serves the Lord. Dan was on the prayer team during the Outpouring and had a number of opportunities to lead students to Christ. In the following months, as chaplain of the baseball team, he experienced the continuing work of the Holy Spirit in transforming the lives of the young men on his team. But Dan's love for college students and the impact he's had for decades almost didn't happen. During the Outpouring, the Lord brought about two events of divine timing within days of each other that blessed Dan's present ministry and reconnected him with an important person from his past.

Dan told me the backstory, which started in 2007. He'd been asked to move with his family to Colorado to be the director of Young Life ministries. Despite the wonderful opportunity, he was weary, struggling with the decision and the prospect of leaving Kentucky. A friend gifted him with a leaders' prayer retreat in London led by Pete Greig. During a time of prayer that week, Pete came over and shared a prophetic word: "You are like a dry, beaten tree in the middle of a desert getting struck by lightning. But God is going to bring to you rivers of living water."

Dan had been unclear whether he should move to be with Young Life, developing work in two states and being on the road a lot, or join a new venture that he had been offered in Kentucky as part of the River Foundation. Then he thought about Greig's words: "The *River* Foundation." He felt this was God's leading, stayed in Kentucky, and moved into a rich new chapter of ministry that connected him to his work at Asbury as well.

Fast-forward sixteen years to February 2023. Dan was in attendance at a Council of Christian Colleges and Universities (CCCU) conference in Florida, representing the River Foundation. The president of the CCCU, Shirley Hoogstra, walked by Dan's booth, stopped suddenly, and invited Dan: "Would you give a quick report on Asbury to start our closing session tonight? And lead us in prayer?"

"Absolutely."

That night Dan spoke to the leadership of many CCCU schools. He felt compelled to say to them all, "I'm bringing you an ember. This is not a report about Asbury. This is not owned by Asbury. This is a movement of God. You receive that ember and bring it back to your school." He then invited them: "If you would feel comfortable, get down on your knees and pray for every campus here."

Everyone got down on their knees and prayed.

Returning home from this remarkable experience, Dan discovered things had changed over the last few days at Asbury. Now there were huge crowds everywhere. Amid all the surprising people showing up, Dan heard that Pete Greig had flown in for literally one day. As Dan put it, "We had been inside an Anglican church when he prayed for me that rivers of living waters would come. It would be cool to talk about what happened. But the chances of actually meeting him or seeing him in Hughes was one in ten thousand."

Yet at one point that day, Dan walked out the back doors of Hughes—and there was Pete Greig! Surprised and delighted, Dan said, "Can I tell you a fifteen-year-old story?" Dan told him, "I'm now an Anglican priest and work for the River Foundation that supports the Dayton School of Business at Asbury teaching the next generation, and I get to be a part of that. And here we are in the middle of an outpouring—like, right here where it is happening." He concluded, "That was an amazing thing."

Dan got to experience the full circle of God's divine timing; from receiving Pete Greig's prophetic word at a time when he needed guidance, to God using his surprise invitation to encourage leaders to humbly seek God and pray for his work on campuses, and finally, by being at the right place at the right time to receive the gift of reconnecting with the man who helped move him toward his next fifteen years of ministry with Asbury students.

All these stories presented here carry the theme of God's leading, our response, and the divine timing of the events that ensued. That timing gave us a glimpse of perhaps how things work in heaven when we are so open and listening that we naturally move in time with God.

Divine Timing in Relational Connections[4]

"Prof. Hamilton, can you pray for me?" became a common refrain over those days. Some students had specific requests, but others just invited me to pray for them. The light of God's presence was so bright among us, we were keenly aware of our desperate need. We wanted what Jesus had to offer even if we couldn't name our needs. This overwhelming sense of humbly approaching our Almighty God prompted us to look around and ask for help from those near us, like those in Acts 2 who marveled at Pentecost over what they were seeing and asked each other, "What does this mean?" and "What shall we do?" (Acts 2:12, 37).

One student brought her sister for prayer and support because she had just surrendered a dating relationship to the Lord. Neither of them could have known it, but I had done the same thing as a student at that very altar nearly thirty years ago. I related parts of my own experience

4. Barbara Hamilton continues from here, describing more ways that God used perfect timing to make relational connections, deepen spiritual insights, and bring healing during the Outpouring.

that God had led me through with the words of Dr. Dennis Kinlaw. Two important phrases still shape my life today: "God never asked of us what He isn't willing to do Himself" and "Whenever God takes something out of your hands, it's because He intends to give you infinitely more." I showed these two women the little prayer, still tucked in my Bible, from all those years ago:

The Sacrificing Your Isaac Prayer

Lord,

Here is the work of my mind, my heart, my hand. Here is the fruit of my womb, Here is the love of my life. I lay them on the altar of sacrifice. I withdraw my hand. I turn my eyes to your face, my One True God. I give this cherished thing up to You the way it was given to me, with love, with love. And gladly.

Amen.

—Author unknown

We marveled together as I shared it with them and guided the young woman through the prayer aloud. That little prayer was close at hand because my husband and I had been praying it anew since the beginning of 2023 as we sought Jesus together in deeper surrender. Little did I know just how many times the Holy Spirit would prompt me to pull out that little weathered index card to share with others across the next several days.

The very first night, I was torn between the timing of all that was happening in Hughes and an invitation from a student to attend her basketball game. Recognizing that God's Spirit is not relegated to the auditorium, I made my way across campus to the Luce Center. I knew many of the players as students inside the classroom, but I marveled over them as I watched them play so freely with such grit, determination, and joy. They were in their element, focused on the ball, calling out encouragement to one another, and ready to pivot on a moment's notice whenever an opponent challenged them. They worked together with precision and hustled the ball from one player to another to find a way to make it to the basket and score. Whether on the court or the bench, they listened to their coach and one another with such synergy. There were other voices calling out from the stands that night, but each player was focused on the game at hand, listening for the coach and each other, as they took the ball up and down the court and back again. Not only did they win their game that night, but they went on to win their NCAA region!

Meagan, a senior math education major, would later remember how they thought it was odd that there were only about ten people in the stands as they were warming up that night. They quickly realized everyone was still in Hughes, so they were eager to get back there after the game and even confessed to questioning whether they should still be playing. Night after night, they continued practicing and playing and then heading right back to Hughes. Meagan recounted how games took on a different feel as they warmed up to worship music, which gave them a renewed sense of being on mission with the Lord on the court. A few days later, they invited the other team back to campus to join them in Hughes. She recalled how the auditorium was so packed that both teams sat on the stage in the newly formed student section, worshiping and experiencing it all together before going out to share a meal. What a bonding experience it proved to be for them as they chose not to keep this experience to themselves but made the most of every opportunity to share the Outpouring.

My favorite memory of that night happened a few hours after the game as some of the team members came bounding up to me in the front corner of the balcony in Hughes, fresh off their win. They were all smiles and had stories to tell. We hugged as I congratulated them on the game and looked around us at all the people filling the floor and the balcony. The atmosphere that night in Hughes proved to be even more festive than a game of basketball, with Jesus at the center of it all. I didn't realize it at the time, but the Lord would use that night as an important illustration of how the body of Christ, the church, exists and is being built together far beyond our human understanding of time and space. Just as these women played together with such joy and focus with their unique gifts, talents, and contributions as a team, they were demonstrating how the body of Christ is meant to function, serving him and one another with the gifts he has given us to embody Christ to a watching world. I began to wonder if the play they were participating in on the court and the opportunities we are given to serve one another in our everyday, ordinary lives are as close as we get to encountering heaven here on earth.

Some attendees of the Outpouring took a little longer to make their approach to Jesus. While some students simply wanted clarity on how to follow Jesus more closely, others brought much deeper trauma. I leaned in to listen to familiar stories of addiction, pain, and abuse hiding just under the surface of seemingly well-put-together students. My eyes welled with tears to hear the realities of the living conditions they were enduring in their thoughts, hearts, and bodies. For some, generational ruins left them carrying around deep devastation, not knowing where to go or what to do.

As I looked into their courageous eyes, risking such vulnerability, I asked the Lord, "What am I even here for, Lord? You've rescued me from such devastation. Am I waiting for permission to tell them about Your power to save?" The Lord gave me increasing boldness to not shy away from telling the harder parts of my story. I would thank students for sharing with me and look back at them and say, "You know you're not meant to just survive the elemental things of this world, right?" I talked about Galatians 4:3–7 and reminded students, "Jesus came in a body like this for a reason—so that we might overcome these addictions, heartaches, and pains in our actual bodies. We are meant to thrive, to bloom and grow *in* Christ Jesus our Lord, so we can keep walking with him toward his Kingdom purposes!"

One evening, with even more of the public in the auditorium with us, a speaker asked those who were younger to find those who were older so that we could pray intergenerationally. As I met three female students from Asbury and the University of Kentucky, I turned to see one of my own students make his way across the balcony to me. I prayed for each of them, and then it was their turn. As I took my spot in the center, they all laid their hands on my shoulders and began to pray. The three students praying in English behind my left shoulder all took turns to pray for me, but during that whole time, Alex had been praying for me in his heart language, Korean. To this day, I have no idea what he was praying, but my spirit certainly did. Even after the three of them finished, he prayed on with deep crescendos and an ebb and flow that made it clear the cues he followed were not his own. With hands open, I wept as our Abba Father's love cascaded over me. These moments were indeed the sounds of heaven breaking through on earth in real time.

Lots of volunteers were needed across those days to help at the altars, the doors, and beyond. Out of the hundreds of people who came to help, my husband and I were amazed to look up night after night and find people we hadn't seen in years due to an abuse of power in leadership at a local church. Here with Jesus at the center, we were blessed to be in ministry with these dear friends once again—something we thought would never happen this side of eternity. God was making all this new, restoring us to serve him together once again. With Jesus at the center, our hurt feelings, past wounds, and confusion did not have the last word. It truly felt like a family reunion as the Holy Spirit gathered us together, walking right through our lived experiences to bring us to this new space and time.

My husband, Glenn, was coordinating food logistics with volunteer vendors, and one volunteer set up his food truck in the semicircle to serve free hot dogs. Later that evening, as Glenn was serving near the front of Hughes, the same man approached him and said, "I notice you're having trouble with your leg. Can I pray for you?" Glenn was not expecting him to literally put his hand on his ankle, but as soon as he did, Glenn felt a sensation of heat flowing from the man's hand, radiating through his leg. When the food vendor finished praying, Glenn thanked him and marveled that the pain was gone. Not only did this man serve food across those days, but he offered prayers for healing. People kept showing up with supplies, and he kept preparing, serving, and praying.

I met another student, Bekah, on the sidewalk one evening, and we shared how we were both learning to navigate the balance between our desire to be in Hughes—where time seemed to stand still—with the needs of our everyday lives. She recounted how she had vacillated the previous weekend over whether to keep a previously scheduled appointment to go wedding dress shopping. As we talked about how she'd navigated this, I shared how I was somewhat reluctant to head home to teach an online class, but in the midst of all the beauty happening in Hughes, we were still a university on an academic calendar with online students eager to hear more. Bekah looked at me with the biggest smile and exclaimed, "You're a whole person, Prof. Hamilton! It's OK to leave for home, just like I chose to keep my wedding dress appointment!" As I walked away so encouraged by this young student, I heard the craziest thing. The Holy Spirit whispered, "That's what I'm doing here, Barbara. I'm wedding dress shopping!" I tucked that impression away until a couple days later when I saw another student, Dietrich, walking briskly past me, faster than his usual pace. When I greeted him, he called back over his shoulder, "Hi Prof. Hamilton! I don't want to be late for premarital counseling!" I turned back around and heard the Spirit say, "That's what I'm doing here, Barbara. Getting my bride ready."

Near the end of the next week, my Asbury alumni classmates wanted to set up a Zoom meeting to hear more about what we were experiencing on campus. With only about fifteen to twenty minutes to share, I asked a student, Sara, to pray for me that I'd tell the stories Jesus wanted this group to hear, not just any random one that came to mind or every story I wanted to tell. I was excited to see my friends and felt nervous about the responsibility of talking with some of my peers who hold positions of leadership in the church around the world as pastors and missionaries. I was ready to wrap up the stories when out of my mouth came the story of meeting Bekah and Dietrich on the sidewalk and hearing the Holy Spirit say he was preparing us, his people, his bride, for himself. I finished and thought how silly that must have sounded with romanticized notions that likely wouldn't translate. Even as I questioned myself at the end of the call, I told Sara what I'd done and surrendered it all to the Lord. A few days later, I woke up to see that one of those friends, Rev. John R. Lane, had penned a post on social media describing how all the ministries of the church are like premarital counseling, preparing us to be God's dwelling:

> One of the purposes of ministry is to prepare the Bride of Christ for marriage. Through all our services, our worship, our Bible studies, our addiction programs, our kids and teen ministries, our outreach programs, we are either inviting or equipping people to be prepared to be the bride of Christ. So they are like pre-marital counseling. Pre-marital counseling prepares people for the rigors and blessings of marriage through teaching, discussion, prayer and preparation. This generation (and perhaps all generations) are simply not prepared to be the Bride of Christ . . . Their experience [in the Outpouring] is one of preparation. They are experiencing a deep inner cleansing through the confession of their sins, their fears, their anxieties, their faults, their worries, their anger . . . What people knew once in theory, they now know in reality. What people once heard of in rumor, their reality has been shaken with the thunderous presence of the living God.[5]

I thanked the Lord that I had been faithful to be his messenger that day. As we continue to bear witness faithfully to all that we have seen and heard, the Holy Spirit continues to translate his love and divine Kingdom purposes here on earth as it is in heaven.

Conclusion

In the book of Acts, Philip said yes, and remarkable events happened at just the right time, in God's *kairos* time. During the Outpouring, we, along with Jim, Alison, Dan, Glenn, and others, experienced many divinely orchestrated events that God initiated among us to bring healing and relational wholeness. It made us wonder, If we lived like that every day, listening and ready for God to move, would our days always be full of similar remarkable stories of God's grace? Our hope in relating these stories is not for them to become history but to remind us of God's powerful presence so that we might continue to live out what we experienced.

5. John R. Lane, "Marriage as Premarital Counseling," Facebook.

CHAPTER SIX

OVERFLOWING GRACE AT ASBURY THEOLOGICAL SEMINARY

Jessica LaGrone

Dean of chapel, Asbury Theological Seminary

On the morning of Wednesday, February 8, 2023, leaders at Asbury Seminary were preparing to begin our chapel worship service just about the time the service at Asbury University's chapel typically ends. But of course, as we would realize later, there was nothing typical about February 8.

As those who were preparing to lead in worship gathered in a small prayer chapel at 10:45 a.m. next to Asbury Seminary's main worship space, Estes Chapel, we went over details for the upcoming service and paused before praying together. I felt prompted to share something with our students that I had noticed in my own prayer time earlier that morning. In Jesus's conversation with the woman at the well in John 4, he tells her that the kind of worshipers the Father seeks are those who worship in Spirit and in truth. I was struck by the idea that the Father was *seeking* worshipers, looking and hoping for them. While we were coming to worship to seek God, it turned out that God was seeking us. The group of lead worshipers seemed encouraged and stirred to worship. We prayed together and then gathered in the main chapel for worship, something we do three mornings a week as a seminary community. We were sensing an undercurrent of the Spirit's movement before we had any idea what that would mean or that it would change our lives forever.

SPILLING OVER OUR BOUNDARY LINES

The relationship between Asbury University and Asbury Theological Seminary can be confusing to those who don't know us well. Students at Asbury University (AU) have joked that ATS (Asbury Theological Seminary) actually stands for "across the street," since the two institutions are divided by a single road, North Lexington Avenue, that runs through the heart of our little town of Wilmore.

People often confuse the two schools, since we have the same name. We're accustomed to getting each other's phone calls and forwarding misdirected mail to the right location. Asbury Seminary was actually born out of Asbury College (now University) one hundred years ago. I don't mean roughly one hundred years; I'm not rounding up or down. The year of the Asbury Outpouring, we were celebrating the one-hundredth anniversary of Asbury College President Henry Clay Morrison's founding of Asbury Seminary in 1923. Dr. Morrison's vision was to start a school to train ministers of the gospel that would share "The Whole Bible for the Whole World" (still our motto today, as written on the seminary's official seal). That was an audacious vision, since the first class at Asbury Seminary had an enrollment of just three students. One hundred years later, we have over eleven thousand living alumni spreading the gospel and stretching all over the world, a definite fulfillment of Dr. Morrison's dream. For several years we had been dreaming and planning ways to make our centennial celebration a big splash. Unbeknownst to us, God had plans that would make a bigger impression than anything we had planned!

As our chapel service ended and the day progressed on February 8 at Asbury Seminary, my phone began to buzz with texts. At first, there were one or two. Eventually, I had to stop in the midst of meetings because the buzzing was almost ceaseless. Students and staff members were texting the news: "Asbury University's chapel is still going on!" "We're heading over to AU's Hughes Auditorium. Are you coming?" "You've got to get over here!" Text after text came in from excited students and staff. By the time I left the main administration building late in the afternoon to join others at Asbury University, our after-hours security person—who was just coming in the same door—asked me, "Where is everybody? This place seems empty!"

Late that first afternoon, when I stepped into Hughes Auditorium, small clusters of people were scattered around the space praying together while a worship band continued to lead singing from the platform. The mood was sweet and intimate. Many familiar faces of seminary students and staff greeted me, as well as neighbors from the Wilmore community, but at the heart of it all were the Asbury University students. These young worshipers had sensed the move of God before anyone else was aware, and as their scheduled chapel finished that morning, they tarried in prayer. They weren't trying to bring about an international event; they were just seeking the God who was seeking them—worshipers who came to him in Spirit and in truth. These young students were still very much the center of all that was happening, but others from our town, the seminary, and local churches were already beginning to get word and gather at the periphery, seeking God themselves. God's presence was palpable in Hughes Auditorium. People described it as sweet or peaceful and assuring, but most of all, it was very, very real.

As other voices here will tell, word kept spreading over the next few days, and the crowds of worshipers began to grow beyond what any of us could have imagined. It was so strange to begin to see actual traffic in our tiny town, as cars lined North Lexington Avenue. Across the street from the center of action in Hughes Auditorium, we at the seminary began joining in prayer early each morning before our chapel service, interceding for the students and the guests, asking for God's will to be done in all that was happening in our little town. During one of our morning chapel services several days later, I remember someone sharing the news that the Asbury University worship (yet unnamed as anything like an outpouring or a revival) was still ongoing and that crowds were growing, and we all turned and faced the university and raised our hands to pray over the growing move of God across the street. We had no idea that soon the crowds would outgrow the normal boundary line between our schools and we would be caught up in it all as well.

Overflowing Grace

That Sunday morning, February 12, I was worshiping at my own local church when my cell phone chimed with a message from my friend Sarah Baldwin, vice president of Student Life and dean of students at Asbury University. Sarah and I had attended Asbury Seminary around the same time, graduated, and then both returned to Wilmore the same year to serve in our roles at our respective schools. We are good friends, so a text from her is not unusual—but the timing and content of this one was: "We are running out of space in Hughes and more are arriving! We need you to open Estes Chapel for overflow worship tonight; can you make that happen?" I sat for a moment in disbelief. This was Super Bowl Sunday, the night of the biggest sporting event watched on TV all year. In all my years as a pastor, I had never planned anything for the evening of the Super Bowl except the occasional church Super Bowl party! Would that many people really come to worship on this night? I texted back that we would do anything we could to help those leading at AU, and then I began texting others to put plans in place to open Estes Chapel on our own campus.

That evening we prepared worship bands of seminary students and welcomed Dr. David Thomas, who had been instrumental in leading the Hughes Auditorium worship, to lead prayer and offer a message. We felt strongly that there should be consistency between what had been happening on the university grounds and what we were offering at the seminary. We weren't beginning something new; we were simply offering our sacred space as a continuous room of worship alongside those leading at Asbury University. As we prepared to open our doors that evening, Sarah texted again: "People are headed for you. Are you ready?" Members of the prayer team arrived and lined our altar just as we opened our doors, and I watched, amazed, as people poured in. That night started a new phase for us of cohosting the outpouring of God's loving presence in Wilmore. I thought of my earlier doubts that people would choose worship over football and laughed. For the many, many people hearing news of this incredible move of God and lining up to worship in Wilmore, this was certainly bigger than the Super Bowl!

At the end of the night, I texted Sarah: "We are sending the last few who are lingering here back over to you. It was a beautiful night in Estes." Sarah texted back, "Thank you, friend. I feel like we have the 'Asbury Outpouring' in two chapels that may bring us together in a new way." I responded, "I agree! This is better than putting together a committee to plan unity!"

I was referring to a joint committee between our two schools that Sarah and I had been coleading for the past eighteen months. Our task was to plan a joint worship service that our two schools would hold together in late April to celebrate Asbury University giving birth to Asbury Seminary one hundred years earlier. We had been meeting together with members of the staff from the two schools to facilitate a working relationship between our corresponding departments, such as communications, technology, student services, worship and chapel leadership, and event planning areas. In some cases, these professionals (in similar roles at the two institutions) had never met one another before the committee had been launched. Our planning meetings had been helpful, we thought, in getting ready for a single large worship service in April. But now we realized that God had been preparing us to work together on another project of his own making! Planning and communication flowed back and forth between our schools in constant conversation and coordination to determine schedules and next steps, to check in on safety and security issues, and to welcome a growing number of guests literally from around the world.

At the seminary, we continued to open Estes Chapel as a place of worship for the many visitors pouring into our tiny town, and as the days progressed, we also opened a second space for worship, McKenna Chapel, and then ultimately our seminary gym. The three spaces had screens broadcasting a live feed from Hughes Auditorium, which continued to be the heart and source of the worship. At first we were concerned that a live feed—instead of being in Hughes Auditorium itself—would somehow seem distant or artificial, but we were amazed at how each room filled with worship that was as strong and fervent as standing in Hughes Auditorium. In each of these spaces, the energy and volume of the crowd singing and praising God was so overwhelming that the worship feed on the screen almost seemed to accompany and confirm what God was doing among us in the room.

A Good Crisis

The weeks during which we helped host the gatherings of worship that February were not always easy. The Outpouring began during the very first week of classes for the seminary's spring term, so we never had a chance to establish a routine. Instead, to accommodate the growing crowds, we put together almost round-the-clock volunteer hosting teams. While our classes were never canceled, normal student life was pushed to the edges to accommodate the unusual events. Our own students, faculty, and staff rose to the occasion to serve and welcome. As I walked through the three worship venues open on our campus, I could see well-known tenured faculty members praying with people at the altar, administrators ushering people to seats, and students filling in wherever they were needed—pushing cases of water on dollies to various buildings and assisting guests who needed directions on an unfamiliar campus. The question "Where are the restrooms?" was answered hundreds of times a day, even with the extra directional signage we had tacked up along our hallways. At the door where people most often asked for restrooms, we constantly stationed a student just to point people down the hall. One evening I walked through that spot and found one of our conscientious students with her head bowed in a textbook, while a sign taped over her head said, "Restrooms are down the hall to the left; please feel free to ask any questions needed." She had found a way to study and serve at the same time.

At the seminary, many of our students lingered in the hallways and classrooms asking deep questions about the events going on around them. "What was God up to? Why was this happening here in our community? Why now?" Theological questions about the nature of God's presence and how he relates to his people are common in a seminary setting, but now the questions being asked had new urgency and relevance. As often happens in our conversations about God, a deeper and more personal layer of questions sometimes surfaced. How does God feel toward me? What does he want for me? Are these events happening for my life or just for the college students and visitors? As conversations went on, many seminary students related that the very nature of this outpouring happening around us was a healing experience for them. Stories about past experiences of hurt in churches and at the hands of Christian leaders were told, and some students (and some faculty and staff as well) talked about how seeing the Asbury Outpouring unfold without manipulation, power struggle, or persons seeking attention or fame brought them assurance of God's true nature and self-sacrificial love. Person after person related stories of healing and emerging hope, and even more admitted they were continuing to process the move of God in awe and wonder, just as Jesus's mother, Mary, had "treasured all these things in her heart" (Luke 2:19).

One day I walked across the street at Asbury University for a planning meeting. As I headed back to the seminary, I looked around astounded at the line, now stretched nearly a mile long, of those waiting to get into Hughes Auditorium. Volunteers were walking up and down the line, handing out water bottles and answering questions. A bank of portable toilets and handwashing stations accommodated people's needs, and as I kept walking, I noticed a food trailer handing out pizza slices. The front of it read "Salvation Army Crisis Relief." It stopped me in my tracks for a moment as I realized that we were in the midst of a crisis. A tiny town filled to overflowing with tens of thousands of people constituted a crisis. But it was a good crisis. I'd never heard of a good crisis before.

Where there was once a clear dividing line of a busy street and our two lawns between the two schools, the crowds now almost merged the two campuses, overflowing onto the open grassy area in front of Hughes Auditorium where people lingered to pray and watch a live feed of the worship inside. Crowds stretched outside of our own Estes Chapel as people lined up for a chance to enter the seminary's worship spaces. People walked back and forth in the street between the two campuses with such frequency that it almost seemed as if the boundary between our campuses was erased, with only the thin line of the road, filled with people, dividing us. The hundred years of history between us was filled with a common purpose and excitement about what God was doing in our midst. Our international students began seeking me out to share excitedly that people from their home countries were calling and contacting them to find out what was happening at their school. One family from India studying at the seminary shared that in their tiny remote village back home, the word of revival at a school called "Ashbury" was spreading and people were openly curious about Jesus. I've sometimes shared over the years that while the city of Las Vegas has a famous slogan of "What happens in Vegas stays in Vegas," ours should be the opposite (for many reasons!): What happens in Wilmore spreads all over the world. During those weeks, the scope of sharing God's love and power around the world was accelerated beyond what we had ever imagined.

During one particular morning in Estes Chapel, before the crowds entered, many of our seminary students were gathered, praying and sharing Scripture and impressions of what God was doing. As people wondered what was next for this ever-increasing movement and how long this would last, one of our students, a young man named Ben, spoke up and said,

> You know, a revival is kind of like a honeymoon. The purpose of a honeymoon is to put aside all your normal daily events and responsibilities; you turn aside from the day-to-day just to focus on the one you love. But no one lives on honeymoon. Eventually honeymoons end, and you return to your daily life together. But you're closer and stronger because you spent that time. The purpose of a honeymoon is to make a home. Revival is kind of the same way. All the daily things seem not to matter as you just focus on growing in love with the Lord. Revivals end, but when this one ends, we will be living in this home we're making with God.

Mountaintop Moments and Daily Life

During the second weekend of the Outpouring, I prepared to leave town because I had been scheduled to speak at a church in a neighboring state. It was a challenge to make sure all our leadership and volunteer positions were filled, all the details were managed, and all the opening hours of our worship spaces were covered. As I drove out of the city limits, I passed long lines of cars headed the opposite direction, all of them trying to get into our small town. These people were hungry for an experience with God, just like the woman in Scripture who just wanted to touch the hem of Jesus's garment. And here I was, leaving. I was overwhelmed with the feeling that I didn't want to leave. It was hard to leave my staff and students taking care of the hosting responsibilities for worship on our campus.

What I think made it harder was that I was going to speak at this church's fundraiser, which was raising money to pay a fee that would allow them to separate from their denomination, with whom they had irreconcilable theological differences. This little church didn't have the money to pay the fee, but they felt strongly that their biblical convictions were leading them to align with another ecclesiastical body. So they were doing everything—a silent auction, a bake sale, and a barbecue dinner where I was to be the speaker—to help drum up support to raise the money. The event had been planned and my part scheduled for almost a year, and although it was almost impossible to leave the move of God in Wilmore, I had to go.

As I left the place where God's Spirit was so thick and drove hours to another state, I felt almost resentful that I had to leave the place where so many people were streaming in to be with Jesus in order to help a congregation go through such an arduous event in their church's life. I thought to myself, Why does this even matter? Why do church politics exist? Why can't we just gather and worship Jesus like we're doing in Wilmore? What's the point of whichever denominations or groups or associations we're aligned with? Why can't we just be the body like this—one big crowd, worshiping together all the time?

Well, as usual, God had a plan for that weekend. That was one of the sweetest churches I had ever visited. They were so kind and gracious. Person after person got up and told stories of how the church had raised them, how their grandmothers had sewed the kneeling cushions at the altar, how many of them had grown up and come to know Jesus right there in the midst of this incredibly Christ-centered, loving group of people. They were so eager to hear news of the Outpouring back in Wilmore, and they told me that even in their worship services, hours away from Asbury, they were feeling the Spirit moving as they talked and prayed over the events. Through the whole experience, I realized again why we need the local church. Mountaintop moments like the one we experienced that February may come and go, but the local church is there week in and week out to share Christ, raise up disciples, and help us grow in the image of God.

When I returned to Wilmore the next day, I found that the road I had used to leave town was now closed to incoming traffic. The police had put up a checkpoint stopping each car. They weren't letting anyone in who didn't live there. You had to show your driver's license with a Wilmore address just to come into town. The crowds had become so great that the town had to completely redirect traffic entering the city limits. Even with everything I had seen with my own eyes, I couldn't believe we had actually reached this point of disruption! I drove into town ever more in awe of God's power and grace. History was happening before our eyes.

Banding Together for the Body of Christ

With all the big crowds that came, most of those who felt drawn to Wilmore were Christians seeking a deeper move of God. They were Christians from all kinds of backgrounds and worship practices and theology. Most of them were very gentle and kind. Waiting in huge crowds to enter the sanctuaries even felt a bit like being in line at Disney World, but this was a space where everyone waited patiently, offered kind words and gratitude, and even let other people go in ahead of them.

But some of our guests, even those who professed faith in Christ, brought with them all sorts of unique beliefs and theology. One of our students, who was pregnant at the time, had a man ask to pray over her, which sounded perfectly fine. But when she agreed, he took her by the shoulders and shook her hard, "praying away any evil spirits" that might be trying to get at her baby. Another of our students at the time was in a wheelchair. As she tried to wheel across campus to go to her classes, she was stopped over and over again by well-meaning people who told her that she hadn't prayed hard enough or prayed in the right way to be healed. Some of them even told her she was sinning and needed to confess so God would heal her and she could walk. She would say, "God and I are good! I'm just trying to get to my class!" Over the course of the days that crowds of worshipers gathered in Wilmore, groups also arrived with picket signs and bullhorns—all of them Christians—shouting harsh statements about who God hated or why certain people were worse sinners than others.

As we enjoyed the presence of God but also strove to keep a peaceful atmosphere in worship and on our campuses with the variety of theological beliefs expressed there, it occurred to me that my resentful thoughts during the beginning of my trip out of town had been misdirected. While all Christians are brothers and sisters in Christ, Christians throughout history have banded together into groups, classes, local churches, and denominations as we attempt to learn the best and healthiest ways to follow Christ and share him with the world. Not only for the local church I visited, but for all of us in the family of God, it did matter who we aligned with and what kinds of teaching poured into our schools and congregations. The act of raising up and training leaders for the local church, one of our primary tasks at Asbury Seminary, suddenly had more urgency and importance than ever. While what was happening in the short span of just over two weeks in front of our eyes was what our seminary president, Timothy C. Tennent, called "a fast-forward miracle," he also reminded us to continue in the "slow-motion miracle" of theological education that would sustain the growth and impact we witnessed for generations to come. And I was thankful—when that comparatively brief period of dramatic outpouring ended—that healthy, strong, vibrant local churches were available for those people to return to for further spiritual growth. Some of these worshipers had just found Christ, while others were renewed in their faith. But these believers could go home to deeply formed churches where they would continue to experience Christ's family and be formed in healthy and vibrant ways into the body of Christ.

So much has happened in our world and in our tiny town since the outpouring of God's presence in 2023. But for those of us who experienced this amazing and unusual demonstration of God's love in real time, life has a "before and after" quality to it. In many ways, what began in February 2023 is still ongoing. God is still pouring out his Spirit, meeting with us in worship settings, classrooms, and conversations. We continue to witness how God's Kingdom can create spaces on earth "as it is in heaven," and our deep desire is that what has happened in Wilmore, Kentucky, will continue to pour out over the earth.

PART TWO

BIBLICAL, HISTORICAL, AND THEOLOGICAL FOUNDATIONS

CHAPTER SEVEN

GOD'S PRESENCE AND EMPOWERMENT IN SCRIPTURE AND BEYOND

Julianne Burnett
Assistant professor of Old Testament, Asbury University

Joy Vaughan
Assistant professor of New Testament, Asbury University

Sam Kim
Assistant professor of Intercultural Studies, Asbury University[1]

The biblical narrative, beginning in the Garden of Eden, depicts a God who dwells perfectly with Adam and Eve. The Holy God created image bearers, Adam and Eve, to know the depths of God's love and his desire to dwell among them. The Garden setting is worth pausing to imagine. John Wesley writes, "We may well suppose it to be the most accomplished place that ever the sun saw, when the All-sufficient God himself designed it to be the present happiness of his beloved creature. The situation in the garden was extremely sweet; it was in Eden, which signifies delight and pleasure. . . . It was beautified with every tree that yielded fruit grateful to the taste, and useful to the body."[2] The Garden depicts a God who is good

1. Julianne Burnett has authored the section on the Old Testament, Joy Vaughan has authored the section on the New Testament, and Sam Kim has authored the section on missiological implications.
2. John Wesley, *Explanatory Notes upon the Old Testament*, vol. 1 (Salem, OH: Schmul, 1975), 11–12.

and who deeply loves and cares for humans, who are also good and made in his image.

The biblical narrative, however, seemingly moves on way too quickly from this blissful utopia. With Adam and Eve's disobedience, the Garden becomes an altogether different experience. When God calls, "Where are you?" (Gen. 3:9), there is no more depiction of delight and loving desire. Instead, fear enters the scene in Adam's voice: "I heard you in the garden, and I was afraid because I was naked; so I hid" (Gen. 3:10). What was once good is now tainted; humanity is "banished from the garden" and driven out. Thank God that the story does not end here! God, acting in unconditional love, does not close the gate and remain apart from humanity forever. Instead, the biblical text reveals a God who has a rescue plan for humanity, a plan that restores what was lost in Eden. In other words, deeply interwoven into the biblical narrative is a theme of God's dwelling; God is unwilling to give up on humanity and will make a way to dwell again in our midst. This chapter aims to walk the reader through the Old and New Testaments to unpack God's faithful desire to dwell among humanity. Importantly, God's story is still being told in our world today. Asbury experienced a piece of this story in the Outpouring. We witnessed God's activity in our world to make himself known in our midst. We have tasted and we have seen with firsthand experiences God's desire to dwell in a special way. Even as we write, what God started at Asbury University is now spreading all over the world. As a result, the final section of the chapter treats missiological implications for outpouring.

Torah and Temple: Spiritual Renewal in the Old Testament

Genesis 1–2 provides the reader with a glimpse into how life with God and one another was intended to be in perfect communion and love. The Lord dwelled with his creation in a way that was tangible to Adam and Eve. But after the banishment of Adam and Eve from the Garden of Eden, things changed. As Victor P. Hamilton states, "They lose what they currently possess: unsullied fellowship with God. They found nothing and lost everything."[3] Humanity was no longer able to inhabit a holy space with the Holy One. The Law, purity rituals, and tabernacle/temple system

3. Victor P. Hamilton, *The Book of Genesis, Chapters 1–17*, NICOT (Grand Rapids, MI: Eerdmans, 1990), 208.

became the God-given means of grace to cleanse an unholy people from sin. Moreover, Yahweh's people are called to keep their covenant relationship with him, which requires full love, joyful obedience, and a posture of love.

We can trace God's covenants in the Old Testament through Noah, Abraham, Moses, and David, but the call to obedience is for all. Yahweh chooses to manifest his presence in physical, tangible ways at different points in Old Testament history and always with the purpose of his people knowing and loving him. These theophanies are powerful encounters with the Holy One where he enters real space and time to make himself known. One important example of this is in Genesis 15:9–21, where the Lord appears to Abram as a smoking pot and flaming torch.[4] Yahweh's promise to him that Abram and Sarai would bear offspring and have a multitude of descendants (15:1–6) is followed by this theophanic experience and covenant. As Sandra L. Richter explains, "Yahweh is inviting Abram to confirm the oaths between them by means of a standard covenant ratification ceremony. How merciful is this God who condescends to Abram's place in time, and helps him to have confidence in the promise."[5]

An additional example occurs with Moses. Yahweh reveals his presence, character, and divine name to Moses in Exodus 3:14 as "I am who I am" or "I will be who I will be."[6] The Almighty One who has been with Abraham, Isaac, and Jacob promises to lead his people into the Promised Land in this profound theophany with the "burning bush."[7] This continues the movement toward a place where Yahweh would dwell among his people.

Exodus 20–31 and 35–40 provide us with the law codes for the ancient Israelites, instructions for the construction of the tabernacle, and regulations for the priesthood. These are partially retold in Deuteronomy and further legal texts, including Leviticus. But significantly, Exodus is recording not simply a group of laws that Yahweh gives but also the fact that

4. Nevada Levi DeLapp, *Theophanic "Type-Scenes" in the Pentateuch: Visions of YHWH* (London: Bloomsbury T&T Clark, 2018), 19–25.
5. Sandra L. Richter, *Epic of Eden: A Christian Entry into the Old Testament* (Downers Grove, IL: IVP Academic, 2008), 78.
6. Thomas B. Dozeman, *Commentary on Exodus* (Grand Rapids, MI: Eerdmans, 2009). Dozeman explains, "The divine name Yahweh is known in tradition as the Tetragrammaton, referring to the four consonants, Y-H-W-H. . . . The NIV, NRSV, NJPS, and most other English versions translate the name Yahweh as 'Lord'" (136).
7. Yahweh also appears to Moses in a pillar of fire and a pillar of clouds in Exodus 13:21–22. For more discussion on the connection between theophanies, fire and/or smoke or cloud, and the divine name, see DeLapp, *Theophanic "Type-Scenes,"* 47.

Yahweh's glory and presence fill the tabernacle (Exod. 40:34–38). The Law is graciously given by God so that the people can be cleansed from sin and impurity and have a relationship with the Holy One.[8] This is the framework in which to understand obedience versus disobedience, the path of life versus the path of death, and the pure versus the impure throughout the rest of the Hebrew Bible.

The Old Testament Torah, or instruction, may seem challenging and even peculiar to many contemporary readers. However, we should understand it as the answer to two main issues—namely, how and where does the Lord dwell on earth, and how can (sinful) humans enter the presence of the Lord? It is through the tabernacle (and then, temple) that Yahweh dwells on earth so that his presence is known to his people at this point in history. But this required careful observation of the Law, joyful obedience, and following the purity and sacrificial system so that a sinful people could be in fellowship with a perfect and holy God. Terence E. Fretheim expounds,

> The book of Leviticus is the center of the Pentateuch. Insomuch as worship-related matters dominate the book, this placement may express a conviction regarding the centrality of worship for the life and well-being of the community. As God had been active in Israel's history, so God promised to be active in and through these rituals. In and through these visible and tangible means, from sacrifices to dramatized festivals, God overcame slavery and death for Israel and bestowed life and salvation. Two different dimensions of God's saving action were made available to Israel.[9]

Thus, both Torah and temple are Yahweh's chosen means of restoring his people to his presence at this point in history.

The Call to Renewal

When we consider spiritual renewal and revival, two examples arise in Israel's history of kings that call for a communal return to loving and joyfully

8. Richard E. Averbeck, *The Old Testament Law for the Life of the Church* (Downers Grove, IL: IVP Academic, 2022), 207–10. "As for holiness (i.e., holy versus common in Lev. 10:10), since God is most holy, the core of holiness in Israel was the tabernacle in which he dwelt in the center of the camp, and the priests who officiated there" (209).
9. Terence E. Fretheim, *The Pentateuch* (Nashville: Abingdon, 1996), 121.

obeying Yahweh, their God: Hezekiah and Josiah. King Hezekiah reigns in Judah during a time after the split of the united kingdom of Israel. We read that king after king "did not do what was right in the eyes of the Lord" and failed to uphold Yahweh's covenant.[10] Sacrifices and worship are offered to other gods, treaties are made with other rulers, and violence and injustice—rather than shalom—are pervasive. In the midst of this, at age twenty-five, King Hezekiah begins to rule in Judah; 2 Kings 18:3 states that he does what is right in the eyes of the Lord. This passage further tells us that he destroys idols and any cultic objects that were not devoted to the sole worship of Yahweh (e.g., the Asherah poles, sacred stones, the Nehushtan).[11] Moreover, Hezekiah trusts in Yahweh and maintains a relationship with the Lord by faithfully obeying the laws and commands given. But by 2 Kings 18:13–16, we read that Hezekiah chooses to enter into a treaty agreement with the king of Assyria rather than trust in Yahweh alone. The result is a dire mistake: removing the silver and gold from the temple and the palace treasury and giving it to the king of Assyria as part of the treaty agreement. These temple items that had been set apart for Yahweh alone were now being freely given away to a foreign power. While Hezekiah's initial actions honored God, it is clear from his later actions that a deeper transformation and renewal is needed in Judah.

By the time King Josiah begins his reign in Judah at age eight, the covenant-law code seems to be a distant memory. There had only been two kings from the time of Hezekiah to Josiah, but in that time, King Manasseh "did evil in the eyes of YHWH" (2 Kings 21:2) and King Amon "did evil in the eyes of the Lord, as his father Manasseh had done" (2 Kings 21:20). When the law code scrolls are rediscovered in 2 Kings 22, Josiah is convicted at the realization that the nation has not been obeying and loving the Lord as they were called to do. Josiah calls the people to a time of repentance and recommitment to God's covenantal relationship through joyful obedience and faithfulness to him. This decision to return to Yahweh rightly results in action. Josiah tears down all the sites dedicated to the worship of other gods, immoral practices, and anything else associated with forbidden activities. This spiritual renewal is not a list of things to perform or avoid. Rather, it is an encounter with the living God that results in repentance and then making radical changes so that the people of God are living into their covenantal relationship with Yahweh.

10. See, for example, 1 Kings 14:8–9, 22; 15:3, 26, 34; 16:7, 19, 25, 30.
11. For the background of the Nehushtan, see Numbers 21:4–9.

Not long after the death of King Josiah, however, we read that Israel's kings choose to trust in their own wisdom more than Yahweh's. Ultimately, this continued willful disobedience results in the loss of the Promised Land (as described in Lev. 18:28), and the people of Judah find themselves in exile. But God had not given up.

A Glimpse of Things Still to Come

During the exile, the Lord gives the prophet Ezekiel words of hope about the return and restoration of the people of God in the Promised Land. Moreover, through visions, Ezekiel sees the promise of the new temple (Ezek. 40–48):

> Then the man brought me to the gate facing east, and I saw the glory of the God of Israel coming from the east. His voice was like the roar of rushing waters, and the land was radiant with his glory. The vision I saw was like the vision I had seen when he came to destroy the city and like the visions I had seen by the Kebar River, and I fell facedown. The glory of the Lord entered the temple through the gate facing east. Then the Spirit lifted me up and brought me into the inner court, and the glory of the Lord filled the temple. (Ezek. 43:1–5)

The hope promised here is that the Lord will once again dwell in the midst of his people and that the people can be in a restored covenantal relationship with him. Without the presence of the Lord, this structure would be simply a building. But this vision affirms that when the glory of Yahweh remains, the people can dwell in his presence and be a restored, redeemed people, once again fulfilling the covenant to which they were called.

This remains true for believers today. While this vision of the temple was not realized under Zerubbabel or Herod's rebuilding of the temple, the promise remains. These glimpses throughout history of how God meets with his people in powerful ways and calls them to spiritual renewal and reawakening are not the end of the story. To more fully understand God's holy presence among his people today, we need to look ahead to the New Testament, to the early church, and how the Lord continues to move across the globe today.

God's Presence in the New Testament

The theme of God's presence develops both temporally and spatially in the New Testament. Temporally, we hear the story of a new covenant that God establishes by sending his one and only Son to give his life as a sacrifice. A new time has come. As previously noted, in the Old Testament, the presence of God was accessible, but only with restrictions for those who wanted to enter the tabernacle. These limits are very real for the OT people of God, and consequences exist for those who do not follow the laws. The God who so deeply wants to live among his people with no separation, like in Eden, dwells in the Holy of Holies. Visits are made by one man—the high priest—who has carefully prepared himself. In fact, that man risks his life if impurity is present. Even so, these limits are not a form of punishment for the people of God. Rather, the Old Testament story realizes the power of God, his essence as holy, and his invitation for his people to walk in relationship with him. This system, while necessary for its time, is not permanent.

The New Testament story flows out of this Old Testament story. In this section, we continue to survey how God dwells with his people, and how the spatial aspect of God's presence develops in new directions. First, we will consider John 1:14 and Jesus as Tabernacle. Secondly, we will consider the Pentecost story, a game changer for the conversation about God's presence. Thirdly, we will reflect on spiritual gifts. Fourthly, we will consider how Paul reflects on bodies as temples. And finally, we will note the promise to come: the New Jerusalem. The reality is that our story is not over. The experience of God's presence, the way he dwells among us, is something we know in part, but the NT offers a promise that one day we will know and experience him in full. From Eden to New Jerusalem, a main theme is God's desire to dwell with his people.

God Dwells with His People

When Jesus enters the scene, God's way of dwelling develops. The Gospel of John illustrates this change: "The Word became flesh and made his dwelling among us. We have seen his glory, the glory of the one and only Son, who came from the Father, full of grace and truth" (John 1:14). Temporally and spatially, a new way of dwelling occurs. The Gospel of John uniquely highlights the connection with the OT narratives. Simply stated, the Logos *dwells* among us. Scholars have often noted the connection to the tabernacle story that John's verbiage conjures up. The verb employed for dwelling, *skēnoō*, carries the connotation of one who takes up residence with his people. He lives among them and settles in their midst. The revelation of God is also taking new form, the form of humanity. The God who dwelled fully in Eden, who continued to appear to his people in the OT despite their disobedience, who tabernacled with them as they journeyed through the wilderness, and who dwelled in their temple in the Holy of Holies now suddenly is accessible to all who encounter Jesus. The Gospel of John celebrates the experience. The author writes, "We have seen his glory, the glory of the one and only Son, who came from the Father, full of grace and truth" (1:14). God's presence and character as revealed in the life of Jesus is further portrayed throughout John's Gospel. Many who come into contact with Jesus are forever changed. They are forgiven, healed, cleansed, cared for, and ultimately experience God and his Kingdom on earth firsthand. Even so, some resist Jesus and do not welcome his presence in their midst.

The Promise of More to Come

The story does not end here. In John's Gospel, Jesus promises a spatial change in the story of how God dwells with his people. Jesus states, "And I will ask the Father, and he will give you another Helper, to be with you forever, even the Spirit of truth, whom the world cannot receive, but it neither sees him nor knows him. You know him, for he dwells with you and will be in you" (John 14:16–17 ESV). In other words, when Jesus ascends, he promises his disciples that they will not be left alone; the Spirit will dwell with them. Verse 18 develops the promise Jesus makes. He states, "I will not leave you as orphans: I will come to you." Further, he adds, "The Advocate, the Holy Spirit, whom the Father will send in my name, will teach you all things and will remind you of everything I have said to you" (14:26 ESV). The message that Jesus sends is that he is going away, but there is no reason to be afraid or troubled. In essence, God's presence does not evacuate earth when Jesus ascends. Jesus has revealed the plan for God's presence to be more accessible among his people, even if it is difficult for the disciples to fully understand.

Jesus's Promise Fulfilled

At Pentecost, Jesus's promise is fulfilled: "And all of them were filled with the Holy Spirit . . ." (Acts 2:4). Just like the crowds gathered around Jesus, God's presence again draws a crowd. This time the crowds are bewildered because the Holy Spirit enabled those who had been filled with the Holy Spirit to speak in tongues. Instantly, every person present is able to understand what is being said in his or her own native language. The barriers to language communication are broken! Various responses follow, both positive (requests for the meaning of the event) and negative (accusations of drunkenness). When Peter addresses the crowd, he makes clear that what is happening fulfills the Scriptures: This is God pouring out his Spirit on all people, as foretold by the prophet Joel. Peter preaches the gospel story, and thousands of Jews embrace the gospel that day. Acts develops this theme and demonstrates that what Jesus promised is fulfilled in the Spirit's coming. The Spirit is poured out, empowers the early church with signs and wonders, leads Jesus's followers in specific directions, enables them to preach and heal, and more!

Pauline Reflections on a Spirit-Led Life and Spiritual Gifts

While Luke narrates the story of the early church's empowerment by the Holy Spirit as a normative part of the Christian life, Paul's letters helpfully reflect on and direct life in the Spirit, spiritual gifts, and spiritual fruit. Living in the Spirit in the here and now embraces the reality that God has already given the Holy Spirit as part of what is to come, our inheritance (2 Cor. 1:22; 5:5; Eph. 1:13–14). In other words, life in the Spirit gives us a taste of what eternal life will be like, God fully with us. Craig Keener helpfully realizes the implications: "Some promises await Jesus' return, but God's presence and power in our lives right now should enable us to live as heaven's people on earth. Can you imagine how it would revolutionize the lives of believers and churches if we actually recognized and believed this reality? We should mean it when we pray, 'Your will be done on earth as it is in heaven.'"[12] The Spirit also gives gifts to believers (Rom. 12:3–8; 1 Cor. 12:8–10; Eph. 4:11–13), and Paul utilizes the term *charismata* for these gifts—a term translatable as "grace gifts." Paul embraces these gifts as part of the church's experience of the Holy Spirit but does not permit misuse of the gifts. Spiritual gifts must edify, exhort, comfort, and build the church as the unified body of Christ. Since the Spirit reveals Jesus to us, any genuine use of spiritual gifts is consistent with the character of Jesus.

12. Craig Keener, *Gift and Giver* (Grand Rapids, MI: Baker, 2020), 35.

Thirdly, when believers live in the Spirit, good fruit is produced. It is critical to remember that the fruit is not produced by trying harder or self-help. Genuine fruit is produced by living in step with the Spirit (Gal. 5:25). Once again, even though the fruit can be produced in the here and now, the fruit also depicts what life in the New Jerusalem will be like. Paul writes, "Against such things there is no law" (v. 23), demonstrating that a fruit-filled life is a life of freedom. One is free in the Spirit to exude copious amounts of love, joy, peace, patience, kindness, goodness, faithfulness, gentleness, and self-control far beyond what is humanly possible. In summary, when we receive the Spirit and live by the Spirit, the power and presence of God are made known in visible ways. Observers can witness and taste fruit and know that God is at work.

Pauline Reflections on Bodily Temples

Lastly, Paul reflects on how God dwells with his people throughout the course of the biblical story. Paul explicitly teaches that this dwelling place is now the body: "Do you not know that your bodies are temples of the Holy Spirit, who is in you, whom you have received from God?" (1 Cor. 6:19). As a result, Paul develops a theology of the body and explains why it matters what Christians do with their bodies: The body is a temple of the Holy Spirit. God has given the Holy Spirit to each believer, and that Spirit dwells in the body. Because of this, Paul exhorts his audience to honor God with their bodies.

In 1 Corinthians 15, Paul further develops his thoughts on these matters. He teaches his audience that the body will be raised in the resurrection; the body sown in death as a seed will be raised to new life. What is sown perishable is raised imperishable, what is sown in dishonor is raised in glory, what is sown in weakness is raised in power, and what is sown as a natural body will be raised in a spiritual body (vv. 42–44). N. T. Wright emphasizes that this resurrection is a bodily resurrection that overcomes death: "Within this framework of thought, death is an intruder, a violator of the creator's good world. The creator's answer to death cannot be to reach some kind of agreement or compromise. . . . Anything other than some kind of bodily resurrection, therefore, is simply unthinkable. . . . 'Resurrection' . . . refers to something that *does* die and is then given new life."[13] Because of this promise, Paul asserts, "Death has been swallowed up

13. Nicholas Thomas Wright, *The Resurrection of the Son of God*, Christian Origins and the Question of God, vol. 3 (Minneapolis: Fortress, 2003), 314.

in victory" (v. 54). For Christians, death is not the end. Rather, the death of the body is simply a seed planted for a great outcome! This outcome is revealed in Revelation 21.

A Promise Yet to Come: The Fullest Dwelling

Revelation 21:1–4 reveals the final outcome of the biblical story of God's presence with his people—God will dwell among his people forever:

> Then I saw "a new heaven and a new earth," for the first heaven and the first earth had passed away, and there was no longer any sea. I saw the Holy City, the new Jerusalem, coming down out of heaven from God, prepared as a bride beautifully dressed for her husband. And I heard a loud voice from the throne saying, "Look! God's dwelling place is now among the people, and he will dwell with them. They will be his people, and God himself will be with them and be their God. 'He will wipe every tear from their eyes. There will be no more death' or mourning or crying or pain, for the old order of things has passed away."

The passage illustrates that one day the Kingdom of God will come in full. At this point, what happened in Hughes, a direct sign of what will come one day, will pale in comparison to the magnitude of the promise of Revelation 21.

In this passage, the New Jerusalem, the Holy City, comes down from heaven. This promise harkens back to the beginning in Eden, where God dwelled among his people without restriction. A loud voice proclaims what the goal has always been throughout the course of biblical history: "Look! God's dwelling place is now among his people, and he will dwell with them. They will be his people, and God himself will be with them and be their God" (Rev. 21:2–3). What follows is the promise of a holy God living with holy people. When God's creation fully reflects his image and the intent of the Creator, there will be no crying, pain, death, or mourning. God, in his perfect justice and mercy, in his perfect holiness, has made everything new. Nothing unholy will remain in God's presence.

Surprisingly, in this city, there is no need for a temple (Rev. 21:22). God is no longer bound in any particular space. God and the Lamb are the temple. Those who dwell in the New Jerusalem are from every nation, tribe, and tongue. They are clothed in white (representing holiness) and dwell with God forever.

Scriptural Implications of the Outpouring

The God who generously gifted Asbury University with his presence in February 2023 is a God who purposes to dwell with his people. The plan began in Eden—God's people dwelled with him in perfection. When sin entered, this experience was no longer the case. However, what did not change was God's intent to dwell with his people. This plan developed from the story of the tabernacle to the temple. With Jesus, a new covenant was established and God himself tabernacled in the midst of his people. Then the Holy Spirit was sent to dwell in bodies as temples. God's dwelling place is no longer restricted to the Holy of Holies. The same Holy Spirit that dwelled in Jesus is now sent to dwell with Christians with no geographical or ethnic restriction. In essence, the biblical story sets a precedent that never changes—God intends to be with his people. And when he is, everything changes. Beginning on February 8, 2023, God dwelled in a special way in Hughes Auditorium at Asbury University. This outpouring of God's presence and God's love has changed our community forever beyond what we can fully imagine. We continue to remain in awe of the depth of God's love and faithfulness. His desire to be with us, to never leave us or forsake us, and to love us is something that we can trust. As we have seen, the biblical story has demonstrated these truths repeatedly.

Missiological Reflections and Implications of the Outpouring

When a powerful manifestation of God's dwelling occurs among humanity, it brings forth his glory and power, instilling new life and holiness that lead to restoration and revitalization. It always evokes a profound reflection of God's nature, specifically his mission to love and reach out to the world. God's relational presence reveals his identity, heart, and will. Experiencing God's presence prompts a person to respond by repenting (turning away from sin and returning to God), embracing holiness, and worshiping, ultimately leading the person to share God's love with everyone.

Building on the contemplation of God's presence throughout the Bible, this segment examines the significance of God's dwelling in relation to the mission of God (*missio Dei*). It explores missiological characteristics, such as centripetal and centrifugal aspects, and the movement of God (*motus Dei*), considering the missiological implications that arise from these impactful and awe-inspiring experiences of the Outpouring.

The *Missio Dei*

The Latin phrase *missio Dei* is connected to the missionary activities of the Triune God. Given that mission is intrinsic to God's nature, the source of the missionary movement lies "in the Triune God Himself."[14] Roger Hahn emphasizes that "God's intention and activity" in his mission is "to restore all creation to the purposes for which He created it."[15] Additionally, Jesus tells his disciples, "As the Father has sent me, so I send you" (John 20:21). The sending of one divine Person by another in the doctrine of the Trinity links the church's involvement to the activity of divine sending into the world. Lesslie Newbigin argues that the church should comprehend mission as "the church's obedient participation in that action of the Spirit by which the confession of Jesus as Lord becomes the authentic confession of every new people, each in its own tongue."[16] Therefore, God's mission stems from his desire to dwell among and live with his people. In this essence, God initiated, acted upon, and fulfilled his mission for the world, empowering his people to engage in his ongoing mission.

In the patterns of the missionary movement of God in the Bible, two distinctive characteristics of God's mission appear: the centripetal and centrifugal dynamic forces. These forces emanate from God's dwelling, drawing his people toward himself and sending them outward into the world.

Centripetal Force

In the Old Testament, God calls Israel to himself and chooses them as a holy nation to bear his blessings to all. This begins with the calling of Abram, making him into a great nation and blessing all peoples on the earth (Gen. 12:1–3).

14. Michael Kinnamon and Brian E. Cope, *The Ecumenical Movement: An Anthology of Key Texts and Voices* (Grand Rapids, MI: Eerdmans, 1997), 339–40.
15. Roger L. Hahn, "The Mission of God and a Covenant People," in *Missio Dei: A Wesleyan Understanding*, ed. Keith Schwanz and Joseph Coleson (Kansas City, MO: Beacon Hill of Kansas City, 2011), 40.
16. Lesslie Newbigin, *The Open Secret* (Grand Rapids, MI: Eerdmans, 1995), 20.

To extend blessings to all, Abram needed to know God intimately and experience his presence in his life. The blessing on Abram is not just for one person or one nation but for all. This blessing within Abram's calling reflects the blessings pronounced by God upon all creation in Genesis 1:22, 28, and 2:3, signifying God's intention to restore the nations to the purpose of creation. As Abram and his covenant descendants are designated as God's chosen people, God desires them to worship him as their God. Yahweh dwells among them, expressing his nature through his words, the Torah, and the temple, calling for renewal and revival. Israel was envisioned as a priestly nation (Exod. 19:6), representing God to the world and the world to God.

In this centripetal force, God desires to call his people toward him, to restore and revitalize them through encounters with him and knowledge of him. This desire is also revealed in the Outpouring. The Outpouring invited individuals into intimate encounters with God, prompting them to recognize God as he truly is and compelling wholehearted submission to God's heart and eternal hope across generations. This acknowledgment of God's greatness, gentleness, holiness, and love through encountering him results in genuine worship and communal healing. In these gatherings, worship naturally arises from a sincere recognition of God's nature, free from manipulation or emotional coercion. Participants engage in continuous worship, repentance, and mutual prayer under the profound presence of God. The greatness of God redirects attention solely to him, transcending personal limitations and weaknesses. This experience serves to revive and rejuvenate spirits and souls, profoundly humbling individuals as they acknowledge their status as God's creatures. Individuals are also led into the holiness of God and the humility of Jesus Christ, resulting in reconciliation with God and the discovery of hope and unity through the Holy Spirit.

Encountering the holiness of God prompts repentance for our inherent sinful nature. For the Israelites, the tabernacle symbolized the dwelling place of God, reminding them to be holy through sacrifices for peace and reconciliation with God, themselves, and their neighbors. Atonement, repentance, and the restoration of relationships were related to the dwelling place of God. The sacred space where God is present brings unity. The Outpouring was also a sacred space for encountering God on both a generational and community level; a diverse assembly of generations—locals and students, young and old, insiders and outsiders—worshiped together, mirroring the gathering of Jews and Gentiles described in Ephesians 2:16–19. Those from outside the campus were welcomed with heavenly hospitality by the local community and university, creating a rich tapestry of experiences in this small county. The space became a unifying ground where Generation Z and others could connect with God.

Centrifugal Force

God's missionary nature draws people to himself and then releases and overflows his love and power to the whole world through the sending of himself and the church. "God is in himself mission through and through. Sending and being sent are integral to his nature, for love is uncalculating in the pursuit of its object. No one falls outside its compass. It perseveres even when opposed, rejected and misinterpreted. Love is centrifugal—it always tends outwards from its center."[17] In the Old Testament, God chose the Israelites as a specific nation to reveal his salvation. However, his intention extended beyond mere selection; it aimed to make them a light to all nations (Isa. 42:6–7; 49:6). This divine purpose persisted into the New Testament, where Jesus summoned his disciples to follow him and entrusted them with proclaiming the good news of the Kingdom of God "in Jerusalem, and in all Judea and Samaria, and to the ends of the earth" (Acts 1:8; cf. Matt. 28:19–20). He dispatched his people, empowered by the Spirit. The presence of the Holy Spirit at Pentecost underscored the significance of the church as the temple of God, bearing revelation and eternal hope. Subsequently, the disciples and the church disseminated the gospel, spreading the message of Jesus's death and resurrection far and wide.

One of the most important features of Jesus's teachings is his focus on the Kingdom of God, which expresses the mission of God.[18] In Mark 1:15, Jesus declares that the Kingdom of God has come near and calls people to be ruled by God's divine kingship throughout his redemptive ministry. Jesus's ministry demonstrates the reality of the Kingdom of God's presence. Jesus's presence has the power to subdue nature, heal the broken, and give salvation to whoever believes in him. He fulfills his mission in his earthly life:

> "The Spirit of the Lord is on me, because he has anointed me to proclaim good news to the poor. He has sent me to proclaim freedom for the prisoners

17. Andrew Kirk, *What Is Mission? Theological Explorations* (Minneapolis: Fortress, 2000), 29.
18. Hahn, "Mission of God," 58.

> and recovery of sight for the blind, to set the oppressed free, to proclaim the year of the Lord's favor." Then he rolled up the scroll, gave it back to the attendant and sat down. The eyes of everyone in the synagogue were fastened on him. He began by saying to them, "Today this scripture is fulfilled in your hearing." (Luke 4:18–21)

By being with the disciples, Jesus reveals God himself. This empowers them to carry out his mission later, through the Holy Spirit.

This Kingdom of God is also future (Matt. 13:24–40). God desires the church to show his presence and cultivate an intimate relationship with him (Ps. 91:14–15). Being God's temple and joyful dwelling place involves worship, fellowship with God, and proclaiming only God, his will, and his words to the world. Consequently, the church is meant to embody and extend God's grace and power for everyone and every generation until Jesus returns to establish the eternal Kingdom of God: "Genesis 12 to Revelation 22 tells the story of God's life-giving mission to reverse all this. Saving people from the guilt they incur for their sinful actions is a part of that mission, but only part. God's larger purpose is to heal and transform people, reconciling them to him, to one another and to God's good creation."[19] From the missionary nature of God, the incarnational ministry of Jesus reveals the Kingdom of God and continues through his disciples and the church as we become the temple of God, reflecting God's presence by the Holy Spirit. In this context, God aims to pour out his Spirit from one generation to the next and from place to place. At the Outpouring, God desired to transform students and others into witnesses and channels, sharing his love and presence to build other outpourings everywhere. Numerous testimonies of God's presence in the Outpouring have spread across states and countries, including South Korea, the United Kingdom, Germany, and beyond. Additionally, countless unrecorded testimonies from students, faculty, and staff have been shared with local churches and friends.

THE *MOTUS DEI*

The *motus Dei*—Latin for the "movement of God"—refers to the dynamic shifts within the Kingdom of God. It encapsulates movements where King

19. Andy Johnson, "Missional from First to Last: Paul's Letters and the *Missio Dei*," in *Missio Dei: A Wesleyan Understanding*, ed. Keith Schwanz and Joseph Coleson (Kansas City, MO: Beacon Hill of Kansas City, 2011), 67.

Jesus is celebrated and the gospel brings about transformative changes in lives and communities. It embodies God's active engagement in his own movement through Christ, working toward the redemption of nations back to himself.[20] In this divine movement, individuals are invited by God through Christ to participate in his mission of redeeming nations and cultivating worship, reconciliation with God, and unity within the community.

The Outpouring marked a profound encounter with God's presence. God revealed his desired direction and imparted the essence of his mission for this generation through this tangible presence. The lessons from the Outpouring prompt us to reflect on various aspects as we chart the future directions of missions.

First of all, God, as he truly is, forms the core of our mission message. Mission is the nature of God. David Bosch affirms, "Mission is not primarily an activity of the church, but an attribute of God. God is a missionary God."[21] God—that is, knowing God and acknowledging God—is the ultimate goal of all our mission activities. Therefore, the heart of the Triune God should be central to today's missions. Our missions become a transformative journey, powered by the Holy Spirit, where believers strive to reflect the attributes of the indwelling God.

Furthermore, our missions should prioritize cultivating a dynamic and genuine Christian community that reflects God's presence among his people. Our missionary work goes beyond mere individual conversions; it involves nurturing and deepening believers' faith within a cohesive community actively seeking God and worshiping together. Andrew Kirk affirms that "God's reconciling activity in Jesus Christ (2 Cor. 5:19) has as its goal not only individuals (Rom. 5:10–11) and the cosmos (Col. 1:20), but human beings with one another."[22]

To create this authentic community that represents God's dwelling, we should emphasize Jesus-like humility and cultivate godly characteristics. This community can then bring reconciliation, healing, and continuity of God's vision across generations. The focus on reconciliation includes addressing geographical and ethnic divisions and fostering a generational calling, uniting every generation in the shared experience of encountering God.

20. Warrick Farah, *Motus Dei: The Movement of God to Disciple the Nations* (Pasadena, CA: William Carey, 2021), 9.

21. David J. Bosch, *Transforming Mission* (Maryknoll, NY: Orbis, 1991), 389–90.

22. Kirk, *What Is Mission?*, 35.

Lastly, a holistic approach to missions, addressing both spiritual and material needs, reflects the presence of God. Compassion for the suffering and oppressed lies at the core of God's work in the world. Jesus's incarnational ministry encompasses every aspect of people's lives. He brings good news to the poor and the needy, proclaiming the Lord's favor (Luke 4:18–21). When God's presence is revealed, his transformative power and love overflow, bestowing upon people "a crown of beauty instead of ashes, the oil of joy instead of mourning, and a garment of praise instead of a spirit of despair" (Isa. 61:3). Our mission endeavors aim to address not only spiritual needs but also physical, emotional, and social aspects, shaping societal values in accordance with God's principles.

Conclusion

When we envision the Outpouring as the dwelling of God among his people, it becomes a transformative force capable of leading individuals and communities into God's presence, facilitating encounters with his glory, and empowering his people to reach out to all nations. Acknowledging that this outpouring is initiated solely by God prompts repentance and catalyzes a shift in the spiritual atmosphere, fostering unity, mercy, love, forgiveness, and a continuous movement of the Holy Spirit.

God's ceaseless works and the manifestation of his grace and love persist in his people. From the calling of Adam and Eve to rule over the earth to Abraham being summoned as a channel of blessing for all nations to the establishment of the tabernacle for purification and holy worship, God's unfolding plan becomes evident. Through the transformative events of the cross and resurrection, God reveals a plan for a living temple, beckoning people to discover new lives through the empowerment of the Holy Spirit. As we encounter Jesus in the New Testament and heed the Great Commission (Matt. 28:19–20), the presence of God extends through time and space, encompassing every tribe and nation.

We can become distracted by the extremity or glamour of these encounters with God, but instead, we must focus on God's gracious calling to surrender ourselves to him through that profound connection with his presence. The God who demonstrated his works in the Outpouring at Asbury University is not confined to a specific place and time; he is present here and everywhere. Let us actively engage in experiencing God's presence and allow him to work marvelously in and among us.

CHAPTER EIGHT

THE ASBURY OUTPOURING AND THE HISTORY OF EVANGELICAL REVIVALS

Kevin L. Anderson

Professor of Bible and Theology, Asbury University

During the nonstop worship and prayer in Hughes Auditorium, more than fifty thousand pilgrims from thirty US states and thirteen countries streamed into the six-thousand-resident town of Wilmore, Kentucky.[1] Students arrived from more than 280 colleges and universities. Capacity crowds of fifteen hundred were in Hughes Auditorium during daylight hours and sometimes deep into the night.[2] Hundreds of people lined up nearly halfway around the campus waiting to get into Hughes Auditorium, at times standing in cold rain. Nearly eighteen hundred volunteers assisted in various capacities. Asbury had more than 280 million hits on social media.[3] These statistics give a snapshot of the Outpouring at Asbury University, February 8–23, 2023.

Revivals are not new to Asbury University.[4] The student body experienced dramatic moves of God's Spirit in 1905, 1908, 1921, 1950, 1958, 1970, 1992, 2006, and now in 2023. Seven of the nine revivals occurred

1. At least one source has suggested numbers as high as seventy thousand visitors, forty US states, and forty countries.
2. Overflow venues also opened up at Asbury Theological Seminary: Estes Chapel (seating 660), McKenna Chapel (seating 375), and Sherman Thompson Student Center gymnasium (seating approximately 1,000).
3. Many of the above figures have been gleaned from Mark R. Elliott, *Taken by Surprise: The Asbury Revival of 2023* (Franklin, TN: Seedbed, 2023), xix, 97, 102, 163–72, and back cover. Others are my own estimates.
4. Asbury College prior to 2008.

in February, including the protracted meetings in 1950 (118 hours), 1970 (144 hours), and 2023 (380 hours). Two occurred in March (1958 and 1992).[5] Revival is in Asbury's DNA. This chapter explores the deeper roots of revival in Asbury's heritage—a lineage of spiritual renewal that reaches back to the evangelical revivals in England and the United States in the eighteenth century.

While the Outpouring in February 2023 was a fresh move of the Spirit, God works within cultural contexts. Divine revelation in both the Old and New Testaments, and especially the Incarnation of Jesus Christ, establishes this truth. God acts in history. So it should be no surprise that the Asbury Outpouring bears a family resemblance to past revivals. This is true regardless of whether the participants were aware of the evangelical history and culture of revivals. The culture of spiritual renewal is woven through the worship music, the practices of prayer and preaching, and the theological framework for Asbury's spiritual life.

A few weeks after the Outpouring, my mother moved in with my wife, Sandi, and me in Wilmore, Kentucky. It has been over thirty-five years since I left my boyhood home, so living in close contact with my mother again has been a learning experience. As an older adult, I am gaining an increased knowledge of how many of my traits and habits have their origins in my parents. The experience has imparted to me a surprising self-awareness of my identity, with both its strengths and foibles. I have also become aware of how my education, marriage, and other life experiences have shaped me in new ways beyond the genetics and nurturing of my parents. Likewise, taking a look at the history, culture, and theology of revival will help us to make greater sense of how God is working both in the light of our past spiritual inheritance as well as in our unique cultural moment. We will gain a self-awareness of how the old spirit of revival still animates our own spiritual renewal, as well as how the fresh wind of the Spirit blows into our communal life to bring about change that looks different from what our spiritual forebears experienced.

The Vocabulary of Revival

The title of this chapter refers to "evangelical revivals." But this raises questions about what the terms *evangelical* and *revival* mean.

5. Matt Kinnell, "Asbury Revival," Asbury University, accessed September 17, 2024, https://www.asbury.edu/academics/resources/library/archives/history/asbury-revival/.

Evangelical, *evangelicalism*, and like terms present something of a moving target. They do not submit to one definition or description.[6] Evangelical identity has also been muddled by US political and ideological rifts.[7] Nevertheless, "evangelicalism" yet serves as a useful banner for a broad Christian movement that exists across the globe. First, it must be noted that the term *evangelical* is derived from the Greek word for "gospel" or "good news" (*euangelion*). Of course, all Christians lay claim to the message about Jesus Christ recorded in the New Testament, which announces God's Kingdom and saving work through Christ's life, death, and resurrection. Evangelicalism aims to preserve and live out the truth of the gospel through four main emphases, as well as a shared understanding of its particular place within the larger Christian family. These four emphases are described by Kenneth J. Collins: "(1) the normative value of Scripture in the Christian life, (2) the necessity of conversion (whether or not dramatic or even remembered), (3) the cruciality of the atoning work of Christ as the sole mediator between God and humanity, and (4) the imperative of evangelism, of proclaiming the glad tidings of salvation to the lost."[8]

Even these four traits are not unique to evangelicalism. Evangelicalism exists as a global movement of orthodox Protestant faith whose origins trace back to the eighteenth-century revivals associated with the work of Jonathan Edwards, George Whitefield, and John Wesley.

This, then, gives us a sense of what evangelicalism is. So what about "revival"? Timothy K. Beougher observes, "The term 'revival' means different things to different people. It has been used to describe renewed spiritual

6. For a survey of viewpoints on evangelicalism, see CT editors, "What Does 'Evangelical' Mean?" *Christianity Today*, January 27, 2020, https://www.christianitytoday.com/ct/2020/january-web-only/evangelical-distinctives.html.
7. Some among the so-called evangelical left have decided to drop the label "evangelical"; see Josiah Hesse, "'Exvangelicals': Why More Religious People Are Rejecting the Evangelical Label," *The Guardian*, November 3, 2017, https://www.theguardian.com/world/2017/nov/03/evangelical-christians-religion-politics-trump. For a study of the evangelical left, see David R. Swartz, *Moral Minority: The Evangelical Left in an Age of Conservatism*, Politics and Culture in Modern America (Philadelphia: University of Pennsylvania Press, 2012).
8. Kenneth J. Collins, *The Evangelical Moment: The Promise of an American Religion* (Grand Rapids, MI: Baker Academic, 2005), 21; for more detailed discussion, see chapter 2, "Evangelical Distinctives." Similarly, Bebbington identifies four characteristics of evangelicalism: biblicism, conversionism, activism, and crucicentrism. See David Bebbington, *Evangelicalism in Modern Britain: A History from the 1730s to the 1980s* (London: Unwin Hyman, 1989), 2–17.

life, a series of evangelistic meetings, unbridled religious emotionalism, wild frontier religion, and fanaticism."[9]

At least two factors come into play when attempting to define *revival.* The first is that numerous terms are used for the same phenomena: *outpouring*, *renewal*, *revival*, *revivalism*, and *awakening*, among others. The challenge is to deploy a coherent vocabulary in which these terms are understood in their relationship to one another. The second factor pertains to whether the most useful definition is descriptive or prescriptive. Descriptive definitions are based on sociological descriptions of revival, but they are often reductionistic.[10] Prescriptive definitions are more useful because they appropriately make theological judgments about the nature and purpose of revivals. A key theological question concerns whether revivals or awakenings are sovereign acts of God or are effected through human techniques that harness the power of the Holy Spirit. Our theological orientation toward the subject of revival will become apparent as we proceed to define terms.

Revival is a biblical concept.[11] In the Old Testament, the verb *revive* or "bring (back) to life" (Heb. *ḥayah*) is used in key texts such as Psalm 85:6 ("Will you not revive us again") and Habakkuk 3:2 ("Revive your work in these years" [CSB]). Various revivals occurred throughout Jewish history, notably under the good kings of Judah (Asa, Jehoash, Hezekiah, and Josiah) and under the postexilic figures of Zerubbabel and Ezra. Revival was a return to the proper obedience and worship of Yahweh after the people had fallen into idolatry.

The New Testament usually employs the language of "revival" in terms of actual resurrection from the dead rather than spiritual renewal—except in the description of the returning prodigal as one who was dead but is "alive again" (Luke 15:24, 32). Yet the entire New Testament is about revival. The opening of Jesus's ministry was a proclamation of the good news of God's Kingdom and a call to Israel to repent and trust in God's new work in Jesus Christ (see Mark 1:14–15). Christ's cross and resurrection are central to the inauguration of God's Kingdom and are emblematic of the spiritual revival

9. Timothy K. Beougher, "Revival, Revivals," *Evangelical Dictionary of World Mission*, ed. Scott Moreau (Grand Rapids, MI: Baker, 2000), 830–31.
10. For example, McLoughlin's definition of revivalism as "professional mass evangelism." See William G. McLoughlin Jr., *Modern Revivalism: Charles Grandison Finney to Billy Graham* (1959; repr., Eugene, OR: Wipf & Stock, 2004), 11.
11. For a longer discussion of biblical precedents for the in-breaking presence of God, see the chapter by Julianne Burnett, Joy Vaughan, and Sam Kim in this volume.

that occurs in believers who share in Christ's death and resurrection and therefore "walk in newness of life" (Rom. 6:4). The resurrection of Christ is also "the firstfruits" of believers' final resurrection from the dead (1 Cor. 15:20, 23). The apostle Paul envisioned the salvation of Jews as nothing short of "life from the dead" (Rom. 11:15).

The indispensable element of revival is the outpouring of the Holy Spirit. The end-time pouring out of the Holy Spirit upon all flesh was prophesied by the prophet Joel (2:28–32) and found its fulfillment in the events at Pentecost (Acts 2). Such outpourings of the Spirit were repeated in the book of Acts, whether to strengthen the early persecuted church (Acts 4:23–31), restore true faith among the Samaritans (Acts 8), effect conversion among Gentiles at the house of Cornelius (Acts 10), or seal the faith of certain devotees of John the Baptist (Acts 19:1–7). Prayers for revival in the eighteenth and nineteenth centuries were pleas for "an outpouring" or "an effusion" of the Holy Spirit.[12] Those in the nineteenth-century Holiness Movement were fond of seeking recurrences of Pentecost in the church and in individuals in order to experience the presence and power of the Holy Spirit for holiness and effective witness to the world.

Consequently, no definition of revival is complete without reference to the outpouring of the Holy Spirit. Melvin Dieter writes, "Revivals are commonly understood to be special periods of religious renewal in which God, through the Holy Spirit and the agency of those inspired and directed by the Holy Spirit, calls men and women to spiritual rebirth and Christian discipleship."[13] Church historian Earl Cairns notes that repentance, prayer, and the Word are important aspects of revival.[14] Intense spiritual experiences accompany revivals. Robert Fleming (1630–94), for example, described a time of revival in 1620s Ireland as "a bright and hot sun-blink of the gospel" and "one of the largest manifestations of the Spirit, and of the most solemn times of the down-pouring thereof, that almost since the days of the apostles hath been seen, where the power of God did sensibly

12. J. Edwin Orr, *The Re-Study of Revival and Revivalism* (Pasadena, CA: School of World Mission, 1981), ii.

13. Melvin E. Dieter, "Revivals, Revivalism," *Historical Dictionary of Methodism*, ed. Charles Yrigoyen Jr. and Susan E. Warrick (Lanham, MD: Scarecrow, 2013), 308.

14. Earle E. Cairns, *An Endless Line of Splendor: Revivals and Their Leaders from the Great Awakening to the Present* (Wheaton, IL: Tyndale House, 1986), 22.

accompany the Word with an unusual motion upon the hearers, and a very great tack,[15] as to the conversion of souls to Christ."[16]

We could multiply such definitions of revival, which accent the necessary coming of the Holy Spirit to manifest the presence, power, and grace of God.[17]

How, then, are we to understand the relationship between such terms as *outpouring*, *revival*, *revivalism*, and *awakening*? *Outpouring*, as we have seen, refers to God's pouring out of the Holy Spirit. Recently, Vickers and McCall have identified "outpourings" as "*those events in which from time to time and in ways that are unscripted and beyond human control, God makes God's presence and power manifest in a manner that is readily discernible, that leads to repentance and deep joy, and that conveys life-changing forgiveness and grace.*"[18] This definition rightly emphasizes God's freedom in pouring out the Holy Spirit when and how he wills to do so, apart from any human planning or determination, as well as in ways that are noticeable, if not unmistakable. The effects of an outpouring (repentance, deep joy, life-changing forgiveness, grace) shade into a definition of revival. Outpourings are not revivals, but revivals may only happen as a result of outpourings. It is only through the work of the Holy Spirit that people may be gifted with divine grace, faith, repentance, forgiveness, life change, and resulting joy. As Orr notes, "Outpourings of the Spirit are exclusively the work of God; but revivals are the work of God with the response of believers."[19]

The terms *revival* and (spiritual) *renewal* are often used interchangeably. Both refer to the reinvigoration of spiritual vitality after it has declined or died away. Therefore, among evangelicals since the eighteenth century, revival has referred to a restoration of spiritual life and Christian devotion in the church or among professing Christians.

15. A Scots word for a catch of fish.
16. Cited in Iain H. Murray, *The Puritan Hope: A Study in Revival and the Interpretation of Prophecy* (London: Banner of Truth Trust, 1971), 32.
17. See H. H. Osborn, *Revival, God's Spotlight: The Significance of Revivals and Why They Cease* (Godalming, UK: Highland, 1996), 16–17; R. E. Davies, *I Will Pour Out My Spirit: A History and Theology of Revivals and Evangelical Awakenings* (Tunbridge, UK: Monarch, 1992), 15–18; R. E. Davies, "Revivals, Spiritual," in *Evangelical Dictionary of Theology*, ed. Daniel J. Treier and Walter A. Elwell, 2nd ed. (Grand Rapids, MI: Baker Academic, 2001), 750.
18. Jason E. Vickers and Thomas H. McCall, *Outpouring: A Theological Witness* (Eugene, OR: Cascade, 2023), 99 (italics are in original).
19. J. Edwin Orr, *The Outpouring of the Spirit in Revival and Awakening and Its Issue in Church Growth* (Bedford, UK: British Church Growth Association, 2000), 6.

The terms *revival* and *awakening* have also often been used as synonyms. It is probably best, however, to draw a distinction between them. The foremost expert on revival, J. Edwin Orr, asserts, "The logic of words suggests 'revival' for the revitalizing of a body of Christian believers, and 'awakening' for the stirring of interest in the related community of nominal Christians or unbelievers."[20] Revivals have a direct effect on the church. A revived church is mobilized for evangelism and social change in the surrounding community. So revival can activate leavening agents in the church that promote a wider awakening in society.[21] Spiritual renewals, though initiated through outpourings of the Spirit, are welcomed and sustained through obedient responses of believers. As a result, there is much variability in whether or to what extent revivals will blossom into larger cultural awakenings. As well, one must realize that in a revival's "effect upon the social welfare there is a time-lag often as long as the lifetime of its converts."[22] We know not when or what seeds of revival will find fertile soil and produce a thirty-, sixty-, or hundredfold yield.

This brings us finally to the meaning of *revivalism*. *Revivalism* may be understood as "the state or form of religion characteristic of revivals," and a "revivalist" is "one who promotes, produces, or participates in a religious revival."[23] However, beginning in the nineteenth century, the language of revival and revivalism came to be conceptually linked if not equated with evangelism. Revivalism became identified with prominent evangelists and mass evangelistic campaigns whose purpose was to reach the lost with the gospel.[24] At this point, revival vocabulary is necessarily

20. J. Edwin Orr, *The Flaming Tongue: The Impact of 20th Century Revivals* (Chicago: Moody, 1973), ix; cf. J. Edwin Orr, *The Eager Feet: Evangelical Awakenings, 1790–1830* (Chicago: Moody, 1975), 127. Elsewhere, Orr points out that "the Oxford Association for Research in Revival has adopted 'revival' for believers and 'awakening' for the community" (*Re-Study of Revival*, iv).
21. Two classic studies document the nineteenth-century evangelical social consciousness and catalyst for social change: Timothy L. Smith, *Revivalism and Social Reform: American Protestantism on the Eve of the Civil War* (1957; repr. Eugene, OR: Wipf & Stock, 2004); and Donald W. Dayton with Douglas M. Strong, *Rediscovering an Evangelical Heritage: A Tradition and Trajectory of Integrating Piety and Justice*, 2nd ed. (Grand Rapids, MI: Baker Academic, 2014).
22. J. Edwin Orr, *The Light of the Nations: Evangelical Renewal and Advance in the Nineteenth Century*, The Advance of Christianity through the Centuries, vol. 8 (Grand Rapids, MI: Eerdmans, 1965), 10.
23. Orr, *Re-Study of Revival*, iii. Orr reports that the terms *revivalism* and *revivalist* began to be used in 1815 and 1820, respectively.
24. Beougher, "Revival," 831.

determined by one's theology of revival. Instead of being "the surprising work of God" in which God sovereignly manifests his glory, revival becomes a staging area for the Spirit to work almost automatically.[25]

No one commended the latter (Pelagian) theology of revival more than the early nineteenth-century revivalist Charles G. Finney. Finney explains his view in a famous passage:

> [Revival] is not a miracle, or dependent on a miracle, in any sense. It is a purely philosophical result of the right use of the constituted means—as much so as any other effect produced by the application of means. . . . In the Bible, the word of God is compared to grain, and preaching is compared to sowing seed, and the results to the springing up and growth of the crop. And the result is just as philosophical in the one case, as in the other, and is as naturally connected with the cause; or, more correctly, a revival is as naturally a result of the use of the appropriate means as a crop is of the use of its appropriate means.[26]

Finney has greatly affected modern evangelical understanding and practice related to revivals. For instance, paradoxically, many churches hold annual revival meetings or services, usually without any breakout of revival. While we may acknowledge prerequisites for spiritual renewal,[27] it is presumptuous to assume that one can produce revival simply by the employment of certain techniques or preplanned events. As set forth above, true revivals are animated by outpourings of the Spirit that are sovereignly administered, even though the depth and continuance of God's work of revival depends on faithful obedience in response to divine grace.

Historic Evangelical Revivals

Revivals and revivalism are characteristic of the evangelical movement, whose doctrinal emphases and spiritual practices were shaped by the revivals in eighteenth- and nineteenth-century America and Great Britain. To be

25. This echoes the title of Jonathan Edwards's *A Faithful Narrative of the Surprising Work of God in the Conversion of Many Hundred Souls in Northampton* (1737).
26. Charles G. Finney, *Lectures on Revivals of Religion*, 2nd ed. (1835; repr., New York: Fleming H. Revell, 1868), 12–13.
27. See the taxonomy of preconditions, primary elements, and secondary elements of renewal delineated by Richard Lovelace, *Dynamics of Spiritual Life: An Evangelical Theology of Renewal* (Downers Grove, IL: InterVarsity, 1979), chaps. 3–5 and chart on p. 75.

sure, spiritual renewal reaches into our fallen world as far back as Enoch, who walked with God. It advances from Abraham's faith and Israel's sin, exile, and restoration, and comes to new life in the ministry of Jesus and the Spirit-filled apostolic church. We can trace revivals of religion throughout the history of the church, yet the unique elements of evangelical revival were forged in modern times.

Therefore, our survey will focus on the historic evangelical revivals in North America and Great Britain. This is not because we wish to neglect the spread of evangelical revivals throughout the world.[28] It is because the global story of revival is much too large a story to tell, and the epicenter of evangelical spiritual energy emerged in the English-speaking world on both sides of the Atlantic in the eighteenth century. Moreover, Asbury University is an heir to the American Holiness Movement, whose adherents were major contributors to the revivalist spirit in the United States and Great Britain in the nineteenth and twentieth centuries.

The Reformation and Revival

There is some debate concerning whether the Protestant Reformation may be properly designated as a revival (or a series of them). After all, it was shaped by not only religious but also political, economic, and cultural factors. Nevertheless, the Reformation marked a tremendous awakening. The doctrinal and ecclesiastical reforms championed by leaders such as Martin Luther, Ulrich Zwingli, John Calvin, and others brought new spiritual life to Europe. Key commitments of Reformed faith—including the authority of Scripture, the focus on Christ as central to spiritual devotion, the doctrine of justification by faith alone, and reliance on the Holy Spirit to illuminate the truths of Scripture—served as the foundation for the later evangelical movement.

Direct Antecedents to Evangelical Revival

Two movements in the seventeenth century were foundational to later evangelical revivals: Pietism among Lutheranism in Germany and Puritanism in Britain and the American colonies.

28. For a convenient summary of revivals in North America, Great Britain, Switzerland and France, the Netherlands, Germany, and the Nordic Lands, see Ulrich Gäbler, "Revivals," *Encyclopedia of Christianity*, ed. Erwin Fahlbusch et al., vol. 4 (Grand Rapids, MI: Eerdmans, 2005), 680–85.

Philipp Jakob Spener (1635–1705) and August Hermann Francke (1663–1727) were the leading lights of German Pietism. Pietism put a greater emphasis on the role of laity in the cultivation of spiritual devotion. They urged people to move beyond mere assent to doctrines and to pursue a personal experience of faith that is focused on the study of the Bible and a lifestyle of holiness.[29] One cannot overemphasize the importance of this radical shift toward personal piety as the key to Christian discipleship. It has been so absorbed into evangelicalism that it is difficult to view it as quite as groundbreaking as it was.

Puritanism, as its name suggests, worked to "purify" the Church of England. The Puritans sought reforms of the church and the sanctification of individuals and society based on biblical teaching. Their biblicism and emphasis on personal piety were matched by their openness to the movement of the Holy Spirit in revivals. It has been said that "the whole Puritan movement should probably be considered as a revival movement."[30] Importantly, at least some Puritan revivals featured emotional outbursts (like the agonizing cry "What shall I do to be saved?") and physical responses (such as swooning under the conviction of sin and lying "slain" on the ground as though dead).[31] These dramatic participatory elements would resurface in the eighteenth-century revivals and would become commonplace in the nineteenth-century American Holiness Movement and twentieth-century Pentecostalism.

The First Great Awakening

The First Great Awakening (or the Evangelical Revival, as it is called in Great Britain) refers to the remarkable revivals that occurred in the thirteen American colonies and in Great Britain in the early eighteenth century.[32]

The First Great Awakening in the thirteen colonies is usually associated with the Congregationalist pastor Jonathan Edwards (1703–58) in Northampton, Massachusetts. But Edwards's grandfather, Solomon Stoddard, had already enjoyed five "harvests" of revival at the Northampton

29. Stanley J. Grenz, David Guretzki, and Cherith Fee Nordling, *Pocket Dictionary of Theological Terms* (Downers Grove, IL: InterVarsity, 1999), s.v. "Pietism."

30. Davies, *I Will Pour Out*, 63, citing J. I. Packer, "Puritanism as a Movement of Revival," *Evangelical Quarterly* 52, no. 1 (1980): 2–16.

31. Osborn, *Revival*, 28; Davies, *I Will Pour Out*, 64.

32. For an overview, see Thomas S. Kidd, *The Great Awakening: The Roots of Evangelical Christianity in Colonial America* (New Haven, CT: Yale University Press, 2007).

church he had pastored since 1670. After Stoddard's death in 1729, Edwards was appointed pastor. Stirrings of revival had also occurred in 1726 through the ministry of the Dutch Reformed pastor Theodore Frelinghuysen in New Jersey. Frelinghuysen, who in his youth had absorbed the influences of German Pietism,[33] pressed upon his hearers the need for an "inner transformation" of true conversion rather than only an outward show of moral uprightness.[34]

The American colonies needed revival. They had experienced a deep spiritual decline. In Congregational churches in New England, the Half-Way Covenant allowed baptized but unconverted persons into membership so that their children would be eligible for baptism. Thus, many nominal Christians populated the churches. Edwards observed that parishioners were formally orthodox in beliefs but in lifestyle were primarily concerned with wealth and property, and their children were given to walking about at night and tavern haunting.[35] On the American frontier, no churches or pastoral care were available for the spiritually impoverished. Commercially, whiskey was liquid gold, and its consumption led to loose living and violence.[36]

The revival in Northampton began in the fall of 1734. Edwards held prayer meetings and preached a series of sermons on justification by faith alone. A young woman's conversion in December led to a revival that ushered more than three hundred souls into the church by May 1735, when the revival trailed off. Other revivals occurred along the Connecticut River valley in more than one hundred communities by 1737. In the 1740s, revival spread in the middle colonies through the fiery preaching of the Presbyterian minister Gilbert Tennent (1703–64) and his two brothers and in the southern colonies through the work of Baptist and Presbyterian ministers.

The Methodist preacher George Whitefield (1714–70) traveled from England seven times to conduct evangelistic campaigns in the colonies, but none was as successful as his tour in 1739–41. Whitefield was a pioneer in mass evangelism, or what was called field preaching—preaching in the open air rather than in a church. In Boston, he preached to five thousand on Boston Commons, with the crowds sometimes swelling to fifteen thousand.

33. Keith J. Hardman, *Seasons of Refreshing: Evangelism and Revivals in America* (Grand Rapids, MI: Baker, 2004), 52.
34. For a discussion of Frelinghuysen's preaching, see Cairns, *Endless Line of Splendor*, 44.
35. Lovelace, *Dynamics of Spiritual Life*, 38.
36. Cairns, *Endless Line of Splendor*, 40.

Through the revivals under Whitefield, 150 new churches were formed in New England, Pennsylvania, New York, New Jersey, and Maryland.[37]

Eighteenth-century Great Britain was also in dire need of revival. People were preoccupied with gambling and amusements like cockfighting, bear-baiting, and attendance at the gallows to watch "hanging shows." Gin houses were doing swift business, and drunkenness was rampant. Politicians were corrupt, and Anglican clergy were materialistic and dull. The intelligentsia were rationalists and Deists.[38]

Britain saw the stirrings of revival as early as 1710 in Wales, but it spread more fully in the 1730s and '40s in all four countries: Wales, Scotland, England, and Ireland. Wales witnessed revivals through Griffith Jones, Daniel Rowland, and Howell Harris. Jones originated the practice of itinerant field preaching and established "charity schools," which taught people to read the Bible. He influenced Rowland, Harris, and others to engage in open-air preaching, which resulted in many conversions and renewals of faith among the Welsh. Scottish churches experienced revivals under George Whitefield's preaching in 1742, with the faithful groundwork of William M'Culloch (1700–1771) at Cambuslang and James Robe (1688–1753) at Kilsyth. The threefold pattern of revival in Scotland involved prayer, preaching about the new birth, and providing spiritual counsel to those who came under conviction.[39] The Methodists, George Whitefield and brothers John (1703–91) and Charles Wesley (1707–88), worked tirelessly to preach the gospel in England and beyond. John Wesley looked upon "the whole world as my parish." He was influenced by Whitefield to engage in field preaching, even as Whitefield had imitated Howell Harris in the practice. Wesley preached some 46,000 sermons from 1738 to 1791 and traveled 225,000 miles on horseback around England, as well as Ireland (twenty-three times), Scotland (eleven times), and Wales (nine times).[40]

John Wesley was profoundly affected by the Moravians—that is, German Pietists who were headquartered in Herrnhut, Germany, under the leadership of Count Nicholas L. von Zinzendorf (1700–1760) and who became missionaries in many places throughout the world. Thus, Wesley's understanding of conversion included the necessity not only to believe by

37. Cairns, *Endless Line of Splendor*, 48.

38. Cairns, *Endless Line of Splendor*, 53–55; Hardman, *Seasons of Refreshing*, 77–79.

39. Cairns, *Endless Line of Splendor*, 61.

40. Cairns, *Endless Line of Splendor*, 81.

faith that one is justified before God through the merits of Christ's death but also to have a personal assurance through the witness of the Holy Spirit that one is saved. Wesley believed that Christian discipleship involved more than outward obedience to God's ordinances. It must include a change in one's affections (from hate, envy, and strife to love, joy, and peace) and ultimately an alteration of one's tempers (that is, deep-seated tendencies or dispositions). One of the strengths (and sometimes a weakness) of Methodism, therefore, has been its attention to the emotional life in both conversion and growth in holiness. This emphasis was supported by music in worship, whose importance is underscored by Charles Wesley's composition of more than sixty-five hundred hymns.

The Second Great Awakening

The Second Great Awakening may have had two phases, 1776–1810 and 1813–46, though the latter phase could be regarded as a fresh movement.[41]

Ground zero for revival in North America was Virginia in 1787, though revival fires had been burning among Congregationalists and Methodists in Canada in the preceding decade. Two colleges in Virginia became the sites of revival: Hampden-Sydney College (which had been founded by Presbyterians in 1776 as a result of the First Great Awakening) and Washington College. At Hampden-Sydney College, the weekly prayer meetings of four young men eventually broke out in revival and yielded the conversion of half of the student body. The revival soon spread to Washington College (now Washington and Lee College).

Yale College in New Haven, Connecticut, was another academic institution that would be revived from its moribund spiritual state, beginning with the accession of Timothy Dwight (1752–1817) to its presidency in 1795. Dwight found Yale in moral and spiritual dissolution. He brought discipline to the institution and, through regular lectures, embarked on a systematic dismantling of "infidel philosophy" (i.e., Deism), which was in vogue among students.

By 1784, when the Methodist Episcopal Church was formally organized, there had been tremendous success under the leadership of Francis Asbury (1745–1816), particularly in the South. Meanwhile, in 1789, Jonathan Edwards's *Humble Attempt to Promote Explicit Agreement . . . in Extraordinary Prayer for the Revival of Religion* was reprinted in Britain, and

41. As does Cairns, *Endless Line of Splendor*, 117.

it sparked "an interdenominational and international movement of prayer" that bore fruit in the modern Protestant missionary movement and the establishment of many societies for social reform.[42] In the western frontier of the United States, the camp meeting was coming into its own. The Cane Ridge camp meeting of 1801 near Paris, Kentucky, in Bourbon County was one of the most memorable. It attracted three dozen Presbyterian, Baptist, and Methodist preachers and between ten and twenty-five thousand campers. Cane Ridge was notorious for its revival excesses, with people shouting, crying, falling down, laughing, barking, and jerking.

By 1830, revival rebounded with great strength, not least through the preaching of Charles G. Finney (1792–1875). Finney, a former attorney, was known for simple, direct, and logically persuasive preaching. He was criticized for his use of "New Measures," including "protracted meetings" and the "anxious seat," which facilitated seekers in repenting and making a decision for Christ.[43] The anxious seat was the forerunner to "the altar call," which became a prominent feature in Holiness camp meetings and was used by many succeeding evangelists, from D. L. Moody to Billy Sunday to Billy Graham.

The Midcentury Prayer Revival (1858–80s)

Timothy Smith called 1858 the *Annus Mirabilis*, "the Miracle Year."[44] Revival happened in major American cities, not due to the preaching of any revivalist, but perhaps because the crash of the New York stock market awakened people to their spiritual need. In New York, and then in Chicago and Philadelphia, noon prayer meetings were held among businessmen, in some cases numbering as many as two thousand attendees. Prominent people were converted, and prayer meetings spread literally throughout the world. In the United States, during a two-year period, a million people joined various churches. Many itinerant evangelists arose, such as Dwight L. Moody and Phoebe Palmer in the United States and William and Catherine Booth in England. Yet laypersons were the driving force for revival, and many organizations and ministries developed in this

42. Davies, "Revivals," 751.
43. Also called "the mourner's bench," "the mercy seat," and in the Salvation Army, "the penitent form."
44. Smith, *Revivalism and Social Reform*, chap. 4, "*Annus Mirabilis*—1858."

period: the YMCA, the YWCA, Salvation Army, the Keswick movement, Sunday schools, Christian unions at universities, and foreign missions.[45]

It is important to point out that in the United States and in Great Britain, the Holiness Movement was a deep current that fed on and perpetuated revival. There is hardly a name or institution mentioned in the previous paragraph that was not impacted by it in some way. Though it was an heir to Methodism and Wesley's doctrine of Christian perfection, its promise of a victorious Christian life made inroads into other Protestant faith traditions, including among Presbyterians and Baptists. Phoebe Palmer refined and promoted the signature doctrine of the movement: a "shorter way" to being entirely sanctified for a holy life and Christian service by putting one's all on the altar and surrendering oneself to Christ in full consecration. Asbury College (now Asbury University), founded in 1890, is a direct product of the American Holiness Movement.[46]

Twentieth-Century Revivals

As a rule, revivals occur against a backdrop of profound spiritual and moral bankruptcy in society and the church. The revivals at the beginning of the twentieth century were an exception. The 1858–59 prayer revival had touched off a wave of evangelical advances that lasted forty years. The end of the nineteenth century was, in the words of J. Edwin Orr, "a blaze of evening glory."[47] Two spiritual movements at the beginning of the twentieth century—the Welsh Revival of 1904–5 and the Azusa Street Revival of 1906–8—would represent a further advance or culmination of the preceding century of revival. They would have a lasting effect on the growth and character of evangelical faith in the new century. Yet many factors would impede twentieth-century revivals from having the same deep cultural impact in the English-speaking world as past revivals did: sustained cultural wars with modernism, kinetic wars among nations (especially the two World Wars), and sweeping social changes brought about by anti-Christian forces from the 1960s onward.

45. Davies, "Revivals," 752.

46. For an overview of the spread of the Holiness Movement, see Randall J. Stephens, *The Fire Spreads: Holiness and Pentecostalism in the American South* (Cambridge, MA: Harvard University Press, 2008).

47. Orr, *Re-Study of Revival*, 41.

The Welsh Revival of 1904–5 started spontaneously in locations throughout the country, but it is associated with the simple "Four Points" message of Evan J. Roberts (1878–1951): put away unconfessed sin, give up doubtful habits, obey the Spirit promptly, and confess Christ publicly.[48] Great outpourings of the Spirit occurred, accompanied by conversions, visions, prophetic words, and all manner of exuberant expressions (cries for mercy, weeping, singing, and the like). The revival was short-lived, as was Roberts's role in it, but its effects were sizable. In Wales alone, church membership increased by one hundred thousand new converts by the end of 1905. Word of the divine work touched off revivals throughout Europe, North America, Australasia, Asia, Africa, and Latin America—winning upwards of five million people to an evangelical faith. J. Edwin Orr called it "the most extensive evangelical awakening of all time."[49]

A second major movement of the Holy Spirit sparked the Azusa Street Revival of 1906–8. In late 1900, Charles F. Parham (1873–1929) led a small Bible school in Topeka, Kansas, that investigated the biblical evidence for the baptism of the Holy Spirit. They concluded that speaking in tongues provided this evidence. Not long afterward, believers there began speaking in tongues. A few years later, Parham opened a school in Houston, Texas, and trained William J. Seymour (d. 1922), who carried this "full gospel" to Los Angeles in 1906. After being rejected by a Nazarene mission because of his Pentecostal interpretation of Acts 2, Seymour eventually held meetings at an old Methodist church building on Azusa Street. Seymour's preaching was electric, and there can be no doubt that a great outpouring of the Spirit occurred. There were reports of miraculous gifts such as tongues-speaking and healing, but also of protracted prayer, heart-searching, and conviction of sin. At first, many in the Holiness Movement welcomed this new work of God. Soon, however, many balked at the notion that speaking in tongues is the evidence of the baptism of the Holy Spirit; they believed that the Pentecostal experience was associated with entire sanctification. The rest is history—a colorful history we do not have space to tell.[50] Suffice it to say that the Azusa Street Revival became the epicenter of the global Pentecostal movement, which birthed the major Pentecostal denominations and missions organizations of the

48. Cairns, *Endless Line of Splendor*, 196.

49. Orr, *Re-Study of Revival*, 41.

50. See especially Vinson Synan, *The Pentecostal-Holiness Tradition: Charismatic Movements in the Twentieth Century*, 2nd ed. (Grand Rapids, MI: Eerdmans, 1997).

twentieth century that are on the leading edge of expanding the Christian faith throughout the world today.

The twentieth century witnessed the perfecting of mass evangelism. Finney had already paved the way with both a theological and practical program of revivalism, but moving forward, American pragmatism would shape the evangelistic enterprise more than theology. In the late 1800s, D. L. Moody (1837–99) applied business sense to his revivalistic endeavors. He perfected the logistics of large-scale, monthslong evangelistic campaigns that he held in urban centers of the United States and Great Britain. William A. "Billy" Sunday (1862–1935), with his rapid-fire and slapdash style, transformed evangelistic preaching into entertainment. The theatrics of Aimee Semple McPherson (1890–1944), complete with props, turned evangelism into a spectacle; but her mastery of mass media—print, radio, and film—set a precedent for later twentieth-century evangelists such as Billy Graham (1918–2018), Oral Roberts (1918–2009), and Pat Robertson (1930–2023).[51]

For our purposes, it is important to note that many college revivals occurred in the twentieth century, both between the World Wars and after World War II.[52] The Asbury College revival of 1970 happened at the same time other currents of revival were taking place, notably the Jesus People movement and the charismatic renewal in Roman Catholic and mainline Protestant churches in the 1960s and 1970s.[53] In the 1980s, the moral failure of televangelists Jim Bakker and Jimmy Swaggart provided heavy ammunition for antirevivalist Christians and secular critics of Christianity. Two revivalist happenings in the final decade of the twentieth century generated controversy: the "Toronto Blessing" at the Toronto Airport Vineyard Church in 1994 and the Brownsville Revival in Pensacola, Florida (1995–2000). They bore many marks of true revival (repentance, the call to holiness, and manifestations of the Holy Spirit), but certain revival excesses (such as the "holy laughter" of the Toronto Blessing) drew criticism.[54]

51. William H. Cooper Jr., *The Great Revivalists in American Religion, 1740–1944* (Jefferson, NC: McFarland, 2010), chaps. 3–5.

52. Edwin J. Orr, *Campus Aflame: A History of Evangelical Awakenings in Collegiate Communities* (Wheaton, IL: Evangelical Awakening Press, 1971); Wesley Duewel, *Revival Fire* (Grand Rapids, MI: Zondervan, 1995), 319–51.

53. The film about this movement, *The Jesus Revolution*, was released on February 24, 2023, the day after the Asbury Outpouring came to its appointed end.

54. As an example of the controversy, John MacArthur penned a broadside against Pentecostal and charismatic revivalism: *Strange Fire: The Danger of Offending the Holy Spirit*

In the twenty-first century, yearnings for revival seem to include expectations for a move of God that is pure, simple, free from slick production and performance, and focused on the sweet presence of the Holy Spirit rather than the pet practices or doctrines of any particular Christian tradition.

Observations on the Asbury Outpouring and Historic Evangelical Revivals

Throughout my experiences of the Asbury Outpouring, I could not help but see comparisons between it and earlier evangelical revivals. This was only reinforced by hearing Asbury students who were firsthand witnesses to the Outpouring either approvingly compare it to the 1970 Asbury revival or wish strongly to refrain from doing so. What struck me most is that the Outpouring bore characteristics of previous evangelical revivals *in spite of* strong inclinations for it to be fresh and different from the past. Assuredly, the evangelical heritage of Asbury University, along with an embedded culture and theology of revival, is bound to put a stamp on our patterns of worship and spiritual renewal.

Here are some of the trademarks of historic evangelical revival and revivalism that were in evidence at the Outpouring:

- Many prayers for revival preceded the Outpouring, and I know of at least one story of someone receiving a vision that revival was going to take place at Asbury.
- The Outpouring took place at a time when the spiritual climate in the United States and throughout the world was at a low ebb. The malaise of the preceding COVID years also contributed to a hunger for spiritual connection with God and others in a genuine Christian community.
- Spontaneous and continuous worship occurred, sometimes rousing and at other times gentle, but nearly always awe-inspiring.
- The Outpouring was marked by contemplation, prayer, seeking the face of God, and repenting in Hughes Auditorium, especially at the altar.
- Participants preached God's Word and exhorted the audience to greater commitment to Christ and the gospel.

---

with Counterfeit Worship (Nashville: Thomas Nelson, 2013). An apologetic response came from Michael L. Brown, *Authentic Fire: A Response to John MacArthur's "Strange Fire"* (Lake Mary, FL: Creation House, 2015).

- Public testimonies were offered, many with raw and vulnerable confessions of sin, pleas for divine help, and expressions of faith and victory over the old way of life.
- The Outpouring was marked by a protracted meeting, beginning on that Wednesday morning after chapel (February 8, 2023) and continuing nonstop for sixteen days.
- The spread of similar outpourings occurred at other Christian (and secular) campuses, such as at Lee University in Cleveland, Tennessee, and Campbellsville University and Northern Kentucky University in Kentucky.
- The presence of the Holy Spirit was almost palpable in Hughes Auditorium, and it acted like a magnet. Once one had experienced it, one had to return again and again. As in past revivals, one could feel suspended in time; the passage of an extended period of time could seem like only a moment.
- News of the Outpouring spread like wildfire, including via major media outlets in print and television. Also, Asbury students testified about the Outpouring informally and formally both during the Outpouring and in the succeeding weeks and months.
- Thousands of pilgrims descended upon Wilmore and lined up to enter Hughes Auditorium to get a firsthand experience of what God was doing.
- The fact that this outpouring of the Spirit occurred largely among young people is thought to be unique, but it is not. Two examples are youth being especially affected by the Great Awakening, according to Jonathan Edwards's remarks, and the participants of the Welsh Revival, including Evan Roberts, who was in his midtwenties. We have also already referred to college revivals that took place in the last two centuries.

All of these have some analog in previous revivals that took place in the last three hundred years.

What, then, are some of the ways that the Asbury Outpouring was unique or did not fit the mold of most past revivals? The first way is communicated by the chosen name: the Outpouring. This seems to be a deliberate attempt to avoid being pretentious and to focus on the Spirit's work rather than Asbury's reputation as a place where revivals happen. A theme stressed repeatedly throughout the Outpouring, by President Kevin Brown and by many speakers, was "radical humility."

In keeping with this central theme, the Outpouring did not coalesce around a single personality or revivalist, as many past revivals have. In fact, the university assiduously worked to distance the Outpouring from attachment to popular Christian leaders or music artists who wished to lend support or capitalize on what was taking place. Respectfully, certain well-known Christian ministers came to bear witness and participate discreetly. Perhaps the Outpouring was, therefore, more like the 1858 Prayer Revival with its organic, lay-level origins.

Music has long been an important feature of revivals. The Wesleys deliberately incorporated hymnody into worship and Christian formation, hymns and gospel songs were integral to the Holiness camp meetings of the nineteenth and twentieth centuries, and every modern evangelist from D. L. Moody to Billy Graham employed a song leader as part of evangelistic services. The music at the Asbury Outpouring, however, had an authentic, unpolished character.[55] It was geared toward real worship, not professional quality or performance. This was a lot like the simpler singing in traditional evangelical churches and camp meetings of the last couple of centuries, but the style of music was not. It is probably no surprise that the "old-time" hymns and gospel songs were not as common in the Outpouring's repertoire as were more contemporary worship songs that are familiar to twenty-first-century churchgoers.[56] Crucially, one might safely say that worship music was more of a driver in the Outpouring than in previous revivals that were centered on preaching.

The internet and social media were factors that had not existed during past revivals. During the Outpouring, livestreaming the services was forbidden, and the only live broadcasts from the university were chapel hours, which were customarily livestreamed anyway.[57] Such prohibitions often went unheeded, so videos and stories about the Outpouring flooded social media and news sites. The sheer existence of this medium of global communication presented a new set of challenges and opportunities that the university had to navigate.

Another feature of Asbury's Outpouring was its multiracial complexion. As this is treated in another chapter,[58] we need not comment at length here,

55. Elliott, *Taken by Surprise*, chap. 3.

56. See the table in Elliott, *Taken by Surprise*, 160–61. See also the chapter by Dan Pinkston in this volume.

57. However, during the last few days, when attendance was largely restricted to youth, livestreaming was allowed.

58. See the discussion in the chapter by Juan Gonzalez in this volume.

except to say that sadly, many past revivals were segregated—even though attempts were made, often unsuccessfully, at achieving racial harmony.

Finally, the university attempted to steer clear of "revival excesses" that have plagued many past revivals. While exuberant and loud singing, jumping, clapping, and other expressions of emotion occurred, the university was determined to rein in overly emotional or physical actions, like jumping up and down in the balcony of Hughes Auditorium, waving large flags, or introducing overtly Pentecostal or charismatic practices like glossolalia. This was not to quench the Spirit but to assure that the Outpouring remained as orderly, nonsectarian, and unifying as it could be.

So was the Asbury Outpouring a revival? Perhaps, in light of the above comparisons. What is most important is that we humbly and gratefully acknowledge the divine visitation that happened on Asbury's campus. And revival will have taken root if we continue to surrender to God's transforming grace in obedience, holiness, and faithful witness so that the fruits of revival can be shared with others both near and far from the little town of Wilmore, Kentucky. We can only pray that the Almighty will bless the world with another Great Awakening before Christ's return.

CHAPTER NINE

HUGHES AUDITORIUM AND A THEOLOGY OF SACRED SPACE

W. Brian Shelton

Professor of Theology and dean of the School of Christian Studies, Asbury University

The significance of place has always marked the history of God's people. While Christians can worship an omnipresent God from any place in creation, some spaces occasionally host the immanent presence of God. Moses ascended to Mt. Sinai to meet with God; the tabernacle curtain separated the holy place from the most holy place. These sacred spaces in turn foster memorials and draw pilgrims to their sites. Joshua coordinated a twelve-stone memorial at Gilgal, and Jewish pilgrims ascended the Temple Mount in Jerusalem as they sang songs of ascent. While the notion of sacred space occurs intermittently throughout the Bible and church history, many Protestants are not aware that their faith operates with a sense of it. In the days following February 8, 2023, some fifty thousand people certainly believed that Asbury University's Hughes Auditorium was a sacred space.

This chapter will develop a theology of sacred place, technically termed *locus*, to explain the dynamics of Hughes Auditorium during the Outpouring. It will briefly examine the biblical notion that God sometimes fills space, visiting his people to bless them at places worth attending and commemorating. Next, a theology of sacred space will be offered. In describing *loci*, scholars distinguish between *topos* as a mere location and *chora* as an energizing location while recognizing the role of music, praise, memory, and hope that regularly characterize the experience. Certainly, Hughes Auditorium became a *locus mirabilis*, a place of encounter with God, a place where despair met hope and anguish met resolution. This theology helps explain its unprecedented draw during the Outpouring, even while many Christians were unaware of their theology of sacred space.

Encountering God in Space

Christians are a God-centered people, able to worship the omnipresent God from anywhere. Yet even in the eleventh century, Anselm of Canterbury recognized how the rousing of the human soul might explain why so many would be drawn spatially to a place where God seemed to be. Imagine Anselm's comment from the point of view of the pilgrim to Wilmore in prayer to God: "He [the pilgrim] yearns to seek You and Your countenance is too far away from him. He desires to come close to You, and Your dwelling place is inaccessible; he longs to find You and does not know where You are; he is eager to seek You out and he does not know Your countenance."[1]

Divine Omnipresence and Limitlessness

Before narrowing in on sacred space, we should note that God is not limited to specific spaces; God occupies all space. The psalmist David knew this, asking, "Where can I flee from your presence?" before considering the breadth of the universe to realize no place escapes divine presence (Ps. 139:7–12). The prophet Jeremiah acknowledged this: "Can a man hide himself in secret places so that I cannot see him?' declares the Lord. 'Do I not fill heaven and earth?' declares the Lord" (Jer. 23:24 ESV). Jesus articulated how we could worship God universally, not merely in the sacred places (John 4:20–24).

In his sermon on God's omnipresence, John Wesley declares, "In a word, there is no point of space, whether within or without the bounds of creation, where God is not."[2] The Reformed tradition shares this understanding of our ability to worship God ubiquitously: "Neither prayer, nor any other part of religious worship, is now, under the Gospel, either tied unto, or made more acceptable by any place in which it is performed, or towards which it is directed: but God is to be worshipped everywhere, in spirit and truth."[3]

Given the universal recognition that God is omnipresent, the draw of pilgrims to Hughes was surprising at first. Yet while God is unlimited in his presence, he at times does not seem to be near. He seems hidden to us,

1. Anselm of Canterbury, *Proslogion* 1, in *Major Works*, ed. Brian Davies and G. R. Evans (New York: Oxford University Press, 2008), 85.
2. John Wesley, "On the Omnipresence of God" I.1, *The Works of John Wesley*, ed. Thomas Jackson, 3rd ed., vol. 7 (Grand Rapids, MI: Baker, 2002), 239.
3. Puritan Westminster Assembly, 1643–49, *The Westminster Confession of Faith* (Suwanee, GA: Great Commission, 1995), 23, chap. 21, para. 6.

and our faith wonders why divine presence seems so elusive. In anticipation of Israel's loneliness in exile, the prophet Isaiah wrote, "Truly, you are a God who hides himself, O God of Israel, the Savior" (Isa. 45:15 ESV). When suddenly the God who hides himself seems to be "over there," his lonely and hungry people run to his manifest presence. Jason Vickers and Thomas McCall recognize the polarity between God's hiddenness and manifestation: "If divine hiddenness and silence are mysteries, so, too, is God's manifest presence and power." This seemed to be the state of the world when thousands began to descend on Hughes Auditorium. In the case of the Outpouring, these two authors themselves realized, "Ultimately, it is a joyous and wonderful thing to encounter the manifest presence and power of God."[4] Understanding this migration of Christians requires a theory of sacred space.

Divine Special Presence

The Bible evidences occasions on which God was especially present for his people. When Jacob beheld a vision of heaven at Bethel, he commemorated his divine encounter with a stone marker (Gen. 28:18–22). Remembering that Moses struck the rock in the wilderness for water, Paul remarks that Jesus himself was the rock (1 Cor. 10:4). On Mt. Sinai, God passed by Moses, who hid in the cleft of the rock (Exod. 33:21–23). When Israel wandered in the wilderness without a place to live, God established a place for them to meet him. The tabernacle became a holy place, a space to meet and hear from God: "There I will meet with you, and from above the mercy seat, from between the two cherubim that are on the ark of the testimony, I will speak with you about all that I will give you in commandment for the people of Israel" (Exod. 25:22 ESV).

In any one of these places, *loci*, God is present in a way and in a moment differently than previously. On one hand, Aristotle insisted that place, *topos*, was as regular a space as any other, without particular influence. Plato, on the other hand, hypothesized how particular places nourished the soul. Belden Lane says, "His fascination was with the capacity of a place to resonate to the immediacies of human experience. Place as *chora* carries its own energy and power, summoning its participants to a common

4. Jason Vickers and Thomas McCall, *Outpouring: A Theological Witness* (Eugene, OR: Cascade, 2023), 43–45, quot. 44.

dance, to the 'choreography' most appropriate to their life together."[5] These ancient Greeks grappled with the special presence of the divine—even if in a non-Judeo-Christian worldview—to recognize powerful potential and distinctions in space. In the biblical record of extraordinary space, the divine *locus* was a *locus mirabilis*, an amazing place.

In these sacred places, God does not descend into the creative realm as much as he intensifies his presence from across creation in one special place. In these sacred places, God blesses his people. The psalmist recognizes this: "In your presence there is fullness of joy; at your right hand are pleasures forevermore" (Ps. 16:11 ESV). The space of the tabernacle is curiously marked by the boundary of its court and curtains as "holy," while the meeting space in the tent is called "most holy," as if distinguishing spaces of more or less sacredness.[6] These spaces seem to mediate contact between God's people and God, as an experience of his presence changes the one who enters.[7] While we tend to think of this meeting with God to be a positive and blessed occasion, sometimes its context is judgment. For example, when God stands beside the altar of the temple in the vision of Amos, his presence is manifest to punish his people, none of whom will escape (Amos 9:1–4). Even as God's faithful go to an altar in a place like Hughes, their sins are subject to his sanctifying power. They should expect to be changed, purified, and made holy. Michael Hundley recognizes how divine presence is inseparable from the manifest holiness of God: "Holiness is more than just a label: it likewise seems to carry some of the dangerously potent divine essence."[8] As Moses led Israel to the foot of Mt. Sinai "to meet with God," thunder, lightning, and a thick cloud marked the presence of God, reciprocated by the people's fear (Exod. 19:16–17). This makes an outpouring a sobering event and an approach to the Hughes Auditorium altar a solemn walk, with the promise that it can be an equally joyous event for the one willing to be changed by the Holy Spirit.

5. Belden C. Lane, "Giving Voice to Place: Three Models for Understanding American Sacred Space," *Religion and American Culture: A Journal of Interpretation* 11, no. 1 (2001): 54.
6. Michael B. Hundley, "Sacred Spaces, Objects, Offerings, and People in the Priestly Texts: A Reappraisal," *Journal of Biblical Literature* 132 (2013): 755–56.
7. Hundley, "Sacred Spaces," 764.
8. Hundley, "Sacred Spaces," 753.

Discerning Divine Special Presence

A theology of sacred space in Hughes Auditorium requires a ruling on the inherent quality of the space itself. But what makes a space sacred? Is it the place itself, or is it what we bring to it? Just as scholars distinguish between *topos* as a mere location and *chora* as an energizing location, they have effectively theorized that such places have an ontological, cultural, or phenomenological quality to them. Answering such logistics of space is important for understanding the dynamics of Hughes Auditorium during the Outpouring.

Ann Taves typifies two models for understanding sacred space. First, the premodern model of *sui generis* describes a space as having its own ontological value and power. Second, the modern model called "ascription" describes a space as having cultural value and power because of what the worshiper and community attribute to it.[9] In the first model, the Asbury University community might expect a special, powerful time when God will work anew in the sanctuary of Hughes Auditorium. He visited there in 1970; the faithful prayed he might visit there in 2023. It might be viewed like the Bethesda pool (John 5:1–7), where the needy gather and wait for the supernatural to appear because God seems to work in this fashion. In the second model, Hughes is sacred because people in need continue to locate there, bringing their hope for a divine encounter in that place. At special times, God manifests in part because of the concentration of prayers and worship ascending from the place. In other words, Hughes is either where God dwells specially and independently of its pilgrims or Hughes is where pilgrims bring their hopes for a spiritual experience and thus often find it.

Lane recognizes that these two options for understanding sacred space require one to choose one cause over another to explain its sacredness. Taves's first cause, which Lane calls the "ontological approach," requires one to join the "supernaturalist folks" who believe in an "inherently sacral character" of a place like Hughes. Taves's second cause, which Lane calls the "cultural approach," stems from community members bringing their expectations of an experience; this approach fails to "exhaust their fullness of meaning" for sacred spaces.[10] Instead, Lane proposes a third, "phenomenological"

9. Ann Taves, *Religious Experience Reconsidered: A Building-Block Approach to the Study of Religion and Other Special Things* (Princeton, NJ: Princeton University Press, 2009), 17–22.

10. Belden C. Lane, *Landscapes of the Sacred: Geography and Narrative in American Spirituality* (Baltimore, MD: Johns Hopkins University Press, 2001), 5.

approach. It combines the esoteric power of God in setting a place apart, the cultural values of a place as special, and a recognition of topography where God's people hope to encounter him.[11] Here, both the transcendent and cultural come together to prevent Taves's options from offering a false dichotomy. This position allows for a combination of divine operation and human participation that still permits measures of the mysterious. Here, one is not forced to call the space magical in its own right nor the pilgrims responsible for the revival.

Without consciously possessing a developed theology of sacred space, this is what evangelicals likely thought when they descended on Hughes Auditorium in the winter of 2023. They combined a sense of bringing their own need to a special place where God was manifest. C. S. Lewis describes our primal desire for knowing as "an imaginative impulse as old as the human race working under the special conditions of our time . . . to visit strange regions in search of such beauty, awe or terror as the actual world does not supply."[12] Jeremy Begbie writes on such unimaginable encounters: "Wonder is a reaction or response to something that arrests our attention. It cannot be self-generated. It also involves a large measure of surprise: it comes upon us with unbidden force, unexpectedly."[13] The national draw to the Outpouring was an endeavor by thousands to go to a place where God seemed to be manifest in a space that was sacred.

This model was made clear to me in the story of one visitor. After a friend expressed to my wife, Sally, her desire to drive six hours to come to Hughes Auditorium, I unsympathetically asked, "But why?" Sally immediately recognized why: "She wants to pray for her children." For this friend, prayers from another state were not being realized, but like the Syrophoenician mother who tenaciously persevered to see her daughter healed (Mark 7:25–29), they both came with hope to where Jesus was. Hughes Auditorium was a *locus sacra*, a sacred space, that fostered a draw to the divine presence.

11. Lane, *Landscapes of the Sacred*, 42–46.

12. C. S. Lewis, *Of Other Worlds: Essays and Stories*, ed. Walter Hooper (New York: Harvest, 1966), 67–68.

13. Jeremy Begbie, "Encountering the Uncontainable in the Arts," in *God and Wonder: Theology, Imagination, and the Arts*, ed. Jeffrey W. Barbeau and Emily Hunter McGowin (Eugene, OR: Wipf & Stock, 2022), 104. The context for this quotation is not revival but the uncontainable potential of the arts to reveal the metaphysical and theological dimensions to the power of creating.

The Draw to Divine Presence

The draw to the place where heaven touches earth is not new. The ancient Celts—both Christian and pagan—held the concept that, in some places, heaven and the creation seemed to intersect. When Patrick went on mission to Ireland, he employed rather than deserted this quality, so the hill at Tara is central to the narrative of his evangelism of the chieftain, and his writings have a nature focus to them.[14] The Celts called these *loci* "thin places," as the veil of heaven seemed permeable and the transcendent God seemed descendant to creation. God's people are drawn to such places out of a love for their God and for supplication to him.

This theology is evident in the ancient and continuing practice of Christians going on pilgrimage. Each year, more than two million pilgrims go to the Holy Land for its sacred spaces. The traveler is drawn toward a *mysterium fascinosum*, a mystery that attracts, as Rudolph Otto describes in *The Idea of the Holy*: "The mystery is for him not merely something to be wondered at but something that entrances him; in this which bewilders and confounds, he feels a something that captivates and transports him with a strange ravishment."[15] Thus, for the pilgrim, standing in the place can arouse a sense of disembodied connection to the God who orders their faith.

The Outpouring was an event of pilgrimage to sacred space. It held a promise to meet God, and this promise drew pilgrims to travel for hours, only to wait in line for more hours. Drawn to the report of the presence of God in a "thin place," Christians came. They came and they came. The line formed around the perimeter of campus for more than half a mile as the faithful waited patiently for the opportunity to enter Hughes Auditorium, which can only hold fifteen hundred people. When all the seats were filled and the rotation of pilgrims did not free enough seats for those still waiting to enter, overflow venues at Asbury Theological Seminary across the street and in nearby churches opened in a way that seemed to extend the sacred space. Overflow venues are difficult to explain in relationship to sacred space, as if human organization can extend the presence of God. It can only be explained by a connected worship in relationship to Hughes itself. These places were viewed as overflows of God's presence without discrimination,

14. Tracy Belzer, *Thin Places: An Evangelical Journey into Celtic Christianity* (Abilene, TX: Leafwood, 2007), 26–29.

15. Rudolph Otto, *The Idea of the Holy* (London: Oxford University Press, 1958), 31. Paraphrased for clarity.

and one might recognize that the line to enter, with its fellowship and patience between worshipful Christians, was an extension of sacred space. Yet the hub was the *locus* where a chapel service and student prayer on February 8 led to an outpouring: Hughes Auditorium.

Encountering God in Hughes

Hughes Auditorium has long been a hallowed building for many Asbury alumni. A university historical monograph, *A Purpose Rare*, calls Hughes Auditorium "the heart of spiritual life on campus."[16] It has a seating capacity of 1,489, with seats around three-quarters of its perimeter, facing center stage.

The Space

The space called Hughes Auditorium is the venue for weekly chapel services, special worship performance events, and religious conferences. Its platform is wide and deep, capable of holding faculty at an academic event or a choir at a musical event. An altar rail with a kneeler lies at the base of the platform. For generations, speakers have brought their spiritual convictions in the form of sermons, testimonies, and lectures to a traditional student population with a complement of visitors, faculty, staff, and administration. In the Wesleyan tradition, an invitation in the form of an altar call draws respondents forward and to their knees at the altar. For those who approached the altar in response, or for those who simply digested the message from their seats, the space imprints their memory of Hughes Auditorium as a place to approach the living God on matters of their soul.

Asbury University director of alumni relations and 1990 alumna, Lisa Harper, remarks how this space comprises "our shared heritage and a legacy for future generations." She elaborates:

> Hughes Auditorium serves as an Ebenezer stone for our alumni. It is a place that reminds us of the promises we made to a Holy God and of his goodness and faithfulness to us. It is a spiritual "home" where alumni come, from all walks of life, to sit in the presence of God. Oh, the stories the altar in

16. Edward McKinley and Jon Kulaga, *A Purpose Rare: 125 Years of Asbury University* (Ann Arbor, MI: Edward Brothers Malloy, 2015), 225.

> Hughes could tell of lives changed over the almost one hundred years as it has been flooded with tears. It is a place of reverence and remembrance, of conviction and compassion, of safety and steadfastness. It is familiar and is water for our dry and thirsty souls.[17]

This experiential memory brought many of the pilgrims to the Outpouring in 2023. For those new to the campus, Hughes became for them the same *locus* of sacred space.

Hughes was also central to the Asbury College revival of 1970. Robert Coleman writes, "In a way awesome to behold, God had taken over the campus. Caught up in the wonder of it, a thousand students remained for days in the college auditorium—not to demand more freedom or to protest the Establishment, but to confess their sin and to sing the praises of their Saviour."[18] Harold Spann describes that revival: "Overshadowing it all is the commanding sense of the Divine Presence. . . . So great was this feeling that when three cultured ladies from Chattanooga walked into the back of Hughes Auditorium, one of them said, 'I must take off my shoes, for this is holy ground.'"[19] Jon Tal Murphree journaled from 1970, "Last night I joined with a thousand worshippers in Hughes Auditorium singing the Diadem arrangement of 'All Hail the Power of Jesus' Name.' It was one of the most magnificent, moving experiences I have ever known. Thank Thee, my Lord, for halls aflame . . . !"[20]

During the Outpouring, Hughes Auditorium became a *locus mirabilis*, an amazing place of encounter with God, a place where despair met hope and anguish met resolution. This theology helps explain its unprecedented draw, even while Christians were unaware of their theology of sacred space.

17. Lisa Harper, interview by author, December 4, 2023.
18. Robert E. Coleman, ed., *One Divine Moment* (Old Tappan, NJ: Spire, 1970), 13–14.
19. Harold Spann, "Crisis and Opportunity," in *One Divine Moment*, ed. Robert E. Coleman (Old Tappan, NJ: Spire, 1970), 99–100.
20. Jon Tal Murphree, *The Twisting Trail: My Failures, God's Favors* (independently published, 2022), 208–9. Murphree was also present in Hughes for the 1958 revival: "Emotion was subdued, but an intimate sense of Christ was far deeper. . . . Without lightning or thunder, we were experiencing a steady downpour that sank deeply into the soil of our souls." Jon Tal Murphree, *Only a Pilgrim: My Blunders and Blessings* (Charleston, SC: Create Space, 2013), 196–97.

The Altar

If sacred space is the spot where human presence meets divine presence, then the altar is often the *locus* where a person meets God. One kneels outwardly as an expression of the humility of the heart. One prays in self-submission to a God who may not be understood, and one prepares to yield and surrender to whatever the divine might require. In the altar call, people leave their unity with the congregation to become individuals again, approaching the *locus* with hope and maybe some trepidation.

The tradition stems from the Second Great Awakening. The preaching of Francis Asbury in Appalachia and Wilson Thompson in Missouri in the early nineteenth century began to create space for mourners before the pulpit, but the custom of the altar call really became established with the camp meeting movement in these early decades.[21] Asbury University shares this Wesleyan heritage practice. Evangelists preached from Scripture in a way that led to a call for sinners to repent by formally approaching the altar.[22] This preaching of the Word has been viewed as a means for the Holy Spirit to bring prevenient grace to the human heart.[23]

A student's diary from the 1970 revival witnessed the centrality of the altar: "700–800 people in Hughes. I don't know that I've even seen the altar area so crowded."[24] Likewise, "a great crowd at the altar. I saw a beautiful sight a few moments ago when an entire family made their way to the altar. I see a man who drove all the way from New Jersey to the altar. All is well."[25] Additionally, historian Joseph Thacker writes of the event, "The presence of the Holy Spirit became so powerful that the students began to move forward in waves [to the altar]."[26]

In a sense, the altar is for individual prayer, while the whole space is for corporate singing. As voices unite in song to fill the auditorium, they seem to sanctify the space even further. As an individual steps into the aisle to

21. For more on this tradition, see Kevin Anderson's chapter in this volume.
22. David Bennett, *The Altar Call: Its Origins and Present Usage* (Lanham, NY: University Press of America, 2000), 10–11, 29, 79, 97.
23. W. Brian Shelton, *Prevenient Grace: God's Provision for Fallen Humanity* (Wilmore, KY: Francis Asbury, 2014), 253–58. For more on this topic, see Suzanne Nicholson's chapter in this volume.
24. Jeff Blake, "A Student's Diary of Revival," *One Divine Moment*, February 7, 1970, 42.
25. Blake, "Student's Diary," *One Divine Moment*, February 8, 1970, 42.
26. Joseph A. Thacker, *Asbury College: Vision and Miracle* (Nappanee, IN: Evangel, 1990), 223.

advance to the altar, he or she seems to leave the body to face God as we all do ultimately, alone with our souls naked before our Creator. However, dealing with God individually does not necessitate doing so alone. One testimony from student Alexandra Presta typifies the activities at the altar in Hughes: "During a call of confession, at least a hundred people fell to their knees and bowed at the altar. Hands rested on shoulders, linking individual people together to represent the Body of Christ truly. Cries of addiction, pride, fear, anger and bitterness sounded, each followed by a life-changing proclamation: 'Christ forgives you.'"[27]

The Echo

The Old and New Testaments evidence the place of song in the congregation of the faithful.[28] Colossians 3:16 names "songs, hymns, and spiritual songs" as expressions of thanksgiving to God, and Psalm 22:3 remarks that "God inhabits the praises of his people." At the Outpouring, song was a prominent aspect of the experience as the Hughes visitors raised their voices in harmony, echoing throughout the auditorium to sanctify the space. John Calvin declares, "We know by experience that singing has great power and vigor to move and inflame men's hearts to call upon and praise God with a more vehement and burning zeal."[29] If the Outpouring pilgrims did anything, they sang with "great power and vigor as hearts inflamed to praise God." They sang with joy, hope, and praise. There was a glimpse of elements of eternity here—a collection of God's people, individuals from many tribes and tongues, and seeming eternal praise, echoing the four living creatures in Revelation: "Day and night they never stop saying, 'Holy, Holy, Holy'" (Rev. 4:8).

A Storied Place

Belden Lane explains that enchanted places about which stories are told become "storied places."[30] The sacred space of Hughes Auditorium is such

27. "The Asbury Outpouring," Asbury University, accessed September 6, 2024, https://www.asbury.edu/outpouring/.
28. Notably the Psalms, but in practice also Acts 16:25, 1 Corinthians 14:26, Ephesians 5:18–20, James 5:14.
29. John Calvin, "The Forms of Prayers and Songs of the Church, 1542, Letter to the Reader," trans. Ford Lewis Battles, *Calvin Theological Journal* 15, no. 2 (1980): 163.
30. Lane, *Landscapes of the Sacred*, 37.

a storied place for every generation of Asburians. As 1997 alumna Heidi Raass Spencer testifies, "We wanted to be there and looked forward to every service. Why? Because the Spirit of Jesus hovered in and around that place. Chapel speakers from all over the world led us to the throne of God through inspiring messages and riveting tales from the mission field. I did a lot of business with God in those old, wooden seats in Hughes."[31]

The stories from the population of the Outpouring include those who remembered Hughes Auditorium from a different day, where they had a formative experience with God that shaped their return. Jean Kingery, 1979 alumna, testifies of both early and Outpouring memories there: "Fall semester 1976 was the first time that I entered Hughes as a transfer student. Upon entering, there was an apparent sweet fragrance that filled my soul. Fast forward forty-seven years later—the third week of February 2023—the fragrance was sacred, different, and overwhelmed my heart with awe."[32] Jeannie Banter, 2006 alumna, testifies regarding both of her dual undergraduate and Outpouring Hughes experiences: "From the hard-wooden chairs, to the back corner on the piano side, to the wooden altar, the entire room is an altar of remembrance of God's faithfulness, goodness, and love in seasons of wilderness and outpourings. When I walk into Hughes, my soul feels at rest."[33]

These stories of the space are perhaps best described as stories of a people and their God *from* the space. Like concentric circles, the story goes first from Hughes into the community. Student Charity Johnson remarked of the Outpouring, "His Spirit changed the atmosphere and went beyond Hughes. The most precious moments I had involved meaningful conversations in the dining hall and meeting new people throughout the city who had a hunger for God."[34] The story goes next into the region, then into the world. Student Isaiah Friedeman accompanied teams that testified of the Outpouring, remarking, "We told our stories of encountering God's presence to youth groups in rural Kentucky and international conferences in London. Every time we humbly and plainly gave testimony to the outpouring of God's presence, He revealed himself in fresh ways."[35]

31. Heidi Raass Spencer, letter, correspondence with Lisa Harper, November 12, 2023.
32. Jean Kingery, letter, correspondence with Lisa Harper, the director of alumni relations, November 10, 2023.
33. Jeannie Banter, interview by author, December 11, 2023.
34. "Asbury Outpouring."
35. Isaiah Friedeman, interview by author, December 11, 2023.

In the end, the story of Hughes Auditorium as a sacred space during the Outpouring becomes a story of the past. However, the story is alive; it is simply extended into the world as attendees take away the story and the legacy that Hughes hosted. They carry in their memory and their sentiment an internal witness to an external sacred space. The breathtaking witness of so many coming to worship an omnipresent God remains an irony that reinforces the faith. The basis for the irony is captured by John Oswalt: "The New Covenant differs from the Old in this one respect. It is internal . . . Now God's will can function from within us; now his nature can flow out of us."[36] Student Eswin Monroy recognized this reality as he said, "My hope is that everyone knows that the same spirit moving in Hughes is the same spirit that is moving all over the world. Hughes became the epicenter of it. But God lives in our bodies."[37]

CONCLUSION

While the Outpouring activities have ended in the *locus* of Hughes Auditorium, the storied testimony of its sacred space continues in the world. Yet we continue to ask questions and posit answers from our theology of God, the church, and sacred space. The same Anselm who recognized the rousing of the human soul above is credited with this notion of "faith seeking understanding."[38] The *why* and the *how* of sacred space remain beyond our comprehension, but its mystery equally offers us assurance of the reality of *what* made it so. It was the great I Am. Yes, he was to Moses the God of Abraham, Isaac, and Jacob (Exod. 3:6). Yes, he was to us the Holy Spirit of the 1970 revival. Likewise, the 2023 Asbury community could claim a divine work in Hughes Auditorium as their own. That he returned to this space to make it a sacred space again ushers in a humility as we reflect on the nature of God: "The great God, the eternal, the almighty Spirit, is

36. John N. Oswalt, *Called to Be Holy: A Biblical Perspective* (Wilmore, KY: Francis Asbury, 1999), 87.

37. Nikolas Lanum, "Asbury Revival Brings 'Beautiful Disruption' and Multi-Generational Community to Post-COVID World," *Fox News*, February 25, 2023, https://www.foxnews.com/media/asbury-revival-beautiful-disruption-multi-generational-community-christian-covid.

38. Anselm recognized the powerful "meditation on the meaning of faith from the point of view of one seeking, through silent reasoning within himself, things he knows not . . ." *Proslogion* preface, 82.

as unbounded in his presence, as in his duration and power."[39] When the unbounded God makes himself manifest, the people are blessed.

In his 1913 commencement address, Asbury President Henry Clay Morrison seemed to anticipate the future Outpouring moments: "Jesus desired to arrest our attention and awaken in us some sort of proper appreciation of the value of a human soul."[40] The 2023 arresting, awakening, and appreciating offered by the sacred space of Hughes continues to tell the story of the place where God poured out his Spirit to touch a generation.

39. Wesley, "On the Omnipresence of God" I.2, 7:239–40.

40. H. C. Morrison, "The Value of a Soul," in *Commencement Sermons* (Louisville, KY: Pentecostal, 1915), 10. The context is Jesus's words in Matthew 16:26: "For what will it profit a man if he gains the whole world and forfeits his soul? Or what shall a man give in return for his soul?"

CHAPTER TEN

SEEKING THE KINGDOM OF GOD THROUGH PRAYER

A Theological Reflection on the Asbury Outpouring

Craig D. Saunders
Adjunct professor of Biblical/Theological Studies and Christian Ministries, Asbury University

The Old and New Testaments provide abundant examples of prayer. Not only does this emphasize the importance of prayer to God, but it leaves one wondering: With so much material on prayer, how does one synthesize a theology of prayer concisely? My hope is to provide the reader with a blueprint of a theology of prayer by examining The Lord's Prayer (Matt. 6:9b–13) in comparison with Jesus's own practice of prayer—demonstrating Jesus's didactive and experiential method of discipleship. Next, I will share some scriptural examples of those who sought God's Kingdom because they thirsted (longed) for God and his presence in their lives. Finally, I will provide a brief reflection on how I witnessed the theology of prayer during Asbury's Outpouring as an altar minister.

On a personal note, my own cognitive understanding of prayer came from being raised in church, yet my practical experience of prayer primarily came through my grandparents, Albert and Lula Moffatt.[1] Through my childhood and early teens, my grandparents exemplified what it means to seek the Kingdom of God through their daily one-hour prayer sessions immediately after lunch. Though I disliked kneeling at the couch and listening to my grandparents pray, I learned the importance of the centrality of prayer in the Christian life. Through their prayers, I also discovered the

1. I dedicate this chapter to the Reverend Albert B. Moffatt (1900–1988) and Lula M. Moffatt (1908–2006).

need to glorify God for who he is and what he has done and the need to pray for others who are in physical and spiritual need. In other words, I learned an important lesson in comprehending and practicing the theology of prayer—prayer is simply *attentive communication with God about one's love for him and one's love and concern for others.*

A Theology of Prayer: Seeking the Kingdom of Heaven

The structure of the Lord's Prayer (Matt. 6:9b–13) is significant in deciphering what Jesus deemed central in his theology of prayer. Verses 9b–10 primarily focus on the nature and will of God, while verses 11–13 emphasize the physical and spiritual needs of others. Scot McKnight has described the Lord's prayer as having two distinct parts—to love God and to love others as ourselves.[2] At least in Matthew's correspondence, such a focus is not surprising, since there are multiple connections and scriptural citations from the Old Testament for the Gospel's primarily Jewish audience. In the Ten Commandments in Exodus 20:1–17, for example, the first section (20:1–11) focuses on the need to love God through worshiping his nature and maintaining a monotheistic commitment, while the second section (20:12–17) focuses on the importance of loving one's neighbor as oneself. Also, both the giving of the Ten Commandments (Exod. 19–20) and Jesus's teaching on the Sermon of the Mount (Matt. 5–7) occur on a mountain—the place where God reveals himself and his will to humanity. In relationship to the Lord's Prayer, McKnight helpfully adds, "True piety for Jesus transcends our relationship with God and becomes relation to both God and others. True piety is about loving God and loving others: prayer is about praying for God's glory and for the blessings of others."[3] Therefore, by teaching his disciples through the Lord's Prayer, Jesus was helping his disciples to fulfill the "entire law and the prophets" through the two greatest commandments: "You shall love the Lord your God with all your heart and with all your soul and with all your mind" and "You shall love your neighbor as yourself" (Matt. 22:37–40; also 5:17–20 and 7:12).[4]

2. Scot McKnight, *Sermon on the Mount*, SGBC (Grand Rapids, MI: Zondervan, 2013), 173. See also Jonathan T. Pennington, *The Sermon on the Mount and Human Flourishing: A Theological Commentary* (Grand Rapids, MI: Baker, 2017), 221.
3. McKnight, *Sermon*, 173.
4. Dale C. Allison states, "Karl Barth was correct to observe that whereas the first three petitions announce God's lordship, the last three reveal that the frail human creature

In Matthew 6:9b–10, Jesus told his disciples to address God as "Father." In Matthew's Gospel, this term relates to a personal relationship with God (a familial term) and a commitment to do God's will.[5] Therefore, those who use God's name in prayer emphasize their love through pursuing him affectionately (as "Father") and obediently (due to his divine and heavenly nature: "the one in the heavens" and "let your name be reverenced/treated as holy"). Later in 23:9, Jesus will instruct his disciples and the crowds by stating, "And do not call anyone on earth 'father,' for you have one Father, and he is in heaven." Jesus's instruction in 23:9 and 6:9b is consistent with the monotheistic emphasis in Exodus 20:1–6, proclaiming that there is only one God that deserves committed love and complete allegiance. Additionally, the emphasis in 6:9 to treat God's name as "holy" is stressed in God's commandment in Exodus 20:7: "You shall not misuse the name of the LORD your God. . . . The LORD will not hold anyone guiltless who misuses his name." Therefore, in Jesus's prayer, the disciples are reminded of their commitment to live in reverence to God (i.e., to bring him glory) and to adhere to his authority as their one and only Father.

Matthew 6:10 stresses that submission to the Father's authority relates to following and obeying God's holy will: "[Let] your will be done on earth as in heaven." In their prayer, the disciples should desire that God's reign (rulership) in heaven be mirrored on the earth. In Matthew's Gospel, such comparison is partially fulfilled through their own participation in "doing God's will" on earth. They are called to "be holy" as God himself is "holy" (Lev. 11:44–45). As stated in Matthew 7:21, "Not everyone saying to me, Lord, Lord, will enter the kingdom of heaven, but only the one who does the will of my Father in heaven." Therefore, even though there is a future eschatological dimension to 6:10—God's will being fully realized at the eschaton (cf. 16:27; 24:30–31; 25:31)—a realized eschatological emphasis is also contained in this prayer. The disciples have a part to play in bringing about God's will on earth; thus, they are called to pray that God will enable them to do so.

Jesus himself clearly exemplified this portion of the Lord's Prayer (6:9b–10) in his own itinerant ministry. In the Garden of Gethsemane, Jesus spent extended time in prayer (Matt. 26:36–46). Interestingly, Jesus

---

depends on that lordship: we cannot live without God to teach us, forgive us, and save us" in *The Sermon on the Mount: Inspiring the Moral Imagination*, CNT (New York: Crossroad, 1999), 114.

5. See 5:43–48; 7:21; 10:32–33; 11:25–27; 12:48–50; 18:10; 25:34–40, 46b; 26:29.

chose Peter, James, and John to have front-row seats to his intense, heartfelt prayer to his Father (26:36–37). In his prayer, Jesus's singular focus was to submit himself to his Father's will—committing himself to help God's will be done on earth as it is in heaven. Though he struggled with the difficult requirements of obedience—"he began to be sorrowful and troubled" (26:37)—he committed himself to bring glory to God by following his Father's will: "My Father, if it is possible, may this cup be taken from me. Yet not as I will but as you will" (26:39, 42, 44). This threefold repetition emphasized his total allegiance to God.

Matthew declares that God's will and glory would be manifested through Jesus's crucifixion, in which he saved his people from their sins (1:21; 20:28; 26:28; 26:53–56). Similarly, the author of Hebrews describes Jesus's obedience in 5:7–9 ESV: "In the days of his flesh, Jesus offered up prayers and supplications, with loud cries and tears, to him who was able to save him from death, and he was heard because of his reverence. Although he was a son, he learned obedience through what he suffered. And being made perfect, he became the source of eternal salvation for all who obey him" (ESV). This example identifies the reality of inaugurated eschatology—Jesus's life was centered on fulfilling God's will and declaring God's reign on earth.

John Wesley similarly describes the focus of those who pray Matthew 6:9b–10: "We pray that we and all mankind may do the whole will of God in all things; and nothing else, not the least thing, but what is the holy and acceptable will of God."[6] This kind of prayer is transformative, as Richard Foster notes: "In prayer, real prayer, we begin to think God's thoughts after him: to desire the things he desires, to love the things he loves, to will the things he wills."[7] Thus, we are instructed to pray to God, our only Father, committing ourselves completely to him as our holy Father and proving our allegiance to him, helping to bring his Kingdom—his will—to earth as it is in heaven. In this way, we proclaim our monotheistic faith and demonstrate our desire to love him with our whole beings.

The second part of the Lord's Prayer (6:11–13) focuses on seeking God's provision for our physical and spiritual needs. Jesus will state a few verses

6. John Wesley, *Thirteen Discourses on the Sermon on the Mount* (Franklin, TN: Seedbed, 2014), 127. In a similar vein, John R. W. Stott states, "In the Lord's Prayer, Christians are obsessed with God—with his name, his Kingdom, and his will, not with theirs. True Christian prayer is a preoccupation with God and his glory" in *The Message of the Sermon on the Mount: Matthew 5–7*, BST(Downers Grove, IL: InterVarsity, 1978), 151.
7. Richard Foster, *Celebration of Discipline: The Path to Spiritual Growth*, rev. ed. (New York: HarperCollins, 1988), 33.

later, "Do not be anxious saying, 'What shall we eat?' or 'What shall we drink?' or 'What shall we wear?' For the Gentiles seek after all these things, and your heavenly Father knows you need them all. But seek first the kingdom of God and his righteousness, and all these things will be added to you" (6:31–33; see also 6:8; 7:7–11). This larger context suggests that in this portion of the Lord's Prayer, Jesus wanted his disciples to pray that God would supply their needs. With his communal focus, it can be implied that Jesus would call people to extend their prayer toward the needs of others as well—demonstrating their commitment to love their neighbor as they love themselves (22:39). John R. W. Stott states, "The three petitions which Jesus puts on our lips are beautifully comprehensive. They cover, in principle, all of our human need—material (daily bread), spiritual (forgiveness of sins), and moral (deliverance from evil). What we are doing whenever we pray this prayer is to express our dependance upon God in every area of our human life."[8] The second part of the Lord's Prayer emphasizes that truly God is enough—his love, power, and presence are evident in every part of our lives.

The first petition requests that the Father provide daily bread (6:11). Some New Testament scholars view this appeal as directed only to physical human need;[9] according to the context of Matthew's Gospel; however, a physical *and* a spiritual view seem to be present. Two good examples occur in Jesus's miraculous feedings of the five thousand and the four thousand (14:13–21; 15:32–38). These narratives include several insights regarding the petition for daily bread. First, Jesus's motive in seeking bread was compassion for the mass of sick and hungry people (14:13–16; 15:32). Jesus's concern was not his own "daily bread" but the physical needs of others. Second, Jesus relied on God his Father through prayer to provide him the power to multiply the bread and fish (14:17–21; 15:33–38). Third, Jesus taught his disciples the importance of active faith. In contrast to the disciples who wanted to send the crowds away to get food due to their lack of supplies—and lack of faith (14:15–17; 15:33–34)—Jesus sought the Kingdom of God and trusted God would provide (see also 16:8–12). Therefore, in these narratives, Jesus taught his disciples that through God's power and provision, *both* physical and spiritual needs could be provided. Similarly, in 26:26–29, Jesus compared bread to his broken body—the

8. Stott, *Message*, 150–51.

9. For example, Stott, *Message*, 148–49; Robert A. Guelich, *The Sermon on the Mount: A Foundation for Understanding* (Waco, TX: Word, 1982), 293; and Pennington, *Sermon on the Mount*, 225.

physical food that would bring *spiritual* nourishment: the forgiveness of sins and eternal life due to his sacrificial death on the cross.[10] Georg Strecker summarized the meaning of "bread" in 6:11 well: "The word *bread* here designates a primary means of nourishment. It represents everything else that can satisfy the material and spiritual needs of humankind."[11] When we pray for the "daily bread"—for ourselves and others—we are seeking physical and spiritual sustenance, and we are demonstrating our call to love others as we love ourselves.

The second petition asks for restored relationships with God and others (6:12). In this request more than any other, we recognize the heart of God—we do not truly love God if we are unwilling to love others. Jesus stated to his disciples that they could only seek the Father's forgiveness for sin *if* they were willing to forgive others who had harmed them. Jesus stated, "For if you forgive other people when they sin against you, your heavenly Father will also forgive you. But if you do not forgive others their sins, your Father will not forgive your sins" (6:14–15). Such a forgiving heart is also implied earlier in the Sermon on the Mount when Jesus taught his disciples to "love your enemies and pray for those who persecute you, so that you may become children of your Father in heaven" (5:43–45), for this is what it means to be perfect "as your heavenly Father is perfect" (5:48). In Jesus's itinerant ministry, he taught Peter (and the other disciples) that there is no limit to forgiveness—disciples are called to always forgive those who sin against you. Those who do not are in danger of eternal damnation (18:21–22, 33–35). Also, Jesus forgave the sins of a paralytic man when he said to him, "Take heart, son; your sins are forgiven" (9:2, 6–7). Finally, as Jesus watched his enemies from the cross—those who had whipped, beaten, and nailed him to a cross—he prayed to his Father, saying, "Father, forgive them, for they do not know what they are doing" (Luke 23:34). Jesus also taught his disciples about a prodigal son who sinned against his father. Yet when he had hit rock bottom, he returned to his father and was immediately forgiven. The father also instructed his older son to forgive the prodigal—emphasizing the desire God has to forgive us of our sins and his call for us to forgive others who have sinned against us (Luke 15:11–32). As Luke 15:7 states, "There will be more rejoicing in heaven over one sinner

10. See also John 6:30–58. According to John 6:35, Jesus himself is the "bread of life"—the only one who can quench hungry and thirsty souls.

11. Georg Strecker, *The Sermon on the Mount: An Exegetical Commentary*, trans. O. C. Dean Jr. (Nashville: Abingdon, 1988), 118.

who repents than over ninety-nine righteous persons who do not need to repent." We demonstrate deep love for others when we are willing to forgive their sins against us so we can experience a right relationship with them and our Father in the heavens.

The third petition requests the ability to overcome temptation and to be delivered from the evil one—that is, Satan (6:13). This request in the Lord's Prayer is centered on spiritual warfare.[12] In the Garden of Gethsemane, Jesus instructed the disciples to conquer temptation through prayer: "Keep watch and pray, so that you will not give in to temptation. For the spirit is willing but the body is weak!" (26:41–42 NLT). Throughout his own itinerant ministry, Jesus relied on the Holy Spirit's power and the truths of Scripture to overcome Satan's temptations (4:1–11). Through the Holy Spirit, Jesus was able to have divine authority to cast out demons (8:28–34; 12:22–23, 28; 17:18–20).

In his High Priestly prayer, Jesus asked the Father to protect his disciples from the evil one (the devil): "I do not ask that you take them out of the world, but that you keep them from the evil (one). They are not of the world just as I am not of the world. Sanctify them in the truth; your word is truth. As you sent me into the world, so I also sent them into the world" (17:15–18). In this same prayer, Jesus lamented over the loss of Judas because Judas had succumbed to temptation and allowed Satan to enter him; he chose money over his allegiance to Jesus (17:12; cf. 6:70; 13:2, 27; Luke 22:3–6). Jesus was aware of the spiritual threat Satan would pose to his disciples, so he prayed that they, like he, would be protected by the Holy Spirit. John Wesley once said, "Every new victory which a soul gains is the effect of a new prayer . . . In the greatest temptations, a single look to Christ, and the barely pronouncing his name, suffices to overcome the wicked one, so it be done with confidence and calmness of spirit."[13] When we pray to the Father to deliver us from temptation and the evil one—for ourselves and others—we are seeking God's protection for others so they

12. In 1 Corinthians 10:13, the apostle Paul reminded the Corinthians (and present-day readers) that God has the ability to provide a way to stand up under temptation so it will not overcome us. By relying on God's power through prayer (as Jesus relied on the Spirit in Matt. 4:1–11), we can have the reassurance that it is God's will and desire for us to overcome temptation and resist the spiritual onslaughts of the devil. God is faithful—he will help us overcome any temptation that threatens to destroy us and our relationship with him.

13. John Wesley, *How to Pray: The Best of John Wesley on Prayer* (Uhrichsville, OH: Barbour, 2007), 35.

will continue in their intimate relationship with him. We are demonstrating our desire to love others as we love ourselves.

The Lord's Prayer provides us with a great template for a theology of prayer, demonstrating how to pray according to our Father's will. E. M. Bounds once said, "We can never expect to grow in the likeness of our Lord unless we follow His example and give more time to communion with the Father. A revival of real praying would produce a spiritual revolution."[14] Let us continue to seek the Kingdom as we dedicate ourselves to praying our Lord's Prayer, and may the spiritual revolution continue in and through our hearts and lives.

Scriptural Examples of Those Thirsting for Living Water

Combined with the practice of prayer—communication with God—is the need for an internal longing for God. Scripture provides examples of those who yearned to be close to God, basking in his holy presence and desiring his life to consume theirs. One metaphor for this longing is thirsting for water. Since water is a prime necessity of life, biblical authors used this metaphor to emphasize that only God could bring true lifelong satisfaction. Space will not allow for a comprehensive treatment, but the following examples illustrate this deep longing for God.

The book of Psalms frequently describes this intense spiritual thirst. In Psalm 42:1–2 NLT, the sons of Korah—who were Temple musicians and assistants—cried out, "As the deer longs for streams of water, so I long for you, O God. I thirst for God, the living God. Where can I go and stand before him?" In the time of exile, the sons of Korah felt separated from God since they were far away from Jerusalem and the Temple. In this psalm, they felt anguish, grief, and discouragement as they thirsted for their God. All they desired was to be close to him again. Yet amid their pain, they chose to worship through prayer and praise. They lifted their eyes toward God and decided to hope in God—to praise him for his steadfast love (42:8 ESV) and his nature as their "rock" of safety and their Savior (42:5, 9, 11). Instead of despair, they prayed to the God who gives them life (42:8). Therefore, instead of allowing the storms of life to engulf them, they recognized God's

14. E. M. Bounds, *The Complete Works of E. M. Bounds on Prayer: Experience the Wonders of God through Prayer* (Grand Rapids, MI: Baker, 2004), 337.

omnipresence and chose to seek the Kingdom of God—they turned to the only One their hearts longed for, thirsting for his holy presence.

King David wrote Psalm 63. Like the sons of Korah, David was in a dark, fearful place. Most likely, he was being pursued by his son, Absalom (2 Sam. 15–18). Not only was David grieved over his son's rebellion against him, he was hiding in the barren wilderness of Judah. As he was in this dry, deserted place, he cried out to God saying, "O God, you are my God, I earnestly search for you. My soul thirsts for you; my whole body longs for you in this parched and weary land where there is no water" (63:1 NLT). It appears that David has chosen to make the wilderness his "sanctuary" in which to seek after God in prayer and praise (63:2–4). He praised God for his steadfast love, his help, and his security (63:3, 7–8). He asserted that his only satisfaction in life is found in the presence of God—more than the abundance of food (63:5). Both day and night, he meditates and thinks about God (63:6). Finally, when in fear, David chose to "cling" to God in faith that his "strong hand" would hold him in security (63:8). In God alone did David place his hope and salvation. No matter what enemy may pursue him, he believed that they would be destroyed (63:10). Therefore, David continued to seek after the Kingdom—thirsting for the only One who could give him hope and salvation (63:11).[15]

In Psalm 84, the sons of Korah—once again far away from Jerusalem and the Temple—celebrated the Temple as the place where God's living presence resided. To these Temple assistants, their greatest joy in life was to be in God's presence. Their longing for God is particularly showcased in 84:1–2, 10 (NLT):

> How lovely is your dwelling place, O Lord of Heaven's Armies. I long, yes, I faint with longing to enter the courts of the Lord. With my whole being, body and soul, I shout joyfully for the living God. . . . A single day in your courts is better than a thousand anywhere else! I would rather be a gatekeeper in the house of my God than live the good life in the homes of the wicked.

15. Commenting on Psalm 63, Beth Tanner states, "Prayer offers a refuge from current troubles and encourages us to trust in God today because of God's aid in the past." See Nancy de Claissé-Walford, Rolf A. Jacobson, and Beth LaNeel Tanner, *The Book of Psalms*, NICOT (Grand Rapids, MI: Eerdmans, 2014), 521.

Though the metaphor of water is not present in this section, longing for God is the central theme. The sons of Korah were unconcerned about *where* in the Temple they were present; they simply wanted to be as close to God as they could (84:3). They desired to praise with joy (84:2, 4), to seek him in prayer (84:8), and to celebrate his character as their "King" (84:3), their "strength" (84:5, 7), and their "sun and shield" (84:11). They acknowledged God as the giver of grace and glory to those who "do what is right" and "trust" in him (84:11–12). Therefore, even though they were living in a dark place in exile, God's presence would be their "blessing" and "a place of refreshing springs" (84:6). Therefore, once again, the sons of Korah chose to seek the Kingdom of God—they thirsted and longed for God's presence to be with them. Their joy was found in relying on him (84:12).

The "thirsting" metaphor also appears in Isaiah 55. Through his prophetic word, Isaiah invited anyone who longed for God to come to him:

> Is anyone thirsty? Come and drink—even if you have no money! Come, take your choice of wine or milk—it is all free! . . . Come to me with your ears wide open. Listen, and you will find life. I will make an everlasting covenant with you. I will give you all the unfailing love I promised to David. . . . Seek the Lord while you can find him. Call on him now while he is near. (Isa. 55:1, 3, 6 NLT)

Through this prophetic word, God offers salvation to all who are willing to do the following: (1) come to him—enter into a covenant with God; his love is unfailing and his requirement is for people to listen to his words (most likely with the intent to obey); (2) seek the Lord in prayer until he is found and call out to him (55:6); and (3) be willing to repent and turn to God—to change their ways, turn away from wickedness and every thought of doing wrong, and receive his generous forgiveness (55:7). The result of such thirsting for God will be worship, celebration, and joy (55:12–13). These words from Isaiah are reminiscent of Jesus's words of invitation in Matthew 11:28–29 (NLT): "Come to me all who are weary and carrying burdens and I will give you rest. Take up my yoke upon you, and learn from me, for I am humble and lowly in heart, and you will find rest for your souls."

John's Gospel encapsulates these themes in Jesus's interaction with a Samaritan woman at a well (John 4:1–42). The author begins by describing the reason Jesus went through Samaria, using an important Greek term, *edei*, meaning "it is necessary"—that is, it is God's will (4:4). The Samaritan woman's encounter with Jesus was divinely orchestrated, emphasizing the opportunity for salvation (as in Isaiah 55) for both Jews and Gentiles. At noontime, Jesus saw the Samaritan woman, who came to draw water from Jacob's well, near where Jesus sat. He chose to have an encounter with this woman—he wanted to initiate a relationship with her. Jesus began by boldly asking her for a drink (4:7 NLT). The woman questioned Jesus: "You are a Jew, and I am a Samaritan woman. Why are you asking me for a drink?" (4:9). Jesus bypassed this ethnic animosity and revealed why he came to Sychar in the first place: "If only you knew the gift God has for you and who you are speaking to, you would ask me, and I would give you living water. . . . Those who drink the water I give will never be thirsty again. It becomes a fresh, bubbling spring within them, giving them eternal life" (4:10, 14). Jesus came to the woman to offer her spiritual life, not physical water—a never-ending, abiding relationship with God her Father through the long-awaited Messiah.

The Samaritan woman asked for the living water Jesus offered, but Jesus asked her to get her husband and return. When she indicated she did not have a husband, Jesus said, "You're right! You don't have a husband—for you have had five husbands, and you aren't even married to the man you're now living with. You certainly spoke the truth!" (4:17–18 NLT). If this Samaritan wanted to have a thirst-quenching relationship with God, she needed to forsake her sinful life,[16] which was the spiritual barrier preventing her from gaining Jesus's living water.

Jesus then taught her the truths about the Jewish faith and his identity as the Messiah—truths that the Samaritan people did not understand (4:20–26). After hearing Jesus's words, she left her waterpot and went back to her village to tell other Samaritans to come and see Jesus (4:28–29). The Samaritans came and believed that Jesus was the "Savior of the world" due to the woman's testimony and their willingness to listen to Jesus's teaching (4:39–42). The Samaritan woman discovered what her heart longed and thirsted for—a relationship with God her Father through Jesus Christ, the Savior of the world.

In Luke 2:25–38, we see a final example of two individuals who longed to be in the Temple to seek after the living God. Simeon was filled with the Holy Spirit and was led by the Spirit to the Temple. Earlier, the Holy Spirit revealed to Simeon that he would not die before seeing the Messiah—Christ, the Lord (2:25–26). As he entered the Temple, Jesus's parents were bringing

16. For the woman's sin in this context, see Leon Morris, *The Gospel According to John*, rev. ed. (Grand Rapids, MI: Eerdmans, 1995), 234–36.

the newborn in so the priest could perform for Jesus the things required by the Law. When Simeon saw Jesus, he took Jesus into his arms and prayed a blessing over him. In this prayer, he declared that Jesus was God's "salvation" prepared for all people—"a light for revelation to the Gentiles and the glory of your people Israel" (2:28–32). Simeon blessed Mary and Joseph, who were surprised by Simeon's words, and then told Mary that there would be mixed reactions to Jesus's ministry—acceptance and opposition—and that a "sword would pierce" her own soul, indicating Jesus's future suffering and crucifixion (2:33–35). As Simeon spoke these words, Anna the prophet approached. She never left the Temple—the *locus* of God's holy presence—but worshiped there with prayer and fasting night and day (2:37). As a widow, it appears that Anna had no other human being to provide her with companionship and interaction, yet she chose to cling to her God—thirsting and longing to live in his presence and bask in his unfailing love. Her heart was open and ready to receive God's revelation. Anna praised God for the advent of the Messiah and immediately spoke of the child to all who were looking for the redemption of Jerusalem (2:38).

Simeon and Anna were both longing for the same thing—the restoration of Israel under the reign of God. Through the Messiah—Christ, the Lord—God's plan for salvation would come to fruition. The longing for God's holy presence is the reason why we should cultivate a life of prayer. From the above scriptural examples, we can be assured that God wants us to thirst for his presence and love in our lives. He desires us to seek after him with our whole beings. He wants our worship, companionship, and to hear the cries of our hearts. As we thirst for his living water, we are drawn into an ocean of love, peace, and hope. May we thirst for God—cling to him—as we perpetually seek his Kingdom through prayer.

Reflections as an Altar Minister at the Asbury Outpouring

E. M. Bounds said, "All true revivals have been born in prayer. When God's people become so concerned about the state of religion that they lie on their faces day and night in earnest supplication, the blessing will be sure to fall."[17]

I had the privilege of serving as an altar minister for many evenings at the Asbury Outpouring of February 2023. Every day I attended and night

17. Bounds, *Complete Works*, 362.

I served, I came to the same realization: thousands of souls are thirsting and longing for God, like David in the wilderness or Anna in the Temple. The atmosphere in Hughes Auditorium was breathtaking—the presence of the Holy Spirit manifested profound peace and unity. People were smiling and rejoicing, weeping and repenting, embracing and praying with one another, and no celebrities dominated the worship. Thirsty people came to the well and drank deeply from the Holy Spirit and found their lives changed as a result. Mark Hall of the contemporary music group Casting Crowns has described this kind of transformation: "When we draw on anything or anyone other than Jesus for contentment, hope, security, peace, and life, we trade the only true Well for a meaningless hole. . . . The more time we take to drink him in and the more we surrender to him and allow him to change us, the more Jesus becomes our Well."[18]

As an altar minister, I witnessed thousands of people seeking Jesus for deep spiritual and emotional healing. They had a deep passion to take the Outpouring experience—the overwhelming presence of the Holy Spirit—to the places where they lived. I had the privilege of praying every aspect of the Lord's Prayer over those in attendance:

- The love of God was demonstrated when children and adults accepted Jesus as their Savior for the first time and when others rededicated their lives to him after a season of spiritual dryness in their relationship with him. Many people came to the altar to confess their sins, sharing how God revealed to them these obstacles in their relationship with him. Others showed their submission to God as they sought the Lord's will and direction for their lives.
- Love for others was demonstrated by students on campus who, through being in God's presence, reconciled with other students with whom they had conflict.
- Petitions for physical, emotional, and spiritual provision arose from those who had experienced deep trauma in their life and desired to be healed from years of pain and suffering. Some came in grief over the loss of loved ones, others dealt with long and short-term sicknesses, and still others desired God's comforting presence and emotional healing due to sexual trauma. As people shared these tragedies with

18. Mark Hall, *The Well: Why Are So Many Still Thirsty?* (Grand Rapids, MI: Zondervan, 2011), 26.

me, we prayed for God's strength, increased faith, and the mending of their broken hearts.

- Others asked for prayer to resist temptation—they wanted to honor God by giving up sinful habits related to sexual immorality and lust and sought God's power and victory over the enemy's work in their lives.

One of the great blessings of serving as an altar minister was seeing the joy on the faces of worshipers as they came to the altar to celebrate the Holy Spirit's presence—thirsty souls being quenched by God's transforming work. Witnessing God moving in the lives of so many people, I received a glimpse of the Kingdom of God. Every person I had the privilege of praying with was thirsting for God—longing for more of him and realizing that he alone is the answer to their every need and desire. God had invited and called people from all over the globe to meet with him in Wilmore, KY, and people responded to his call. Then God reminded them of his deep desire to have an intimate relationship with him. Finally, God called people to a lifelong pursuit of holiness—a deep desire to obey his Word and pledge their allegiance to him alone. They came thirsty and left spiritually refreshed.

This process of transforming humanity is described by John Oswalt: "God is calling them to share his unique character, one that will alter how they approach every aspect of their lives . . . the goal of salvation is fellowship with God within the parameters of his character and nature."[19] Such "outpouring" can happen at any time, though, if we are open to the Holy Spirit's call for intimacy and transformation (e.g., Matt. 5:6). May each day of our lives be consumed with a desire to seek after the only One who can ever satisfy our thirsty, needy souls.

19. John N. Oswalt, *Called to Be Holy: A Biblical Perspective* (Wilmore, KY: Francis Asbury, 2000), 33.

CHAPTER ELEVEN

VIEWING THE ASBURY OUTPOURING THROUGH A WESLEYAN LENS

Suzanne Nicholson
Professor of New Testament, Asbury University

The Wesleyan movement was born out of revival. Even though John Wesley had grown up in a Christian home, was ordained in the Anglican church, and had already taken a mission trip to the American colonies, it wasn't until his heart was "strangely warmed" at the Aldersgate Street meeting on May 24, 1738, that his life and ministry turned in a vibrant new direction.[1] His journal from this day declares that "an assurance was given me that [Christ] had taken away my sins, even mine, and saved me from the law of sin and death." Wesley goes on to describe his continuing prayers and the calling to share his experiences publicly: "I began to pray with all my might for those who had in a more especial manner despitefully used me and persecuted me. I then testified openly to all there, what I now first felt in my heart."[2] These experiences were mirrored by many of those attending the Asbury Outpouring: students felt called to trust in God alone, received assurance of salvation, prayed intensely, experienced deep transformation, and testified to the goodness of God.

Wesley's ministry continued for more than fifty years as he proclaimed the gospel to anyone who would listen. His theology and passionate beliefs shaped churches and institutions to the present day, including Asbury University, which was founded by Methodist pastor John Wesley Hughes. When God poured forth his Spirit on those gathered in Hughes Auditorium

1. Certainly the Holy Spirit was at work in Wesley's life prior to this. Nonetheless, his Aldersgate experience was pivotal in his being swept up in the Evangelical Revival.
2. Wesley, *The Works of John Wesley*, 3rd ed., vols. 1 and 2 (1872; repr., Grand Rapids, MI: Baker, 2002), 103.

in February 2023—nearly 285 years after Wesley's Aldersgate Street experience—God abundantly blessed those present, regardless of their denominational affiliation. Nonetheless, Asbury's Wesleyan theological heritage has been foundational in helping many of those present to make sense of their experience.[3]

Sin, Prevenient Grace, and Repentance

Wesley's theology is thoroughly grounded in Scripture, which he encouraged others to interpret through "the analogy of faith." He described this concept as "the connexion and harmony there is between those grand, fundamental doctrines, Original Sin, Justification by Faith, the New Birth, Inward and Outward Holiness."[4] For Wesley, one could only understand the truths of God within the framework of the overarching story revealed in Scripture.

A key aspect of this story is the recognition that, although originally created good, humanity has been fundamentally warped by the sin of Adam and Eve. Original sin has so affected humans, according to Wesley, that apart from the grace of God, "'every imagination of the thoughts of his heart is' still 'evil, only evil,' and that 'continually.'"[5] Even human actions that may be considered good on the surface nonetheless have selfish motivations: "The other-oriented, self-giving nature was replaced by bondage to a self-consumed heart."[6]

Humans do not have the power or the will to escape this bondage on their own, nor can they free themselves from the condemnation they justly

3. One does not need to embrace Wesleyan theology in order to understand the Outpouring. In what follows, those of other theological leanings likely will find significant overlap with their own theological vantage points. My hope is that this conversation will help visitors to the Outpouring to process and clarify their experiences, as well as help the curious to consider the possibility of a loving God who desires to bless humanity through the call to repentance, salvation, and holiness.

4. John Wesley, preface to *The Explanatory Notes upon the Old Testament*, Wesley Center Online, accessed September 24, 2024, https://wesley.nnu.edu/john-wesley/john-wesleys-notes-on-the-bible/preface-to-the-old-testament-notes/.

5. John Wesley, "Original Sin," sermon, Wesley Center Online, accessed September 24, 2024, https://wesley.nnu.edu/john-wesley/the-sermons-of-john-wesley-1872-edition/sermon-44-original-sin/.

6. Ryan Danker, ed., *The Faith Once Delivered: A Wesleyan Witness to Christian Orthodoxy* (Franklin, TN: Seedbed, 2024), 30. Also available at the John Wesley Institute, accessed September 6, 2024, https://nextmethodism.org/summit-document/.

deserve. Sin separates a person from God, who is holy and cannot be tainted by sin. Wesley emphasized, however, the incredible love of God that refuses to leave us in our sin and condemnation. Rather, God gives us prevenient grace—that is, the grace that goes before—so that humanity can begin to respond to God. Apart from this grace, we are so warped by sin in our thinking and hearts that we cannot respond to God. But with prevenient grace, God partially restores us—that is, we are enabled to choose to follow God or not.[7] Wesley described God's offer of prevenient grace as similar to someone who enters a prisoner's jail, takes off the prisoner's chains, and opens the cell door but does not force the prisoner to leave. The choice is up to the prisoner.[8] This grace is described beautifully in the fourth verse of Charles Wesley's famous hymn "And Can It Be":

> Long my imprisoned spirit lay,
> Fast bound in sin and nature's night;
> Thine eye diffused a quick'ning ray—
> I woke, the dungeon flamed with light;
> My chains fell off, my heart was free,
> I rose, went forth, and followed Thee.

When a person responds to God's prevenient grace, they begin to comprehend their sin and can choose to repent. That is, one recognizes that they have sinned and turned away from God, and they now desire to turn around and follow God's perfect will. Wesley distinguished between repentance prior to justification and repentance after justification. Prior to salvation, sinners repent of their sinful acts and corrupted nature; after salvation, believers repent of lingering sin.[9] This salvation is effected through the perfect sacrifice of Jesus Christ, whose death on the cross paid the penalty for sin—death—and thus we are now able to approach the living God through faith in Christ.[10] His resurrection assures us that sin and death have indeed been defeated through his perfect sacrifice.

The outpouring of the Holy Spirit in Hughes Auditorium in February 2023 demonstrated both prevenient grace and deep repentance of sin.

7. W. Brian Shelton, *Prevenient Grace: God's Provision for Fallen Humanity* (Anderson, IN: Warner, 2014), 7.
8. Shelton, *Prevenient Grace*, 99–100.
9. See Danker, *Faith Once Delivered*, 48.
10. Danker, *Faith Once Delivered*, 48–49.

Students who remained in Hughes after chapel that day felt the powerful presence of the Holy Spirit. As they responded to what God had initiated, they became more deeply aware of their sin. Students began experiencing a profound sense of repentance, and they proclaimed publicly the sins they had struggled with for so long—addictions to pornography, doubts about God as the result of struggles with anxiety and depression, anger and resentment originating from difficult relationships and traumatic experiences, and so much more. The overwhelming love of God experienced in that auditorium brought those present to their knees. Students did not demand that God show up; rather, they experienced the presence of God and responded to the grace that God offered. Some students came to repentance for the first time and embraced the salvation offered by Christ; others were renewed in their faith as they repented of lingering sin and embraced the goodness of God.

Justifying Grace, Assurance, and the New Birth

Those who believed in Christ for the first time, trusting in him alone for their salvation, experienced the justifying grace of God. Wesley says, "The plain scriptural notion of justification is pardon, the forgiveness of sin."[11] Many of those present in Hughes Auditorium experienced a profound sense of the forgiveness of their sins. Wesley explains the nature of this justifying grace:

> To him that is justified or forgiven, God 'will not impute sin' to his condemnation. He will not condemn him on that account, either in this world or in that which is to come. His sins, all his past sins, in thought, word, and deed, are covered, are blotted out, shall not be remembered or mentioned against him, any more than if they had not been. God will not inflict on that sinner what he deserved to suffer, because the Son of his love hath suffered for him. And from the time we are 'accepted through the Beloved,' 'reconciled to God through his blood,' he loves, and blesses, and watches over us for good, even as if we had never sinned.[12]

11. John Wesley, "Justification by Faith," sermon, Wesley Center Online, accessed September 24, 2024, https://wesley.nnu.edu/john-wesley/the-sermons-of-john-wesley-1872-edition/sermon-5-justification-by-faith/.
12. Wesley, "Justification by Faith."

Not only are sinners justified through the blood of Christ, but they receive assurance that they have indeed been forgiven. This is not merely a theological conviction, but it is "the direct witness of the Holy Spirit in assuring grace, a conviction that we can be certain—not just mentally but experientially—of God's pardon and acceptance. We can know that God's pardon has been granted to us and his renewal work has begun in our hearts."[13] Many of those who prayed in Hughes described receiving a deep sense of peace from the Holy Spirit. As sins were laid at the altar, spirits were freed from bondage and condemnation, and the Spirit caused great rejoicing in response.

John Wesley, too, experienced powerful movements of the Holy Spirit at various points in his ministry. On January 1, 1739, for example, he recounts in his journal that he and about sixty other believers were celebrating a Love Feast at the Fetter Lane Society, when "the power of God came mightily upon us, insomuch that many cried out for exceeding joy, and many fell to the ground. As soon as we were recovered a little from that awe and amazement at the presence of his majesty, we broke out with one voice, 'We praise thee, O God; we acknowledge thee to be the Lord.'" Similarly, on June 16, Wesley recorded, "In that hour we found God with us as at the first. Some fell prostrate upon the ground. Others burst out, as with one consent, into loud praise and thanksgiving. And many openly testified, there had been no such day as this since January the first preceding."[14]

Certainly, one does not need to experience an outpouring or revival in order to receive assurance of the pardon of God. Nonetheless, these outpouring experiences often provide an intensity of assurance like no other.

More than assurance, however, is offered by God's Spirit. Having been justified by faith in Christ, the believer experiences what Wesley called the new birth. Whereas justification refers to the work God does *for* us, the new birth refers to the holiness that God begins to work *in* us as God renews our fallen nature. The new birth is the beginning of sanctification. Wesley describes it this way:

13. Danker, *Faith Once Delivered*, 49.

14. Douglas Fox argues that meetings at the Fetter Lane Society were more spiritually impactful on Wesley than his Aldersgate Society experience the previous May. See "Aldersgate or Fetter Lane?" *Firebrand*, April 20, 2021, https://firebrandmag.com/articles/aldersgate-or-fetter-lane.

> It is that great change which God works in the soul when he brings it into life; when he raises it from the death of sin to the life of righteousness. It is the change wrought in the whole soul by the almighty Spirit of God when it is "created anew in Christ Jesus;" when it is "renewed after the image of God, in righteousness and true holiness;" when the love of the world is changed into the love of God; pride into humility; passion into meekness; hatred, envy, malice, into a sincere, tender, disinterested love for all mankind. In a word, it is that change whereby the earthly, sensual, devilish mind is turned into the "mind which was in Christ Jesus."[15]

Many of those at the Outpouring experienced this kind of radical transformation. Students who had been at odds with one another reconciled, others gave over their addictions in submission to God, and still others renewed their faith and devoted themselves anew to Christ. Healing led to hope, and hope led to new life.

Means of Grace

Wesley believed that the life of a Christian after justification must be imbued thoroughly with the grace of God. Only through this continuing grace is the believer empowered to live the holy life, a life that reflects love for God and neighbor. Wesley believed God had provided numerous means of grace, which he defined as "outward signs, words, or actions, ordained of God, and appointed for this end, to be the ordinary channels whereby he might convey to men, preventing, justifying, or sanctifying grace."[16] He urged believers to make use of these means as often as possible: prayer, searching the Scriptures, fasting, partaking in the Eucharist, and works of mercy (such as caring for the poor), to name but a few. As believers participate in these means of grace, "we place ourselves in the posture of receiving God's transforming work. The many varied means of grace allow us to live out the Great Commandment to love God and neighbor (Matt. 22:36–40)."[17]

15. John Wesley, "The New Birth," sermon, Wesley Center Online, accessed September 24, 2024, https://wesley.nnu.edu/john-wesley/the-sermons-of-john-wesley-1872-edition/sermon-45-the-new-birth/.
16. John Wesley, "The Means of Grace," sermon, Wesley Center Online, accessed September 24, 2024, https://wesley.nnu.edu/john-wesley/the-sermons-of-john-wesley-1872-edition/sermon-16-the-means-of-grace/.
17. Danker, *Faith Once Delivered*, 60–61.

Those who attended the Outpouring participated in multiple means of grace. Rather than a celebrity speaker leading worship, visitors were invited up front to read their favorite scriptures. Those in their seats were called regularly to pray with those near them, and intercessions were lifted for families and students and churches, the young and the old, for those in the next seat and those across the world. The community worshiped together, offering praise to God in a unified voice. This praise was a response to the grace experienced in community as the Holy Spirit revealed the goodness of God. Jonathan Powers notes that this revelation cannot be forced. "Instead, it is by the power of the Holy Spirit that God is made accessible by faith so the church might be granted an epiphany of his beauty, goodness, and majesty. As the church begins to know and understand the character of God, the rightful response to his revelation is loving worship."[18] The Holy Spirit graciously initiated worship, and worship itself became a channel of further grace. Such is the love of God for humanity.

Sanctification and Christian Perfection

Wesley has described the Christian life using the metaphor of a house. A person approaches through the front porch of repentance and enters the house through the door of justification. But living in the rest of the house—to which repentance and justification give access—involves holiness of heart and life.[19] We were made to live the sanctified life.

As with every other aspect of the life of a believer, holiness is enabled by grace. We cannot become holy of our own accord. Rather, we respond to the grace that the Holy Spirit provides, and as we cooperate with the Spirit, we begin to bear the fruit of the Spirit: love, joy, peace, patience, kindness, generosity, faithfulness, gentleness, and self-control (Gal. 5:22–23). Thus, through the Spirit we begin to reflect the likeness of Christ and demonstrate the love of God. We receive what God always intended for us—a life of flourishing with God and neighbor—and become what God desires us to become: "Be holy, for I am holy" (Lev. 19:2; 1 Pet. 1:16).

18. Jonathan A. Powers, "Liturgy and Worship in the Emerging Methodism," in *The Next Methodism: Theological, Social, and Missional Foundations for Global Methodism*, ed. Kenneth J. Collins and Ryan N. Danker (Franklin, TN: Seedbed, 2021), 231.
19. See John Wesley, *Principles of a Methodist Farther Explained* (London: W. Strahan, 1746), 6.

This process of sanctification begins with the new birth. Our priorities and desires change as we are "inwardly renewed by the power of God."[20] This initial sanctification transforms a person from a life directed toward sin to a life directed toward holiness. God continues to pour out grace, and as the believer responds, the process of becoming holy—becoming Christlike—continues. Utilizing the means of grace, as noted above, is key to living the holy life and being shaped by God.

In addition, social holiness is crucial to our formation. In response to those who prefer to isolate themselves from others in order to draw near to God, Wesley declared, "Whereas, according to the Judgment of our Lord, and the Writings of his Apostles, it is only when we are knit together, that we have Nourishment from Him, and increase with the Increase of GOD. Neither is there any time, when the weakest Member can say to the strongest, or the strongest to the weakest, 'I have no need of Thee.'"[21] Instead, Wesley argued that community is necessary for the development of our faith. We need Christian fellowship and accountability: "The Gospel of CHRIST knows of no Religion, but Social; no Holiness but Social Holiness. Faith working by Love, is the length and breadth and depth and height of Christian Perfection."[22] Accordingly, Wesley developed—and required Methodists to attend—society, class, and band meetings for their discipleship. These groups encouraged corporate worship and prayer as well as small-group confession and accountability.

This process of sanctification ultimately ought to lead a believer to entire sanctification, also known as Christian perfection.[23] Wesley makes it clear that this does not mean freedom from ignorance, mistaken judgment, infirmities, or temptation.[24] (For example, the continuing presence of temptation in this world means it is possible to fall from perfection once attained.)

20. John Wesley, "The Scripture Way of Salvation," sermon, Wesley Center Online, accessed September 24, 2024, https://wesley.nnu.edu/john-wesley/the-sermons-of-john-wesley-1872-edition/sermon-43-the-scripture-way-of-salvation/.

21. John Wesley and Charles Wesley, preface to *Hymns and Sacred Poems* (London: William Strahan, 1739), vi.

22. Wesley and Wesley, *Hymns and Sacred Poems*, viii. Emphasis in original.

23. For an excellent overview of this doctrine, see Kevin M. Watson, *Perfect Love: Recovering Entire Sanctification—the Lost Power of the Methodist Movement* (Franklin, TN: Seedbed, 2021).

24. Danker, *Faith Once Delivered*, 51. See also John Wesley's *A Plain Account of Christian Perfection*, Wesley Center Online, accessed September 24, 2024, https://wesley.nnu.edu/john-wesley/a-plain-account-of-christian-perfection/.

Rather, as Kenneth Collins has helpfully summarized, "entire sanctification, then, is love replacing sin, holy love conquering every vile passion and temper."[25] The believer has become rightly related to God, and the image of God has been restored. Collins continues, "Christian perfection, then, is another term for holy love. It is holy in that believers so marked by this grace are free from the impurities and the drag of sin. It is loving in that believers now love God as the goal of their being, and they love their neighbors as they should."[26]

If God intends to sanctify the people of faith, then we should not be surprised when the Spirit pours forth in powerful ways, calling the faithful into deeper relationships of holy love. To be clear, these kinds of revivals are not the only way in which God operates. The normal avenue for deepening our relationship with God is through the means of grace. As the psalmist declares, those who delight in the law of the Lord are like trees planted by streams of water, which yield their fruit in its season. In all that they do, they prosper (Ps. 1:2–3). But at times, those streams of water become floods of spiritual nourishment, intensifying and quickening the process. This is what we experienced at the Asbury Outpouring. Repentance and recommitment occurred in response to a powerful experience of God's holy love. Relationships were healed, and the faithful produced new fruit of the Spirit. Together, in community, we encouraged and strengthened one another. Even after the Outpouring, the Spiritual Life staff at the university encouraged students to join band meetings to further engage in discipleship and process what they had experienced. In many ways, this pattern reflects the prayer of Paul in 1 Thessalonians 5:23–24: "May God himself, the God of peace, sanctify you through and through. May your whole spirit, soul, and body be kept blameless at the coming of our Lord Jesus Christ. The one who calls you is faithful, and he will do it."

"The Fruits Test" and Free Will

Nonetheless, experiencing such a powerful manifestation of God's presence does not guarantee sanctification. Wesley takes a synergistic understanding of sanctification in which humans cooperate with God to become holy. To be clear, God is always the initiator in offering grace; as Collins states,

25. Kenneth J. Collins, *The Theology of John Wesley: Holy Love and the Shape of Grace* (Nashville: Abingdon, 2007), 302.
26. Collins, *Theology of John Wesley*, 302–3.

"this working together with God does not grow out of human initiative but emerges out of the *response* to divine prior action."[27] We cannot make ourselves holy on our own—but we do have a choice in responding to what God offers. We can choose to remain in step with the Spirit, or we can choose to go another direction.

This understanding helps to make sense of questions that may arise about the authenticity of the Outpouring. Some critics have questioned whether what occurred at Asbury was "real." Occasionally the suggestion has been made that "the fruits test" will make it clear whether this truly was a movement of God. In other words, if those who attended the Outpouring bear fruit for the Kingdom by transforming the world through evangelism, holy living, and the like, then we can judge the Outpouring to have been an authentic act of God. On one level, this is a valid consideration. Charlatans leading self-interested "revival" services will not be able to produce the lasting transformation of hearts and minds that only the Holy Spirit can empower.

But if Wesley's view of cooperant grace is correct, then the "fruits test" provides insufficient evidence of the authenticity of a movement of God. When the people whom God calls fail to respond, then God can be moving authentically without long-term fruit appearing among his people. Thus, we should not be surprised if some of those who attended the Outpouring falter afterward, returning to previous patterns of sin. The apostle Paul describes the Christian life as one in which the believer must walk (also translated as "live") in step with the Spirit (e.g., Rom. 8:4; Gal. 5:16, 25). As the Spirit moves, so we must also move. The relationship with the Spirit is continual and active. We must daily follow the leading of the Spirit, who is continually calling us closer to Christlikeness. Thus, one act of transformation alone does not guarantee lifelong faithfulness.

Perhaps no better example of this exists than the people of Israel themselves. Even after witnessing God's plagues upon Egypt and miraculous deliverance through the Red Sea, the people returned to a lackluster faith. Instead of trusting God's goodness, they feared dehydration and starvation in the rough circumstances of the desert, and they accused Moses and Aaron—and by implication, the God who led them—of bringing them to the wilderness to die (Exod. 16:3; Num. 20:4). Even when they neared the Promised Land, they were afraid of the people there and accused God of

27. Collins, *Theology of John Wesley*, 289, emphasis in original.

planning to destroy the Israelites (Num. 14:3). They now accused the God who had saved them of trying to kill them! The psalmist describes this tension in Psalm 106 when he proclaims that his ancestors have sinned by not considering God's "wonderful works" and forgetting "the abundance of your steadfast love" (vv. 6–7). As a result of their repeated sinfulness in the desert, all the first generation died before seeing the Promised Land—except Caleb and Joshua, who remained faithful (Num. 14:20–30; Deut. 1:34–40).[28]

If onlookers had applied "the fruits test" to the people of Israel, they would have concluded that God had not really been present in the desert, for those who witnessed the "mighty acts of God" had not remained faithful. Nonetheless, Scripture is unequivocal in its description of the powerful presence of God, who led the Israelites in the desert in a pillar of cloud by day and a column of fire by night (Exod. 13:21–22; Deut. 1:32–33), who fed the people manna and quail (Exod. 16:4–35), who provided water from a rock (Exod. 17:1–7), and who defeated the surrounding nations (Exod. 17:8–16).

Similarly, the early church struggled to maintain lives of holiness, despite the infilling of the Holy Spirit and the testimony of the disciples who witnessed not only Jesus's teaching and miracles but also his resurrection. Jason Vickers describes these tensions:

> The members of the earliest churches often disagreed with one another, failed to differentiate between the true gospel and false gospels, took one another to court, hoarded their resources, struggled with a lack of courage in the face of persecution, considered returning to Judaism, dabbled in pagan rituals, mismanaged funds, and wrestled with all manner of sin and corruption. Nevertheless, they somehow banded together and, with the help of the Holy Spirit, worshipped the Holy Trinity and bore witness to the life, death, and resurrection of Jesus in word and deed throughout the world. Indeed, when we consider the many failings of the earliest churches, it is exceedingly hard to account for the survival and gradual spread of

28. Readers of this story should not ignore the continuing grace of God. As the psalmist notes, despite Israel's repeated rebellion, God heard their cry when they were in distress, remembered his covenant, "and showed compassion according to the abundance of his steadfast love" (Ps. 106:43–45). God stands ready to welcome the penitent sinner home, as the parables of the lost sheep, the lost coin, and the prodigal son attest (Luke 15:1–32).

> Christianity in the first and second centuries apart from the ongoing presence and work of the Holy Spirit.[29]

Gauging the authenticity of the presence of God, therefore, cannot be based solely on individual responses to what God appears to be doing. One could point to Peter and Paul, or one could point to Ananias and Sapphira. Rather, we must also look closely at the phenomena present in these holy spaces and ask whether what we are experiencing is consistent with Scripture's witness to the power and presence of the Triune God. In the early church, a variety of activities commonly occurred when the Spirit was present: "tarrying, praying, welcoming and celebrating the Holy Spirit, repenting, baptizing, learning from the apostles, breaking bread together, combining and sharing resources, worshipping together, and most importantly, bearing witness to Christ crucified, resurrected, and exulted."[30] In the book of Acts, Luke describes a variety of responses to God's work and presence: "amazement, awe, rejoicing, joy, praise, and prayer."[31]

At the Outpouring, repentance, prayer, Scripture reading, and proclamation of the gospel of Jesus Christ rose to the forefront of the activities. Resources were shared as Wilmore residents offered their homes to visitors, churches and individuals donated food for the hungry, and Christ's name was praised through joy-filled corporate worship. Many of those present experienced transformation, responding to the call to live a holy life. A common description of the spiritual presence in the room was that of a sweet, gentle spirit. The apostle Paul described this kind of peace among those who lift everything to God in prayer and supplication with thanksgiving: "And the peace of God, which surpasses all understanding, will guard your hearts and your minds in Christ Jesus" (Phil. 4:6–7). These phenomena point to a genuine experience of the Holy Spirit.

29. Jason E. Vickers, *Minding the Good Ground: A Theology for Church Renewal* (Waco, TX: Baylor University Press, 2011), 34–35.

30. Vickers, *Minding the Good Ground*, 35.

31. Beverly Roberts Gaventa, *Acts*, ANTC (Nashville: Abingdon, 2003), 41–42. In the story of the Ethiopian eunuch, for example, after the Ethiopian is baptized, he goes on his way rejoicing (8:39). Gaventa notes, "That remark bristles with significance, since it later becomes a hallmark of the response of Gentiles to the gospel (13:48; 15:31)" (145). Thus, even though individual responses to the work of the Spirit may vary, when the Spirit is present, rejoicing tends to be present among the community.

Conclusion

After John Wesley's powerful experience at the Aldersgate Street meeting, he served as an evangelist for more than fifty years and led the emerging Methodist movement. During that time, he developed a theology emphasizing the holy love of God, a love that continually initiates relationship by offering grace to sinners and believers alike. As people respond with repentance, demonstrating faith in Jesus Christ and walking with the Holy Spirit, God transforms them, making believers holy. This is the goal of God, that humanity would perfectly love God and neighbor and thus reflect the likeness of Christ.

What we experienced at the Asbury Outpouring in February 2023 was a microcosm of this theology. A powerful movement of the Holy Spirit called us to draw near to God, to "taste and see that the Lord is good" (Ps. 34:8). As we cooperated with the Holy Spirit's divine initiative by our repentance and faith, we were transformed. Our natural response to the goodness of God was worship, praising the name of the Father, Son, and Holy Spirit. We were given a gift—a vision of what life with God can look like. Now, in the normal time of everyday life apart from such a profound divine outpouring, we must continue to cooperate with the Holy Spirit, who is still ever-present and ever-accessible. While the spiritual floodwaters may have receded, we must continue to stay connected to the streams of living water God so readily provides.

PART THREE

PRACTICAL CONSIDERATIONS

CHAPTER TWELVE

UNCERTAINTY, MISSION, AND HOLY IMAGINATION

Order and Orchestration in the Outpouring

Kevin Brown
President, Asbury University

During the Outpouring, someone commented to me that my administrative tenure—which began in 2019—had now experienced two *outbreaks*. In response, I said I liked the second one better. While comparing the Asbury Outpouring to a global pandemic is fraught with challenges, both required university leaders to manage through conditions of uncertainty.

In the time since the Outpouring, I have remarked that there is no particular formula for manufacturing what we saw and experienced in February of 2023. Nor can we distill the experience into a set of leadership maxims. Navigating the social and spiritual significance of the Outpouring is not reducible to managerial principles or organizational best practices. In retrospect, however, there were visible guideposts that allowed leaders to navigate the uncertainties of what was unfolding before us. This chapter is my attempt to describe those guideposts—not as a set of techniques to replicate and scale, but as commitments, temperaments, and a spiritually formed imagination that fostered and sustained both the complexity and power experienced during the Outpouring. Specifically, I want to describe the importance of institutional mission, the power of holy imagination, and the shared sensibility to "strive upward."

The Importance of Mission

I was in my assigned seat in the south side balcony in Hughes Auditorium for the regularly scheduled chapel service. It would be fair to say that I

> was in a normal attitude of worship. I remember listening to the speaker with appropriately reverent attention but not expecting anything out of the ordinary until a student stood up among the senior class below and asked to give a testimony. Others followed with testimony and confession and the altar was quickly filled. . . . Confession and repentance was followed by songs of praise and testimonies of gratitude to God.[1]

This testimony, given by Asbury student David Williamson, is consistent with the mood and manner of what took place on the campus of Asbury University in February 2023. The only difference is that David's testimony is from the 1950 Asbury Revival, nearly three-quarters of a century ago.

Throughout its history, Asbury has made space for spiritual spontaneity. We have never sought to be a school that relegates spiritual matters to chapel or church and intellectual matters to classrooms or labs. Rather, there is an intellectual and spiritual porosity between all campus spaces. The symmetry between the intellect and the soul is captured in our mission: "Academic Excellence and Spiritual Vitality."

After the Outpouring, and speaking to our institution's commitment to the spiritual dimension of full formational education, one of our faculty members remarked, "Asbury is like a riverbed. When water comes, it knows where to flow." Over the decades, these grooves have been formed by faithful women and men who have been sensitive and responsive to God's presence. Unsurprisingly, then, making space for spiritual revival is not an interruption; it is welcomed—even expected.

But while the Outpouring was fundamentally spiritual, that does not mean it was immune from complexity. During those sixteen days, there were moments of great inconvenience and fatigue and periods where our humanity and associated limitations showed up. I have described the Outpouring as a crisis marked by overwhelming goodness. But it was still a crisis.

Consider, for example, the challenges created by the broad range of visitors. While the overwhelming majority of visitors were "fruit of the Spirit" Christians eager to have a spiritual encounter, we also saw pockets of street preachers, prophets, attempts to exorcise demons, and shofar-blowing expressions of faith. Some visitors banged upon the doors of student dorms in the middle of the night seeking shelter (and unnerving students). Other visitors used the Outpouring as an occasion to draw attention to their

1. David Williamson to Mark Troyer, email forwarded to author, March 11, 2023.

personal social media platforms. Although most of our students participated in the Outpouring to some degree, many felt alienated from their own space.

While we were awestruck by the overwhelming display of spiritual hunger from earnest pilgrims flocking to our campus, we were equally mindful of the need for porta-potties, increased security, infrastructure challenges like parking and traffic flow, bursting sewage pipes, food availability, the need to coordinate multiple facilities to absorb incoming visitors, and crippling fatigue.

Importantly, while a spiritual outpouring is a product of our mission, it is not our singular mission. Asbury University is just that: an institution of higher education. Our accrediting body does not hold us accountable for revival-type events. As grateful as members of our board of trustees were for the Outpouring, they operate as stewards of Asbury's rigorous intellectual and formative spiritual training of students. Indeed, the spiritual disruption of the Outpouring complicated student academic schedules (testing, studying, art exhibits, recitals, etc.), on-campus events (athletic competitions, mandatory chapel), and residential life (tens of thousands of visitors on your doorstep). In the middle of the Outpouring, and in a room with multiple administrators and directors, I asked how many had reallocated time and resources from their respective departments to sustain the Outpouring. Multiple leaders raised their hands.

As welcome as the Outpouring was, it complicated the continuity of our university life. The Outpouring could not continue indefinitely unless our mission adjusted to something like that of a church or mission-agency outpost. But to continue in our calling as a school whose purpose is to form and educate students, we had to establish a horizon to shift back to more conventional and traditional practices of our mission as an institution of higher education.

Three factors, all in varying degrees, played a role in bringing our services to a close. First, as mentioned, was the desire to resume the rhythms and practices of a Christian university that takes both of those descriptors—"Christian" and "university"—seriously. The sacrificial above-and-beyond effort I saw from staff and faculty is, to this day, the greatest act of collective hospitality and godliness that I have ever witnessed. But it was not sustainable. The leadership, authenticity, confession, repentance, testimony, and worship of our students was awe-inspiring. But it, too, was not sustainable. The various ministry and education leaders who partnered to give order and structure to the Outpouring demonstrated an embodied, contextualized adaptation of Galatians 3:28: No longer insider or outsider, young or old, administrator or administrated—"all are one in Christ Jesus." But even that structure, in all its beauty, was not sustainable. Mission is what allowed us to say yes to what unfolded from February 8, 2023. And our mission equally compelled us to protect and provide for our students, elevate the experiences of Gen Z, and establish a horizon for returning to our normal schedule.

The second factor in bringing our services to a close originated from a conviction that whatever was happening before us was the genesis of something else, something larger. "Behold," says the King in Revelation 21:5 (ESV), "I make all things new." A group of leaders used the metaphor of fire to help frame this thought. Specifically, a fire is brightest when it is tallest. In this sense, we experienced an unparalleled spiritual bonfire from February 8 to February 23. However, and almost counterintuitively, a fire is hottest when it is smoldering. Even though it would eventually begin to look like the Outpouring was "dying down," we collectively wondered aloud whether we were seeing a holy smoldering with an outward trajectory. This fostered a new instinct to go out, share, and testify. We desired embers to flare with a searing hot flame for years and years to come—a campus marked, a people changed, and a flame advancing.

A third and final factor informing our decision to close was the Collegiate Day of Prayer (CDOP) scheduled for February 23. The idea of using Asbury University for the CDOP venue began in 2021. "As the students go, so goes our nation!" reads the vision of the CDOP.[2] This vision accorded with the spirit of the Outpouring—particularly, the shared emphasis on "making room at the table" for Gen Z teens and young adults. Thus, it seemed fitting to end the multiweek outpouring with a nationally and internationally simulcast CDOP service that focused specifically on college-aged students.

Holy Imagination

One of the most significant dimensions of the Outpouring was the holy imagination present within the community. On February 8 chapel ended, but students lingered. Later, more students came. And while it is impossible to impose a comprehensively explanatory grid upon all dimensions of the Outpouring, it is my belief that the imaginative capacity of various

2. "Vision for the Collegiate Day of Prayer." Collegiate Day of Prayer, accessed September 9, 2024, https://collegiatedayofprayer.org/about/vision-collegiate-day-of-prayer/.

community members played a role in shaping and sustaining those sixteen days of spiritual abundance.

For example, consider the holy imagination of our Gospel Choir that prayed over individual seats in Hughes Auditorium late into the evening of February 7. Or the holy imagination of Asbury's student development staff to provide space for chapel participants to linger after the service. It took a spiritually inclined imagination to encourage me, as president, to send an email to our faculty, staff, and students inviting them to come and pray as they were available on the afternoon of February 8. Later that evening, it was holy imagination that encouraged a group of leaders to suggest Hughes should remain open throughout the night. And over the next few weeks, godly women and men exhibited spiritual maturation and imaginative capacity to provide both order to foster what was unfolding and enough space to step back and let the Spirit move. Put differently, it takes a holy imagination to let go.

Another expression of holy imagination could be found in what I have described as "uncoordinated humility." As more and more Asbury students, Asbury seminary students, and Wilmore community members began to occupy Hughes Auditorium in the early days of the Outpouring, Asbury's Strategic Communications office made the decision not to post any social media, university messages, or any other digital communication that would draw attention to the school or what was happening. Similarly, our advancement office instructed all gift officers to suspend fundraising and gift conversations. To protect the integrity and purity of what was happening during that time, our university communications team had the insight not to livestream Hughes Auditorium (including the request that no smartphone livestreams occur) while simultaneously limiting media exposure inside worship spaces.[3] Indeed, the character of our time ran opposite of common instincts toward aggrandizement and promotion. There were no celebrities. No influencers. No renowned musicians. No marketing campaigns. Before taking the stage, worship teams inhabited a consecration room of prayer, not a greenroom. No titles were offered when a student, minister, or university leader introduced themselves or addressed the crowds.

Whatever was taking place before our eyes, members of our community did not want to be the ones to define it. There was a strong sense of creating

3. See Abby Laub's chapter in this volume. In the last few days of the Outpouring, we did make the decision to livestream after Wilmore announced that it could no longer support incoming visitors due to the stress placed on city infrastructure.

order, but not necessarily orchestration. In other words, great effort went into establishing an environment that fostered the work of God's Spirit, which could never be manufactured or manipulated on our own. Leaders did not construct; they accommodated.

This spirit of humility even influenced the name "Outpouring." I remember a group conversation about avoiding the word *revival*—at least for the moment. Asbury has had several revivals throughout its history. In February 2020, we celebrated the fifty-year anniversary of Asbury College's 1970 revival. Using the description "revival" would immediately invite comparisons, which seemed like an unnecessary distraction. In contrast to words like *revival*, *renewal*, or *awakening*—labels that carry nuanced theological significance—*outpouring* has enough space to harbor a variety of interpretations but is neutral enough to avoid defining something prematurely.

In contrast, various news and social media commentaries seemed preoccupied with assigning the appropriate moniker for what was occurring. Was this a revival? A renewal? An awakening? The desire to assign the proper nomenclature to such a visible spiritual inflection is reminiscent of the story of the blind beggar in John 9. Recall the question raised of this poor man and his blindness: "Who sinned—this man or his parents—that he was born blind?" (9:2). After Jesus miraculously healed him, the Pharisees summoned the beggar, interrogated him, and asked for his own testimony about who Jesus is and whether *he* is a sinner. "Whether he is a sinner or not, I don't know" the man replied. "One thing I do know. I was blind but now I see" (9:25). Similarly, the holy imagination of the community members present at the Outpouring displayed an uncoordinated unwillingness to box and compartmentalize the untamed spiritual bonfire burning before them. What would happen next, what the long-term ramifications would be, or whether to call this a revival—they could not, and would not, answer. They did not know. But like the blind beggar, they could say, "Here is what I do know." We know that fifty thousand hungry-hearted people came to a space to seek Jesus. We saw God respond to that hunger. There was a movement among us. We know it was sweet, gentle, beautiful, good, right, and true. We know people were freed from crippling strongholds in their lives. We know God showed up in a way we could not ever have anticipated or manufactured.

A holy imagination recognizes our country's soul-starved vacuum of meaning, marked by hunger and desperation. It also recognizes Jesus's words in Matthew 5:6: "Blessed are those who hunger and thirst after righteousness—for they shall be filled." A holy imagination meant that no one stopped and said it was time to go. No one clamped programmatic architecture upon the worship space. No one sought to disingenuously benefit from the Outpouring to enhance their platform. No one wanted anyone to be left out. Those attributes are not just a function of kindness. They are made plausible and embodied through a cosmic God-narrative that has burrowed its way into the imaginative landscape of those who shepherded the Outpouring while coloring the spiritual possibilities and expectations of their world.

"Strive Upward"

One of the more moving and salient attributes of the Outpouring was a "vertical" instinct; that is, a shared orientation to "seek the things that are above, where Christ is," as Paul writes (Col. 3:1 ESV). As some have put it, "Jesus was the only celebrity in the room." This impulse to look up (Ps. 121:1) is beautifully captured in St. Dionysius the Areopagite's expression to "strive upward as much as you can towards union with him who is beyond all being and knowledge."[4] Moreover, striving upward is an alternative narrative to the day-to-day realities of our modern life and the challenges characterizing the moment in which we find ourselves.

For example, the spirit of the Outpouring was sweet and gentle. One of our community members called it a "holy hush." A visiting student characterized his time as "a soft and sweet song to the seekers of God."[5] It seemed to be a collective reception of Jesus's invitation for shalom: "Come to me, all you who are weary and are carrying heavy burdens, and I will give you rest" (Matt. 11:28).

The Outpouring was apolitical. In marked contrast to a society that increasingly applies a political grid to nearly all of its dimensions, it would have been difficult to map those weeks in February 2023 onto a politically hued horizontal axis of left, middle, or right. Rather, the Outpouring was a collection of hungry hearts directionally oriented to God. There was but one political statement: "Jesus is Lord."

4. Pseudo-Dionysius (the Areopagite), *Pseudo-Dionysius: The Complete Works*, trans. C. Luibheid (New York: Paulist, 1987), 135.
5. J. T. Reeves, "'All You Want to Do Is Worship': A Student Reflects on 8 Months after Asbury," Gospel Coalition, October 19, 2023, https://www.thegospelcoalition.org/article/8-months-after-asbury/.

The diversity of God's Kingdom was pervasive during the Outpouring. It was age diverse. Economically diverse. Denominationally diverse. And it was ethnically diverse. To the last point, a beautiful picture of Revelation 7:9—every tribe, tongue, and nation in communal worship—was continually apparent.[6]

Perhaps counterintuitively, striving up meant looking to our students. Specifically, the Outpouring naturally prioritized our younger generation of teens and young adults. It is easy to pathologize and dismiss today's Gen Z cohort (born between 1997 and 2012).[7] But during the Outpouring, there was a collective sense to make space for them. It was, as I like to say, "in the water"—an unspoken priority at the forefront of our consciousness.

Finally, and importantly, the shared instinct to strive upward allowed for unity—the kind Jesus prayed for in John 17. Missional unity occurs when we collectively fold into a common aim, value, or purpose independent of ourselves. In one of his most famous sermons, "Catholic Spirit," John Wesley references 2 Kings 10:15: "If your heart is as my heart—take my hand." Missional unity is a function of directional unity—specifically, the direction of a cross-shaped doorway, a self-giving, self-emptying life. The direction of Christ. The spiritual self-sacrifice of a cruciform life is an invitation to a new, abundant reality because Christ says, "Whoever loses their life for me will find it" (Matt. 16:25). Perhaps this is why one student called the Outpouring "a beautiful graveyard." Here we found, and will continue to find, unity.

Conclusion: A Watchful Spirit

There is much to say regarding what I witnessed at the Outpouring. In fact, when it comes to telling stories about what we experienced in February of 2023, I often describe it as a door that, once opened, is difficult to shut. Luckily, much has already been written. Asbury has created a repository of stories, pictures, documentaries, and articles describing what happened.[8]

But what about the aftermath of the Outpouring? Specifically, what does it ultimately mean? What is the significance? I have been asked this

6. For more on the diversity apparent during the Outpouring, see the chapter by Juan Gonzalez in this volume.
7. As a generational cohort, Gen Z is less religious, more skeptical of institutions, marked by anxiety and depression, and has been raised on phones and social media.
8. "The Asbury Outpouring," Asbury University, accessed September 6, 2024, https://www.asbury.edu/outpouring/.

question numerous times since February 2023, and answers broadly fall into one of two categories.

Andy Crouch makes a helpful distinction between impact and influence.[9] Impact, he says, can be characterized as a burst of force over a short period of time. And there are plenty of data points to speak to the Outpouring's impact. For salient examples, one could reference social media views, visitor counts, conference panels, sermons preached, podcasts produced, witness teams launched, and articles printed. These highlights, and many others, chronicle the notable and measurable impact of the Outpouring. But impact, a common barometer of our modern attention economy, is the wrong metric. Among other reasons, chronicling the impact of the Outpouring is misleading because it implies that what happened in February 2023—and what happens in its wake—is something within our realm of control. But this is not something we control. We don't create this; we respond to it. This is not something we manufacture; it is something we participate in.

In contrast to impact, the final chapter of the Outpouring will be recorded in terms of its influence. Influence, says Crouch, is a low-wattage force over a long period of time. To describe influence, he uses the example of gardening ("you can't *impact* gardening"). The influence of the Outpouring involves a different set of questions. What is the long-term transformation? What counterliturgies are borne out in the days ahead? What scales will fall from our eyes? What positive freedoms can we testify to? How might our imaginative landscape be broadened to new and holy horizons? How might we embody different habits and practices? Where might we bend the universe in a Godward direction? Is the cause of the neighbor, orphan, widow, and alien advanced by virtue of our existence? By virtue of what we do? This is not mere "impact." Now we are talking about *awakening*. We are talking about a new humanity. Now we are talking about a Spirit-filled, Spirit-empowered people.

I suspect that every February I will celebrate the Outpouring. I want to deliberately honor those unforgettable days. I want to faithfully narrate what happened. I want to testify to what I witnessed and experienced. But the worst thing that could happen is, at some point in the future, we look back and merely remark that something interesting happened in February of 2023—only for us to regress into the status quo. Praising a past

9. Curtis Chang, host, "The Impact Fetish (with Andy Crouch)," *Good Faith Podcast with Curtis Chang and Friends*, Redeeming Babel, April 1, 2023, https://redeemingbabel.org/podcasts/the-impact-fetish-with-andy-crouch/.

that has no meaningful bearing on our present or our future strikes me as tragic. So while I will forever be grateful for the Outpouring, my prayer is that in two, five, and ten years, we will look back on that time and say, "That was nothing compared to what we see occurring now." My hope is for a growing spiritual fervor and future "outpourings" that eclipse what we experienced in those days. My prayer is that in the time ahead, we will locate the Outpouring in a broader unfolding of spiritual awakening across our country and our globe.

I end with this. In addition to the commitment to mission, holy imagination, and the shared sensibility to "strive upward" that marked the Outpouring and allowed leaders to navigate its complexity, we do not celebrate an event relegated to the past. My heart is not simply filled with sentimentality. My words are not merely nostalgic. I am overwhelmed with gratitude. And I am positive, hopeful, and watchful for the days ahead.

CHAPTER THIRTEEN

"THEN LET US HIS PRAISE SING ON"

Lessons in Humility and Musical Worship from the Asbury Outpouring

Dan Pinkston

Worship pastor at New Community Church, Spokane, WA

> Christian musicians know of the obligation to make music as agents of God's grace. They make music graciously, whatever its kind or style, as ambassadors of Christ, showing love, humility, servanthood, meekness, victory, and good example . . . as an act of worship, in direct response to the overflowing grace of God in Christ Jesus.
>
> —Harold Best, *Music through the Eyes of Faith*

It seems like every recounting of the Asbury Outpouring starts with the statement "It was just a normal Wednesday." No one felt anything out of the ordinary was about to happen as students filed into their Wednesday morning chapel. As a professor of worship arts at Asbury during spring semester 2023, I attended chapel regularly, since the musical leadership was most often provided by my students. But on February 8, I stayed home. None of the bands I supervised were leading that day, and I didn't teach until the afternoon.

Around 3:00 p.m., I received a text from a student with a grainy video of people singing in Hughes Auditorium with the caption "Chapel is still going." I thought this was great, and when I got to campus, I joined the worshipers in Hughes for two to three songs. On stage was a mixture of students from the worship arts program and some leaders that I recognized from the broader community. The spirit was sweet and simple, with still no indication that this was going to grow.

As we all know, what was happening in Hughes Auditorium grew rapidly and exponentially due to word of mouth and especially sharing on social media. By Friday, it was obvious something big was happening, something good, something fresh.

And while the spirit in Hughes Auditorium was sweet and peaceful, what was happening inside me was not good. By Saturday afternoon, I found myself feeling some unpleasant emotions—I was becoming jealous. I was wondering why I wasn't up there leading, why as the professor of worship arts and a longtime professional musician and worship leader I had not been called on to lead whatever this was that was happening at Asbury. To make matters in my heart more complex, I also had a conversation with a student who said something that hurt my feelings, which has rarely happened during my twenty-five-year career in Christian higher education. So that night I told my wife how I was struggling, and I spent some time praying. I confessed that my jealousy was keeping me from joining fullheartedly with the worship in Hughes Auditorium.

On Sunday morning, I asked the Lord to change my heart. I recognized that not only was this not about me, but it also wasn't about any of the worship leaders. It didn't matter who was on the platform of Hughes; what mattered was what God was doing. I confessed my jealousy, asked the Lord to forgive me, and pledged to support those leading in the days to come. Theologian Tom McCall described historical "outpourings" as being marked by repentance, and what was becoming the Asbury Outpouring certainly prompted my own personal repentance.[1]

What happened next is truly remarkable. Five minutes after I had admitted to God the frailty and pettiness of my emotional struggles and surrendered to God, I received a text: "Can you come lead the worship in Hughes this afternoon?" And then I found myself on the platform, seated at the piano, leading worship with several thousand people singing along with passion and full commitment. This went on for three hours, broken up only by Scripture readings and a few testimonies.

Over the next sixteen days, I was privileged to lead the music for about ten hours of the Asbury Outpouring. At times this was when Hughes Auditorium was jam-packed with enthusiastic worshipers, where the gentle

1. Thomas McCall and Jason Vickers, *Outpouring: A Theological Witness* (Eugene, OR: Cascade, 2023), 7.

roar of their singing could literally take your breath away. Other times I led at 6:00 a.m. with only two or three people in the room—total strangers singing, praying, and worshiping in stillness.[2] Both contexts were beautiful and special. There was nothing better about leading thousands of people in praise than leading a handful. The difference was the sense of power that I felt when leading the large crowd.

Stewarding the Power of Praise

When one performs any kind of music—classical, pop, jazz, and so forth—it is never a sure thing that all who are listening are supporting you or with you. They could be judging your musical abilities or not enjoying the style, song choice, or volume of the music. People have strong opinions about music and which music is best for worship, opinions often influenced by one's formative experiences in church and the types of music one connects with emotionally. But during the Asbury Outpouring, those of us who were musical worship leaders experienced a remarkable buy-in of those worshiping. Any song we started would be joined by the crowd, and they would joyfully follow the dynamics and direction modeled by the leader. This further heightened the sense of power I experienced: My choices had a direct and real impact on how people were experiencing these remarkable moments. This is not to say that we worship leaders were fabricating anything artificial or that God was not moving people to a more surrendered worship, but it does acknowledge the influence of those in positions of leadership.

This reminds us that all worship leaders in these types of contexts have power, or at least are given a heavy responsibility to lead people in their worship of our Lord. This power can be abused; people can be manipulated emotionally and spiritually through music. The challenge and caution here for worship leaders is to understand this potential for abuse and in humility steer away from practices that manipulate congregants.

One of the most beautiful things I observed during the length of the Outpouring was how the leaders, musical and otherwise, consciously stewarded this power in ways that were not manipulative or driven by individual agendas. We were consistently reminding ourselves of the need for humble

2. After the initial days of the Outpouring, leadership decided to close Hughes Auditorium for portions of the early morning so that cleaning could take place. During these breaks, worship nonetheless continued with a few people in the room.

leadership and the offering of our musical talents and abilities to the service of the people.

I also believe that our choices in terms of instrumentation and technology were intentional acts of modeling our theology of worship and our pursuit of humility. The song of the people is the musical priority in worship at Asbury University, and the stripped-down, barely amplified, and acoustic textures of the Asbury Outpouring removed many of the potential distractions that drums, keyboards, electric guitars, screens, and twenty-first-century technology can bring, especially in churches that feel a pressure to have the latest technology and most up-to-date musical sounds. Of course, this started organically at the Outpouring and was not planned, but as the days of continuous worship continued and the situation grew remarkably large, we continued to offer the simplest of musical accompaniments. Further, we placed the musical leaders at the side of the Hughes Auditorium platform, removing them from the center visually and thus symbolically embodying our core convictions about the nature of worship. Without seeing people in the center of the stage, and without having screens to look at, the worshipers were drawn into worship in one of the most communal ways I have ever experienced.

My personal need to humble myself prior to the Lord using me at the Outpouring was echoed in the experiences of the other people serving in musical leadership. Many of us have articulated that it is easy to lead worship from a place of routine in which we trust in our own musical abilities and experience. The Outpouring was a radical wake-up call for worship leaders to embody the principle that the worship of God is a holy act. To that end, a consecration room was set up for worship leaders to center themselves, receive prayer, and read Scripture before they led worship in Hughes Auditorium. This consecration room was not a mystical, overly sacred-looking space. It was a conference room usually used for academic meetings; but in this space worship leaders reminded themselves to pursue a posture of humility, service, and gratitude as they prepared to lead during the Asbury Outpouring.

Musical Observations

Most participants in the Asbury Outpouring have remarked on how congregational singing was the central activity throughout the sixteen days of continuous worship. The majority of the Outpouring was spent singing, and this reminds us of how important music is in the worship of the Christian church. This rings true to Asbury University's Wesleyan heritage, to its understanding of church history, and to the ethos that our chapel program seeks to shepherd. As a music theorist, I have pondered why contemporary worship music was so central to the Outpouring. What follows is a discussion of some of the key characteristics of this music that facilitated the character of the worship at Asbury University in February 2023.

The Priority of Congregational Singing

Asbury University is an institution in the Wesleyan tradition, a movement that itself was "born in song,"[3] especially congregational song. Methodism produced an outpouring of song that, according to hymnologist Carlton Young, "exceeds any previous or subsequent Christian movement."[4] Perhaps this is because Wesleyanism is "a distinctive heart movement with a unique theology—a heart repentant, assured, and forgiven; a heart overflowing in joyous response."[5] The Wesleys' embrace of hymns in vibrant congregational song was a radical, countercultural development that produced radical "spirit-filled" Christians.[6] According to musicologist Nicholas Timperley, not until the Wesleys "brought a wave of folk tunes into the churches would genuinely congregational singing be heard" in the English-speaking world.[7]

In this spirit, Asbury University has long cultivated rich congregational singing, and the student body is known for their fervent singing in chapel and other worship gatherings on campus. This is part of the heritage that flowed into the 2023 Outpouring and certainly was characteristic of other revivals at Asbury. In this light, the Outpouring grew out of a culture and tradition that had long prioritized congregational singing in worship of the Lord.

The Significance of Contemporary Worship Music in the Asbury Outpouring

When I was in seminary, our training focused exclusively on "traditional" church music—that is, hymnology, organs, choirs, conducting, and the like.

3. Preface to the *1930 Methodist Hymnal* (New York: Methodist Book Concern, 1935).
4. Carlton Young, *Music of the Heart* (Carol Stream, IL: Hope, 1995), 31.
5. Young, *Music of the Heart*, 12.
6. Young, *Music of the Heart*, 27.
7. Nicholas Temperley, *The Music of the English Parish Church* (Cambridge: Cambridge University Press, 1979), 99.

An insightful professor, however, noted that my generation was the first that could both lead traditional church music and function in the newly emerging genre then called "praise and worship." Playing by ear, reading chord charts instead of musical notation, and excelling in the primary instrumental colors of the rock band (i.e., drums, guitar, and bass guitar) were new practices. Contemporary worship music has grown in significant ways since then, and while it has mixed results in encouraging congregational participation, one could argue that the rise of contemporary worship music recaptures the congregational ideals of the Wesley brothers. The intent of contemporary worship practices is congregational participation and vitality, and this can be achieved in the hands of skillful worship leaders who understand how to empower the congregation to sing. This is not to say that traditional American and European hymnody was not focused on congregational singing, but rather it is clear—and was evident during the Asbury Outpouring—that contemporary worship music is the dominant musical repertoire of the global church in the twenty-first century. It has become the lingua franca of the Evangelical church. While many older hymns still resonate in a contemporary context, others have moved into the museum. They are worth keeping, studying, and learning from, but they no longer speak to a large number of Christians in modern times.

Theological Features of Outpouring Songs

The repertoire of music sung at the 2023 Asbury Outpouring included songs from a variety of sources, including African American gospel ("Every Praise"), classic or "vintage" choruses (the 1970s "I Love You Lord"), a few well-known hymns ("Amazing Grace," "Come Thou Fount of Every Blessing") and occasional songs from the global church (such as the Ghanaian "Baba"). But the overwhelming majority of music selections sung during the Outpouring were contemporary worship songs in the traditions of Chris Tomlin, Matt Redman, Hillsong, Bethel, Elevation Music, and so on. While the genre has at times been rightly criticized for shallow theological content and a reliance on subjective and emotional content, many songs featured during the Asbury Outpouring revealed that the genre has grown in both poetic quality, theological depth, and musicality. "King of Kings," for example, tells the gospel story and responds to the salvific work of Christ in Trinitarian praise. "Christ Be Magnified" dwells on the lordship of Christ and includes the telling line "I won't be formed by feelings. I hold fast to what is true," acknowledging that our worship goes beyond the emotional. In my analysis, the increased theological and poetic depth of recent worship music was a factor in supporting sustained continuous worship for the sixteen days of the Asbury Outpouring. The emotional fervor of the Outpouring was nourished by songs with significant theology and poetry.

Musical Features of Outpouring Songs

Several musical features and aspects of contemporary worship music made the genre ideal for leading worship in a context such as the Asbury Outpouring. It was almost as if the stylistic features of the repertoire were primed to allow the Outpouring to happen from a technical perspective. These features, detailed below, allowed complete strangers, from various denominational, linguistic, ethnic, generational, and national origins to worship together—with no screens, handouts, or hymnals. It even allowed strangers who had never met or played music with each other to lead the musical worship together.

First, the formal structures of contemporary worship music, modeled on the popular song genre, are predictable and formulaic in a positive way. The Association of Popular Music Education recognizes contemporary worship music as a subgenre of popular music—these worship songs are essentially short pop/rock songs with Christian content. In this context, the verse-chorus structure of pop songs allows musicians and worshipers to quickly learn new songs and participate easily in congregational worship. There is a parallel here to blues or jazz, where predictable, stereotyped song forms allow strangers to "jam" together, to join bands spontaneously. And like with blues and jazz, this predictability does not detract from the artfulness of the genre; rather, on top of predictable structures, skillful and tasteful musicians can perform extremely expressive and powerful music. Significantly, the melodies of contemporary worship music are easier for amateurs to sing than those from blues and jazz traditions, facilitating congregational participation.

The various sections of these songs—including bridges, intros, outros, and the ubiquitous verses and choruses—can be combined in various orders in an ad-lib fashion. This was demonstrated many times during the Asbury Outpouring as worship leaders brought back a bridge, chorus, or other section in an unexpected place. These improvised returns of various sections added commentary or theological emphasis to the worship in Hughes Auditorium. In fairness, the structures of traditional hymnody are also predictable and easy to participate in, but hymns typically don't have as many contrasting sections as a contemporary worship song, making them harder to stretch out to fill extended time periods. It is much harder to extend a three-stanza hymn, such as "Great Is Thy Faithfulness," into a ten-minute experience of intimate worship than it is to extend a song like Cody Carnes's "Firm Foundation (He Won't)." And since the worship at the Outpouring went on continuously for hours, days, and weeks, the ability to lengthen contemporary worship songs in the moment was crucial in facilitating these extended times of congregational worship.

Another interesting feature of formal structures improvised during the Outpouring was the combining of sections from different songs. For example, the chorus of "10,000 Reasons" was repeated in the middle of "Open the Eyes of My Heart Lord"—songs were reimagined as commentary on each other, moving the worshiper into different liturgical moments. In some cases, the refrain or first stanza of a nineteenth-century hymn would be sung as an added section to a twenty-first-century worship song—for example, the refrain of "It Is Well" appended to "Goodness of God."

Contemporary Harmonic Language

The harmonic language of the contemporary worship music sung during the Asbury Outpouring is another significant technical aspect of the genre that facilitated the extended times of worship. Essentially, contemporary worship songs make more prevalent use of minor chords and contain more colorful chords than traditional hymnody.[8] This in turn heightens emotion, connection, expressions of devotion, and a sense of adoration. As an example, Fanny Crosby's classic hymn "Praise the Lord" (1875) uses no minor chords, and the music is very upbeat, presumably to express joyful praise. But "Great Are You Lord" (2016), a song repeated many times at the Outpouring, cycles again and again through the minor vi chord and the dominant sus4 chord at a slow tempo and in a hypnotic compound meter.[9] These harmonies are crucial to the identity of the song and add a level of emotional connection and harmonic interest that many hymns don't have in their original forms.

8. "Colorful chords" are those that have notes added to them beyond the basic three notes of traditional minor or major chords.
9. The verse and chorus of this song repeat the following cycle of chords: G Bm Asus; the tonic chord, D, is not heard until the bridge.

The harmonies in "Great Are You Lord" delay resolution until the bridge of the song, a minimalistic feature that also heightens the emotional effect of singing this song in worship. When the resolution does come, it is paired with the psalm-inspired line "All the earth will shout Your praise." The delayed arrival of the tonic chord is paired with this praise in response to the character of God outlined earlier in the song.

A key feature of the chords used in most recent popular music, including worship music, is the use of an "added note" and unprepared "suspended" chords. Usually this involves adding the musical interval of a second or a fourth above the chord root in traditional major or minor triads. These chords are then more colorful and have a sense of time being suspended, particularly due to the pedal points that are now possible. As an example, if the I, IV, and V chords in the key of C (C, F, and G) are used without these colorations, it is impossible to connect all three with common tones. But in contemporary music, if a Cadd2, Fadd2, and Gsus are substituted, then the chords all are connected by common tones "C" and "G." The experience of the Asbury Outpouring for many worshipers was that of the "interruption of spatio-temporal bearings,"[10] a sense of the loss of time. While this was unique to the Outpouring and is not something that can be re-created in a typical worship service, the phenomenon was nonetheless aided by the pedal-point techniques common in contemporary harmonic practice. These pedal-point, or drone-like, aspects are not unique to contemporary worship music, as they are found in traditions as rich and varied as Scottish bagpiping, North Indian classical music, and Indonesian Gamelan, but they certainly are not a feature of traditional English and American hymnody. Perhaps by adopting this static approach to harmonic connection, the music used during the Asbury Outpouring points to a global perspective on music in worship and not simply a North American one.

Contemporary worship songs also feature much slower harmonic rhythms than traditional hymns. In other words, chords change much less often in popular music than in most hymnody.[11] Historically, if one looks at the hymn arrangements of someone as venerable as J. S. Bach, one finds a relatively fast harmonic rhythm, often one chord per beat or even per syllable. Nineteenth-century American gospel hymns/songs often slow down

10. McCall and Vickers, *Outpouring*, 24.

11. The word *hymn* is used here to refer to historic Christian song, but in truth, contemporary worship songs are in fact hymns, just hymns in a soft-rock style.

the harmonic rhythm, but not at the rate that contemporary worship music does.[12] For example, "Glorious Day," a song that celebrates the power of Christ's resurrection, has many stretches where one chord is sustained for four full measures, much longer than one would find in traditional hymns. In "Glorious Day," the tension that this slow harmonic rhythm imparts only heightens the effectiveness of movement and resolution that accompany the lyrical celebration of Christ's resurrection. These slower harmonic rhythms give less of a sense of rushing toward a musical (and theological) goal and instead more of a sense of hovering on an idea, a theological thought, or an expression of love for God. This imparts a sense of timelessness to the best contemporary worship music. This stylistic feature allows the music to seem to stand still in certain moments, to be a metaphor for transcendent and eternal experiences.

Mass Media and Contemporary Worship Music

Another aspect of contemporary worship music that had a direct impact on the Asbury Outpouring is the fact that new worship songs are disseminated and learned via mass media, especially Christian radio, YouTube, and various streaming services. One no longer needs to read music or own a hymnal to learn the latest songs for the contemporary church. Technology has allowed Christians from a wide range of denominational and theological perspectives to learn and sing the same songs in worship. As the Outpouring demonstrated, this extends internationally and across many languages. It was remarkable that people came to Asbury from all around the globe, many without much facility in the English language. Nevertheless, the vast majority of visitors knew many of the songs being sung, demonstrating that contemporary worship music is not confined to North America or to congregations that worship in English. In some cases, the chorus was sung simultaneously in multiple languages during the Outpouring, which some have described as symbolic of the Kingdom of God spreading across the world into every nation and tongue.

12. The term *gospel hymn* in this context does not refer to African American gospel but rather to the large body of American hymns from the nineteenth century that include a memorable refrain. Examples include "How Great Thou Art," "Blessed Assurance," and "And Can It Be."

Countercultural Worship

As mentioned earlier, the music at the Outpouring focused exclusively on grand piano, acoustic guitars, and light percussion such as a cajon. This was spontaneous at first; no one made a conscious decision not to use drums, electric guitars, or keyboards, but this became an intentional element of the worship as the hours turned into days and weeks. The simplicity of this instrumental accompaniment expressed a theology of worship that prioritizes the praise of the people rather than the performances of professional instrumentalists and singers. The instrumentation of the Outpouring modeled a supporting—rather than leading—role for musicians. Considering the last thirty years of megachurch, seeker-influenced worship trends—where technology, professionalism, and performance have been seen as the key to church growth—the Asbury Outpouring was a countercultural event. Perhaps it was even a call to the church to simplify, get back to what matters, and develop congregational worship over high-tech spectacle.

That being said, the flexible and amateur-driven aspect of the instrumentation of contemporary worship music in general is another feature that makes it an ideal genre for the contemporary church. The same repertoire of songs can be played well with just one guitar or one piano, but they can also be performed with a full band. I recently witnessed a worship band from a Hispanic congregation in Los Angeles lead worship with acoustic, electric, and bass guitars, two keyboards, drums, auxiliary percussion, trumpet/flugelhorn, and seven singers. Many of their songs were the same ones that were featured at the Outpouring with just piano and one or two singers. The genre’s flexible instrumentation allows churches with limited resources or a small pool of volunteer musicians to worship with the same songs that bigger churches use. And this allows worship leaders to be creative and feature a wide range of musical timbres (colors) and textures.

The “play by ear” aspect of contemporary music also allows for great variety in instrumental color. During my years as worship leader at a Nazarene church in California, we were able to use a number of instruments outside the typical bass/guitar/drums/keys paradigm. These included accordion, melodica, banjo, mandolin, cello, violin, flute, and glockenspiel. In each case, the players improvised by ear, meaning there was no need for the worship leader to compose or purchase orchestrations.

Conclusion

Musicians who know the grace of Christ and who are trained to think critically about God's world have a high responsibility. We must be both pragmatic and aesthetic, contemplative and useful. In the Asbury Outpouring, as in all worship leading, we needed to cultivate humility, both personally and corporately. My own struggle with my ego at the outset of the Outpouring is typical of the struggles that church musicians often must prayerfully address. The humble leadership that was modeled during the Asbury Outpouring is one of its lasting legacies and reminds us that character and authenticity are more important than talent, the latest techniques, or celebrity.

While the musical features of contemporary worship music lend themselves to extended times of worship with a sense of timelessness and meditation, we must recognize that these songs did not create the Outpouring or call down God's Spirit. The Lord is present, and our actions during the Outpouring were an acknowledgment of God's constant presence and work in our lives. We were celebrating extravagantly what we believe is true every day of our lives. In turn, God overwhelmed us with his love and the peace that only his Spirit brings.

Harold Best, longtime dean of music at Wheaton College, quotes Charles Wesley's "O for a Thousand Tongues to Sing" in the following call for creativity among Christian musicians:

> Christian music makers have to risk new ways of praising God. Their faith must convince them that however strange a new offering may be, it cannot out-reach, out-imagine, or overwhelm God. God remains God, ready to swoop down in the most wonderful way, amidst all of the flurry and mystery of newness and repetition, to touch souls and hearts, all because faith has been exercised and Christ's ways have been imitated. Meanwhile, a thousand tongues will never be enough.[13]

To echo both Wesley and Best, the fifty thousand or so voices that joined in singing during the Outpouring were overwhelming, powerful, beautiful, and peaceful, but they were not enough. Certainly, Asbury University and the throng of Outpouring worshipers would testify that God is bigger than songs, our gatherings, and our worship, no matter how extravagant. To

13. Harold Best, *Music through the Eyes of Faith* (San Francisco, CA: HarperOne, 1993), 8.

sum up the lessons learned during the Outpouring and what it reminded us about the nature of worship, I am drawn to the following words from a hymn by Fred Pratt Green:

> When in our music God is glorified, and adoration leaves no room
> for pride,
> It is as though the whole creation cried: Alleluia![14]

14. Fred Pratt Green, "When in Our Music God Is Glorified," Hope Publishing, 1972.

CHAPTER FOURTEEN

SURPRISE

Stewarding Unprecedented Media Coverage during the Outpouring

Abby Laub

Director of Strategic Communications, Asbury University

On a gray, blustery Friday night in late February 2023, I sat in a chair in my bedroom on top of an unfolded pile of clean two-week-old laundry and stared at my computer screen. After countless round-the-clock, on-camera media interviews, hundreds of phone calls, and thousands of texts, it was the first time I'd been on my laptop trying to write something coherent in more than two weeks. The topic of my tired typing? Measles. After hanging up from a video call with the Jessamine County Health Department and reading statements from the state's infectious disease experts, I was tasked with writing a press release and website statement—required by the health department—about a potential spread of the contagious virus that evidently was present in a guest during the Outpouring on Asbury University's campus.

As the university's Strategic Communications director, I spent two weeks coordinating media and sharing words with the world that felt like they were not my own; they came from the Holy Spirit. A measles announcement was an unforeseen turn—a comical and humbling ending to something that took all of us by complete surprise. We'd all witnessed an undeniable outpouring of the Holy Spirit, a revival, an awakening, a move of God so extraordinary that I'm confident history will deem it a *revival.* How we communicated that to the world in a very practical and faithful way was an adventure.

Media tried in vain to contact me for a measles quote. Calls and texts from reporters who were just trying to get a saucy headline for the evening news were met with a statement to contact the health department. Long before measles, and from day one of the media coverage of the Outpouring, it was abundantly evident that God had his hand all over Asbury and the news coverage. But our media team had some very practical issues to consider, decisions to make quickly, and an abundant amount of praying to do to know how to handle the scenario we were managing. We all knew that faith and the traditional news media often are a complicated mix.

Initially, we were very uneasy about media attention. We certainly did not seek it out, but we knew it was a possibility. One of the other members of a small group that convened in the basement of Hughes early on, Dr. David Thomas—from Seedbed and a friend of the university—looked Vice President of Enrollment and Marketing Jennifer McChord square in the eyes and said, "Don't be surprised if media shows up."

Almost hourly for two weeks, it seemed, we—Jennifer, Vice President of Athletics and University Communications Mark Whitworth, a micro army of Strategic Communications staff and student workers, and I—had to make judgment calls and rely on the Holy Spirit for wisdom. Coincidentally, our crisis communication plan was already in place prior to this, and we followed the protocols that had been set in that plan.

Who Will Speak to the Press?

This began with knowing who speaks to the media. The university's communications director is the official spokesperson, and the crisis communication plan also designates several others who can take on that role as needed. Thankfully no live interviews were needed about measles, but in the two weeks prior, we fielded hundreds of requests for interviews on live television, on the phone, via text, in newspapers, on the radio, on podcasts, on Zoom, and in about every other media imaginable. This included reporters from around the world quite literally showing up on our doorstep, and our first task was determining who needed to go on the news on behalf of Asbury.

In the beginning, when a few local reporters showed up—with whom we already had great relationships—it was no problem, and our students were willing to share what God was doing. After a few days, our president, Dr. Kevin Brown, was happy to give selective interviews, and we worked to ensure everything was a great fit. The requests picked up and quickly elevated to national media (including high-profile Christian influencers and media personalities) and then to major global news outlets. The demands grew exponentially, and although we stuck to our plan, we needed to expand who we allowed to speak on behalf of Asbury to share faithfully and accurately what God was doing. Lists of willing students, faculty, and staff whom we could call were created quickly. For those two weeks, all interview requests—arriving by phone, text, email, social media, and in person—were fielded by the team, filtered by Mark, Jennifer, and me, and then granted or denied. Reporters needed to have permission. Our "crisis" plan worked well.

God proved merciful with the reporters he sent early on because they helped set the tone positively for the coverage that followed. One was an Asbury student working part-time at Lexington's CBS affiliate, WKYT. She was surprised that chapel had gone on that long and sensed something much bigger was happening. She had felt it herself. College kids don't linger in chapel, and God also was working in her heart. "Something is going on," she told her assignment editor, who reluctantly agreed to send her out to cover the nonstory about students singing around the clock at a small college in the next county.

Jennifer's daughter, a freshman at the time, also sensed something happening in Hughes. She sent a text to Jennifer at 1:05 p.m. on February 8 that read, "Worship and prayer are still going on from chapel! Revival is coming!"

All of this was a great interruption to a busy time in higher education, with intense schedules and ambitious goals. Plus, we all had our own sets of personal challenges and areas of needed growth. God had plans for us in addition to the tens of thousands of others who visited campus in February and the millions impacted around the world.

"When he has something that he wants you to hear or experience, he will get your attention," recalled Jennifer. "Riley's 'Revival is coming!' text rang in my ears as I made the drive back to Wilmore from lunch with my son, Davis, a freshman at the time at the University of Kentucky. But I was skeptical of Riley's text. The picture she included in the text had about twenty people scattered throughout Hughes seemingly praying together. I knew that wasn't normal for sure, but revival?"

In the next day or two, God took time to work on many of us—which was critical, as so many students and communications staff would very soon need to talk to the press and visitors about what was going on at Asbury. Throughout our daily responsibilities and work, the real work God was doing right before our eyes was undeniable. I knew I needed to spend some time in Hughes, pronto, to be able to accurately share my limited human understanding of what God was doing.

As the days and the interviews increased—and this was obviously all about students—we had to assume a posture of sharing how God was moving while also protecting our students. We wanted God to use their voices for his glory, but what student wanted to speak with a news reporter about a spiritual event in their life, oftentimes a deeply personal encounter with Jesus? Ultimately, we had faith he had it in his control.

How to Tell This Story: What Is the Story?

What is happening? That was the key question early on. A lot of Christian media and influencers showed up, so they had a base understanding. But how exactly could we share with secular media members—some of whom had never stepped foot in a church or understood what worship meant—what was happening in Hughes and among our students?

Early on day two, before I even knew I'd have to speak about it to dozens and dozens of media outlets for days in a row, I honestly wondered if I could relay what was happening to friends and coworkers without sounding skeptical and jaded. In all transparency, I was quick to raise my hand in doubt mixed with curiosity when I heard "Chapel never ended." Really? Asbury loves revivals. God is moving? I'll believe it when I see it.

I sneaked into the back of Hughes on Thursday, February 9, at 7:00 a.m. while the magnificent morning sun streamed in the windows, and I believed it. God showed it to me. Students clearly had stayed all night. The group was still small, but they worshiped openly, had the Bibles open from the back of the chairs in Hughes, prayed with one another, and stood up without prompting or fanfare to confess sins. They verbalized very difficult, pernicious things without fear—pornography addiction, abuse, relationship turmoil, anxiety, depression. They were laying it before Jesus and receiving healing and transformation. Eyes were opened, hearts were changed, a generation of students was crying out for something vastly different than what the world was giving them, and they were turning to God—and *that* was the story.

There was no need to embellish this. We had to identify students willing to speak about their experience and share how their life was changed. We all saw students change before our eyes. I remember at first we asked, "Should we even have reporters here? Should we just turn them away? Is this exploitative? Is this taking away from what God is doing?"

It was a sunny, unseasonably warm day, and I was standing on the semicircle near Hughes, thinking, and the Holy Spirit clearly spoke to my heart. "*You can just talk about me on the news.*" But what's the story? "*I am the story.*"

Then I went into Hughes while a friendly local TV reporter waited for me to find someone to talk with, and there in the aisle was student newspaper editor and reporter Lexie Presta, who was on assignment with her camera. "*Her.*"

She gave an amazing interview about *the* story. It was about the changes happening in the lives of her friends and on campus. The deep hunger among students all around the world for Jesus, for something different. The nonstop worship. It was a story that needed to come from her and not a school spokesperson or even the university president.

In the coming days and weeks, it was almost always obvious to us who should do interviews, and we needed to help coordinate those stories. For anyone from local newspapers to bloggers to Fox News to *The New York Times*, God made it clear, and he was honored in every interview. The story was never in question.

How Do We Protect Our People?

But with that came the knowledge that considerations needed to be made. Never did any of us think we were the ones making the "outpouring of news media" happen. It was truly remarkable! I still can hardly believe it. We never initiated calls to reporters; we simply provided a welcoming place for them to tell the story—to receive the story. In fact, in our extreme fatigue as the long days got longer, I remember thinking, "I am so, so tired! Are they still coming!?" Yes, they were.

At Asbury, we value excellence, order, and thoughtfulness. These are holy traits and were very much needed as the crowds swelled to see what was happening and to experience the presence of God. Text messages from security and other Asbury staff rolled in. "Hey, so-and-so just pulled up. What do you want me to tell them?" "Send them to the press check-in."

We received hundreds of emails, phone calls, social media messages. It was beyond what we could imagine and quickly neared "out of control" territory. I feared that the media would start sensationalizing or editorializing—or worse. So we had to pray and make some practical decisions to protect our students, our guests, and Asbury, and to honor what God was doing.

With this sense of the need to protect came tough decisions: What should we do with our livestream? What do we say on our social media platforms? Do we post on social media about what's happening? Do we keep the livestream running so people can "participate" where they are?

Even that first evening, February 8, Jennifer recalls some serious questions quickly arising without a playbook to reference: "The pressure turned on from very well-meaning alumni and staff members asking me why we hadn't posted what was happening on social media. Why wasn't the livestream on in Hughes?"

The building is equipped with video cameras and microphones that livestream chapel three days a week. "People know we have this capability and understandably wanted to share and invite people into Hughes," she continued. "However, I felt convicted that this was a special, intimate time for our campus. I watched as students were confessing and being freed by God from major things such as addictions, abuse, and many other things that weren't intended for public spectacle." Jennifer noted that the texts and questions didn't stop; they only intensified by the hour. "Our 'control' of social media was questioned by many," she said. "I heard many times that we *should* be sharing this on social media and letting people know what was happening. We were convicted that was not what we needed to do for the moment."

These principles were determined through many discussions and prayers for guidance. Some of the answers soon became clear, and some were just common sense—like saying no to the livestream—and we strongly asked that people not livestream on their own feeds from their phones because this was not a spectacle or meant to gain people followers, especially since there were times of testimony and confession. Selective livestreaming by Asbury was resumed near the end of the two weeks. We said no to certain media platforms asking for Asbury interviews or interviewees and no to Asbury creating social media posts because then it would appear that we were manufacturing this or prodding it along in some way.

Another part of protecting the story was simply organizing reporters. We knew we needed to welcome them, talk with them about their assignments, and ask them what they wanted to focus on for their audiences. This sometimes proved difficult when many reporters arrived at the same time, at all hours of the day and night.

We also needed to know when to deny requests. As the fatigue caught up and students tried to stay focused on their studies, many of them were feeling tapped out. Some days or some afternoons, I banned all student interviews, and we were very careful about how often to ask students to appear on the news. Press requests were denied in some of these situations. Dr. Brown was shielded from additional interviews for periods, too, barring a few key outlets, so he could stay focused on his role leading the institution and be present with students, faculty, and staff.

We assembled a press tent and created dated media credentials. Reporters who were coming were asked to spend time in Hughes soaking in the atmosphere and experiencing the peace before they began conducting interviews or recording their shots, and they were always accompanied by designated people from the communications team. I remember multiple times when God used Mark to simply spend time with reporters who truly had questions about Jesus and what was happening and needed time to digest what they were seeing in a thoughtful way. We'll never know the impact of those encounters on this side of heaven.

The secular media overwhelmingly responded, "It is so refreshing to cover a positive story!" and this was so encouraging. We all knew God was in control, but protecting our students and the university was critical in the media relations efforts. It's in our job descriptions. That could be as simple as reminding students that reporters will quote them from phone calls, text messages, or social media. We encouraged students to make their social media profiles private. For some, they needed some practice answering questions on the spot; for others, we helped them understand how some outlets would likely twist their message and make it something it shouldn't be.

Leadership established more concrete rules for the press, including that no interviews could take place inside Hughes during services, reporters should spend some time in Hughes simply observing before they conducted interviews, video collection could only happen from the back or balcony, and no cameras were allowed to be in people's faces in Hughes. We created official Asbury media galleries to share with media outlets that didn't send a crew. Our most important rule was that we were to let our students speak and share. With that, we had to tactfully and quickly remind our entire campus community that all interview requests on behalf of or representing Asbury must go through the Strategic Communications office.

Spirit-Led, Gut-Level Decision-Making

Even with our daily preparations, there were times when decisions had to be made in seconds or in tender situations. And at times we needed to trust our instincts. We needed Spirit-led wisdom and discernment because it was prime territory for Satan to attempt to undercut our decisions and plant seeds of chaos, doubt, and destruction. I told a few people that I was very glad in these moments that God created me with a healthy dose of skepticism. Left unchecked, this can quickly lead to cynicism, but in a few instances, I was enormously thankful for this trait, because we did encounter some media outlets or reporters who could have created inaccurate or unfair representations of what was happening, and those were not platforms for interviews with Asbury people.

It also helped to have people we trusted who worked at Asbury and were on-scene. For example, one member of our team, Jeremy Simmons, was stationed at the media check-in table. He and others provided a welcoming face to reporters who arrived expecting to be pointed in the right direction. His job was to text me the media outlets as they arrived—sometimes multiple at a time—and if we didn't recognize the outlet, his job was to look them up on the internet or social media, read their "About" sections or mission statements, see some of their recent stories, and help determine quickly if they were a good fit for credentials. Even the faith-based outlets we had to consider carefully. I could trust his opinion and quickly got a thumbs-up, a thumbs down, or a not sure. If we weren't sure, someone would have a conversation with them and find out about their background and the angle they wanted to take on their story. This helped tremendously, especially on some of those busy days when we'd sometimes have multiple reporters and photographers lined up outside of the press tent trying to get a story. Jeremy, our graduate assistant Madison Anderson, several student workers, Jennifer, and others who worked as the media welcoming team were crucial to the story of the Outpouring.

I can close my eyes and go back to the slightly controlled chaos of those peak days of media response and remember our reactions and the variety of decisions we made on the spot:

This is not a credentials-for-all situation. They all need to be approved.
Pray.
He's sharing his colleague's press pass from yesterday—he needs his own.
I'm sorry, you can't take your desk and computer in to broadcast.
We can't give you credentials, but please, feel free to interview the visitors from around the world standing on the semicircle; they're amazing.
We need daily color-coded press passes.
My favorite media outlet is here—whoa, fan girl!
No one from AU goes on that outlet.
Please remind the students to check with me before they talk to press.
Yes, they'll quote you from your DMs.
There's an entire documentary crew from Christian Broadcast Network here.

What else does *Time* magazine need for its feature?
The New York Times is here.
Talk about Jesus.
That whole church is praying for us.
What happened to my office last night!? Oh, they broadcasted from there. Cool.
No, we can't grant press passes to people who are trying to avoid the eight-hour line.
For Billy Graham's people? Yes, of course.
That reporter was moved. Thank the Lord!
No, that's fake news.
Yes, all this food was donated.
Yes, we are working closely with the City of Wilmore.
This will all be translated for listeners in South America.
The churches in the Netherlands are responding to this.
I cannot remember where I parked my car this morning!
Coffee.
Yes, I can Zoom with you at 7:00 a.m. Just fell asleep a few hours ago.
We need some messages on the website to answer all these questions for the public.
Let me connect you with the prayer team.
Yes, everything is orderly. There is order in the Kingdom of Heaven.
Yes, those people over there are all volunteers.
We did have to pay for the porta-potties.
We are thankful.
God loves this generation.
God is good.

I didn't ever really understand supernatural strength and energy before these sixteen days. It was extremely humbling.

Answering the Logistical Questions and Moving Forward

Throughout the Outpouring, some of the challenges included simply answering logistical questions and practical considerations for participants and press. They wanted to know if Hughes was open all night, where they could get food or stay the night, where to park, whether classes were continuing, how long the line was, when the next service would start, and so on. Some questions were deeper: "I can't come to Wilmore. Can you pray with me on the phone?" "Can I talk with someone there?" "Is the Holy Spirit there?"

The number of questions was sometimes crushing. But Asbury has an amazing culture of hospitality and worked to remedy this, whether by relaying information effectively on-site or creating digital communication to help people. The Strategic Communications team quickly put together a web page that linked directly from our home page, answering the most common questions about the Outpouring and sharing service times. We also instructed the incredible switchboard operators regarding what to communicate and provided cell phone numbers for key media points of contact. At times when I managed to pass by the switchboard for a quick run into my office, I got a stack of sticky notes put in my hand with names and phone numbers to call back.

We received probably thousands of direct messages on our social media channels about what was happening, with some prying about why we were not shouting from the rooftops what God was doing!

A few days passed, and Jennifer and I decided to start very selectively sharing some of the stories on Instagram in the temporary feed—not posts—to help show people what God was doing and answer the barrage of questions that were flooding our team, the Asbury switchboard, and others. These were being viewed by tens of thousands of people, and we decided to use this to help strategically get out messages and let others speak for us in a way that answered questions and glorified God. But we had to limit these, sharing only from credible sources and people we knew. By default, anything we "share" on social media essentially has our stamp of approval, so great care was taken. However, we recognized it was great news that should be communicated, and it was helpful to people who had questions about what was happening in Wilmore.

As the days passed, social media was taking on a life of its own, and we all watched—with mouths hanging open—as #AsburyOutpouring and #AsburyRevival received hundreds of millions of views all over social media. There was no way to control it, of course. We were being tagged in Instagram stories left and right in firsthand accounts of people experiencing the transformative love of God. TikTok was exploding with Jesus. Google searches turned up endless pages. Unbeknownst to us at first, we had "gone viral" and found that our number of followers was climbing exponentially, right along with the hashtags and mentions. *Jesus* had gone viral, and we couldn't help but chuckle in disbelief at what we were seeing!

We all watched in disbelief as tens of thousands of people viewed the Instagram stories that we chose to share when our posting was otherwise silent. Anytime I felt conflicted about what we were seeing on social media and the media presence we fielded, God reminded me clearly, "*Keep sharing me.*"

Our last post before the Outpouring began was on the morning of February 8, prior to chapel. It was a full ten days later before we posted an official university statement from Dr. Brown, with subsequent video updates from him on February 19 and February 21. It was obvious God was guiding Dr. Brown's messages to those gathered in Hughes that we then shared, knowing full well they'd be received around the world very quickly. Even though that first social media post and website update took place around 11:00 p.m., it was picked up by the press within minutes. I remember sitting in our Strategic Communications suite with a group of key communication professionals and breathing a sigh of relief once the message was out.

Those posts received tens of thousands of impressions. The final Outpouring logistical update came on February 23, and then no more official Asbury social media posts were made until March 2. Great care was taken to keep stewarding the story God was telling and the work he was doing without turning it into a social media opportunity. In the following weeks that spring, most of the posts provided Outpouring testimony. Plus, we made the decision never to post Outpouring-related news articles, to make it abundantly clear this was not remotely related to publicity.

Slowly, we made steps to begin sharing the story with the world in the correct contexts—whether it was working with podcasters, news outlets, or small groups to share the stories—with humility and in awe of God's goodness. Outpouring teams were created to travel the United States and the world to share about what God had done and is still doing.[1] Follow-up news stories, podcasts, social media, and blog posts continued for months around the world.

After the last day of the public services in Hughes on February 23, our earned media value from the Outpouring surpassed $5 million, Asbury's website had received 285 million visits, and our combined social media tags and impressions were nearing a billion. The way that God personally

1. For more information on these teams, see Bridgette Campbell's chapter in this volume.

showed up for me in this way made me smile, because prior to February 2023—when I was still new at Asbury—one of my key goals for our department was to boost the university's media presence. Before February 2023, we weren't often in the news, website visits per week were in the tens of thousands, and our social media accounts had a modest and sometimes disengaged following. I think God likes to surprise us, and my best-laid marketing plans couldn't compare with how he moved. God officially took over the Strategic Communications department.

CHAPTER FIFTEEN

NO PLACE TO PARK

Problem-Solving with City Officials

Harold L. Rainwater
Mayor, Wilmore; Equine Ambassador, Asbury University[1]

City officials often receive training for managing various crises—what to do when a tornado strikes your city, how to manage a financial shortfall, or how to find innovative ways to draw new businesses to town. But no one receives training for how to respond to a spontaneous work of God that increases the population of your city nearly tenfold within a matter of days. In this chapter, we will consider the tensions between stewarding a profound outpouring of the Holy Spirit and providing for the needs of a small community stretched beyond capacity.

EARLIER LESSONS AND NEW SURPRISES

I am not new to a town stretched to capacity. I served as the mayor of Wilmore through most of the years of Ichthus, a Christian music festival that at times caused nearly twenty-five thousand people to flock to Wilmore. The difference between that event and the Outpouring was that Ichthus was planned from year to year. We knew the impact of twenty-five thousand people in Wilmore, where the traffic would flow, where people would park, and when they would leave. Vans and buses transported people to the location in groups of twelve to fifty at a time. So there were larger vehicles, but fewer vehicles. One of the reasons Ichthus moved from its East Main Street location (near downtown Wilmore) out to US 68 (on the outskirts of town) was to provide efficient traffic flow. There was never a question of

1. At the time of the Outpouring, Mayor Rainwater served as director of the Equine Program at Asbury University.

whether there was a place to park once you arrived on the grounds. The question in those days was getting on the grounds—a question that visitors to the Outpouring also found themselves asking.

One of the differences between this event and Ichthus was that the music festival had an entrance and an exit strategy. That was fairly successful until mud and weather conditions complicated the route. Praise God, during the Outpouring in February—when terrible weather is always a possibility—conditions remained good. It was a considerably warmer and drier February than normal. Since we didn't have to worry about muddy conditions, on the last Sunday, more than three hundred cars were able to park in the university-owned field where we cut hay for the Asbury Equine Program.

With Ichthus, we had a year to plan each festival and a year to plan for contingencies. The outdoor music festival sometimes experienced terrible weather, and the best-laid plans required flexibility to keep visitors safe. The Outpouring, however, was a spontaneous act of God. We had absolutely no notice that people were going to begin pouring into town.

The congestion we experienced was different from previous revivals. In February of 1970, another revival occurred. I had graduated from Asbury College the year before, and I had bought the Dine a Mite restaurant, located where the Kinlaw Library stands now (next to Hughes Auditorium). It was a very popular gathering spot for students because it was considered "off campus." On this particular morning, I had my normal fifty-to-one hundred honey buns on the counter, orange juice, coffee, and milk ready to go for students to come in after chapel—and no one came. After a few minutes, someone came in and said, "I guess chapel is going over today, and there are a lot of people at the altar, so they are going to cancel the next hour of classes," which was quite rare at Asbury College. One hour turned into a day, which turned into many days. The difference in that event was that we did not have social media, and the world did not hear about that revival as quickly. For the most part, the only people who came were the seminary students from across the street after they heard that the event was happening. The world later learned about that revival because our students traveled from Asbury to various universities, churches, and other locations to tell the story of the 1970 revival.

Fast-forward to 2023: As we began to have a few cars pull into town on the first day or two of the Outpouring, there was not much congestion. We really did not know that anything was happening in the town. There were a few more cars, but they were all absorbed on university property; then they began to flow over to Asbury Theological Seminary (ATS). Then they began to flow over to a few churches. Then they began to flow over to a few business lots along Lexington Avenue and Main Street. Then they began to flow over to Fitch's IGA (our local grocery store), and the rest is history. "No place to park" became the tagline of people coming to Wilmore. As I look back and reflect on it, I do not know that we could have planned for where people could park.

The Growing Public Safety Challenge

The first two days of the Outpouring were relatively quiet as far as the city was concerned. It was not until Friday, February 10, that the university first reached out to the city and to me through our police department. David Hay, assistant vice president of campus security, initially requested one officer for Hughes Auditorium from 6:00 p.m. until 8:00 a.m. on Saturday, February 11, and Sunday, February 12. We had the first responder present for any medical emergencies. The university agreed from the very beginning to pay all the officers. That is one thing that is very important to note: This was not an expense to the City of Wilmore. The university paid for all the services that they received. On Saturday, Eric Walsh, the safety supervisor of Asbury University Campus Safety and Security, requested officer presence through Tuesday, February 14, and we had one officer remain on campus the entire time. Asbury started metering guests at the front of Hughes to prevent the auditorium from going over capacity.

By Sunday, February 12, the rapid escalation in attendance caused the revival to no longer feel like a college event, but more like a local or regional event. The Wilmore Police Department continued to provide coverage that the university had requested. On Monday, February 13, the increasing attendance resulted in the university requesting a second officer in Hughes for the following evening's service. They also asked for our officers to remain on campus until Wednesday, February 15. Again, we were planning from day to day. On Tuesday, February 14, university officials requested a third officer for roaming patrol on campus. We also received a request from the seminary across the street for an officer to be present in Estes Chapel and McKenna Chapel, since these venues were to be opened to use as overflow sites for simulcast of the events in Hughes. Our officers provided the coverage at ATS, and they were also paid by ATS.

Interagency Cooperation

We began safety discussions with Johnny Adams, director of Jessamine County Emergency Management (JCEM), and on Wednesday, February 15, we began setting up a command post with Major Nelson Shrout (now the Wilmore police chief), running it on behalf of the city. David Hay requested that three officers remain on campus at all times. At approximately 12:00 p.m., Major Shrout contacted the Jessamine County Sheriff's Office (JCSO), and within the hour deputies began arriving to assist. The Wilmore Police Department (WPD), Nicholasville Police Department (NPD), and JCSO provided on-site police presence. David Hay also hired security guards to be present on campus to assist around the clock. On Wednesday, February 15, ATS officials also requested more officers at Estes Chapel and McKenna Chapel, as overflow sites were continuing to grow.

The cooperation of multiple law enforcement agencies was necessary to meet the growing needs of the community. By 7:00 a.m. on Thursday, February 16, the command post was fully set up with dispatcher assistance, and we began 24/7 coverage at the command post. WPD, NPD, JCEM, and Jessamine Emergency 911 loaned the equipment, including radios, computers, traffic cones, and so on, to the command post for the overall operation.

Officers helped with a variety of tasks on campus. Security continued, even as the university decided that services would temporarily end at 2:00 a.m. each night. The university had instituted a "no bag" policy in Hughes, and all allowable bags were searched by university staff and volunteers. A police officer was present for security. Announcements were made to the crowd that no weapons were allowed in Hughes; anyone with weapons should take them back to their vehicles. We continued to operate on Thursday, February 16, with three officers/deputies on campus near Hughes.

Traffic began to increase on Thursday, February 16. There were a large number of vehicles, but traffic was still flowing. We first began to receive parking complaints regarding privately owned parking lots such as at Fitch's IGA and ATS. These private properties were trying to advise people not to leave their vehicles continuously in their parking spots.

The demands only continued to grow. On Friday, February 17, David Hay requested more officers on campus. The university requested multiple officers to be on campus at all times. We put three to four on the morning shifts and four to eight on the two evening shifts. That was stretching us past the ability of the WPD, so we began to bring in other police departments. On Friday, we utilized a new program called BACKUPPS (Bluegrass and

Central Kentucky Unified Police Protection System) because of the growing crowd and the increasing numbers that we anticipated. We had to bring in other police departments to help us manage that. The BACKUPPS program facilitates interagency cooperation, and it was crucial for responding quickly to an ever-changing situation. We contacted the University of Kentucky Police Department, Georgetown Police Department, Scott County Sheriff's Office, and Versailles Police Department, and they began to come. In total, we had thirteen law enforcement agencies involved in providing public safety during the Outpouring.

Not only did the use of the BACKUPPS program provide greater coverage on the university campus, it allowed WPD officers to continue to provide coverage for the city as a whole. All the WPD police officers were taken off the Asbury revival detail and then began to only respond to calls in the city because we had been stretched so thin. Nonetheless, WPD officers were instructed to respond to calls for assistance from BACKUPPS officers so the WPD would take the lead and have the responsibility to follow through on any issue that arose. This would prevent departments from across central Kentucky from incurring complicated follow-up issues.

Managing Traffic

On Saturday, February 18, the university placed steel-barricade fencing at multiple sites along Macklem Drive (in front of Hughes) to direct and limit the increasing pedestrian traffic. I had two council members advising me at my house, since I had broken my ankle and was on crutches and wearing a boot. Thus, my command central was my home. Because of all the traffic issues, the BACKUPPS officers were placed on N. Lexington Avenue (the main road, which runs between the college and the seminary) to prevent drivers from stopping and taking pictures of the cars lining the road all the way out to the edge of town. Occasionally, someone would pull up and a passenger would leave the car to get into the pedestrian line for Hughes. During the late afternoon shifts, we learned that the officers placed on N. Lexington Avenue were no longer effective. People were parking anywhere they could park. At 11:40 p.m., "No Parking" signs were placed between the entrance and exit to Macklem Drive. Parking had become an issue, and people were parking improperly and illegally. In cooperation with command central at the university, we developed a parking plan utilizing space at Wilmore Free Methodist Church (WFMC) on the northern edge of town. We ran the operation on Sunday and Monday.

In order to manage the flow of traffic, we planned a one-way loop for revival attendees. On Sunday, February 19, JCEM placed message boards—and Kentucky State Police Troopers—along US 68 near the northern intersection leading into Wilmore and directed all revival goers to proceed instead to KY 1268 on the west side of town. Thus, we basically pushed all the traffic on US 68 coming to Wilmore to enter from the west and leave heading north. It worked for the most part, but some local residents were upset. Residents who needed to travel to Wesley Village (a retirement community) or Thomson-Hood Veterans Center—both on the north side of Wilmore—found themselves caught in the traffic that took the long way through the revival loop, through Wilmore, and back up through the revival traffic on N. Lexington Avenue, back out to the north side of town. We did try to help Wesley Village and Thomson-Hood Veterans Center employees by giving them a pass to get through, but confusion occurred regarding how that was to be handled, since three state troopers were blocking the road. Rumors came out that Wilmore was shutting down. That was not true, but that is what the television stations were putting on the news. The message board did not clearly communicate that it was not that Wilmore was shutting down; rather, the revival was going to change the focus back to students only.

With the massive crowds on Sunday, we planned to manage parking by directing all revival visitors to campus parking first, then to fill all the green spaces on campus. Then we planned to fill Centennial Park (a thirty-two-acre city park more than a mile from campus); passenger vans owned and operated by WFMC transported people to campus. The church canceled their evening service so they could help. We parked three hundred cars—directed by two council members and myself on a crutch—in the field behind my house on Corbitt Drive, near the park. The miracle is that we could pack three hundred cars in the grass in the month of February and no one would get stuck in mud. These people could have waited on transports by the WFMC, but many parked their cars and started walking. One man said it was no big deal—they had been driving for six hours and needed to walk. Most of the visitors were singing hymns and praying as they walked back to their cars. To our surprise, the parking plan had worked. When you can absorb three to four hundred cars into a new area, that considerably lessens the impact of cars parking on the streets. Traffic decreased significantly. We were all of the opinion that traffic and parking would most likely take care of itself, and so we stopped directing the traffic and let the traffic flow. All officers posted on US 68 and KY 1268 cleared out and allowed traffic to flow as normal. All roadways were open by 8:00 p.m. that evening. No other parking or traffic issues were reported that day.

The last public service took place on Monday, February 20. For the rest of the week, services were only open to Gen Z (sixteen- to twenty-five-year-olds) beginning at 7:30 p.m. each evening, with screening and doors opening at 7:00 p.m. All the BACKUPPS officers scheduled to work were kept on campus each day due to continued visitor interest in the Outpouring. No other issues with traffic or parking occurred on Monday, and this operation continued as planned until Thursday, February 23, 2023.

Managing Protesters

When large events take place, not everyone agrees about the meaning and purpose of the occasion, and protests sometimes develop. On Thursday, February 23—the last day of services—the Jesus Preacher Ministries (JPM) arrived at 12:30 p.m. to begin demonstrating. They set up on the east side of Lexington Avenue to protest. The group fluctuated between four and eight participants throughout the afternoon. All BACKUPPS officers were on the front lawn of the university, a total of nine officers. Two of those officers were staged in front of Estes Chapel at the seminary's request. Patrol officers were also alerted when the protesters arrived. At approximately 2:00 p.m., someone walked over and asked the JPM speaker to quiet down and move because he felt the speaker was being disruptive. The speaker began saying over his bullhorn that he was being threatened: "He's threatening to break my neck," and "He's threatening to break my equipment." Several of the Wilmore Police officers spoke to the allegedly threatened JPM speaker. They made a report for terroristic threatening, and the JPM speaker was referred to the Jessamine County Attorney's office if he wished to pursue criminal charges, which is standard practice. The JPM speaker did not like this answer and demanded that the subject be arrested. Nonetheless, we continued to follow procedure and monitor the situation, which did not escalate further.

We received one official complaint that the protesters were disrupting classes and meetings when they were demonstrating. The group leader agreed to turn the volume down on the bullhorn; several citizens and passersby asked why nothing was being done about this group. In managing these kinds of situations, however, we must balance First Amendment rights: both the right to worship freely *and* the right to speak freely. Police explained that the group was exercising their First Amendment rights; those who complained seemed to understand and chose to ignore the protesters. The JPM members eventually moved to the university side of Lexington Avenue and continued their protests. The BACKUPPS officers continued to monitor the situation, but no new incidents were reported.

Winding Down

It's important to recognize that just because an event has officially ended does not mean that visitors immediately stop arriving in town. Continued security presence is needed until interest finally wanes. On Friday, February 24, the BACKUPPS officers remained on campus as scheduled. There were no revival-related events on campus, which went back to its normal routine of regularly scheduled classes. Even though university security had placed temporary fencing in front of Hughes to discourage anyone from attempting to enter, visitors continued to arrive sporadically, and security had to ask them to leave.

On Saturday, February 25, our BACKUPPS officers remained on campus as scheduled. The command post remained in operation until midnight. All officers and dispatchers cleared the campus at that time. On-duty police officers were advised to provide extra patrol throughout the night.

For the next two weeks, the university retained an extra officer to remain on campus during overnight hours, due to the continued interest in entering Hughes. In addition, the university requested another officer to remain on campus in the Glide-Crawford Residence Hall area—the female dorm near Hughes. By the time the need for increased security presence wound down, a total of ninety officers had participated in providing security for the Outpouring.[2] All this protection was paid for by the university.

Minimal Other Impacts

One might expect that other city services would be disrupted significantly by a sudden influx of thousands of strangers; the answer, however, is less

2. WPD provided ten officers; JC911, fourteen; JCSO, fourteen; NPD, eleven; Boyle County Sheriff's Office, two; Danville PD, seven; Garrard County Sheriff's Office, three; Georgetown PD, one; Lancaster PD, one; Mercer County Sheriff's Office, three; Scott County Sheriff's Office, one; University of Kentucky PD, seven; Versailles PD, fourteen; and Woodford County Sheriff's Office, two.

dramatic than we might imagine. I talked to several city employees about how the Outpouring affected the city. Fire Chief Jimmy Powers stated that he did not think anything needed to be changed in regard to the fire department's involvement with the Outpouring. That may be in part because they were not involved with the command center, which was operated more from the vantage point of security. City Hall did not have any issues. I also talked with Jeff Moberly, Public Works/Utilities supervisor, who stated that they normally empty the dumpsters once or twice a week, but they had to dump them daily during the event. Public Works/Utilities Director Dave Carlstedt stated that there was no substantial increase at the Wastewater Treatment Plant; they ran the Water Treatment Plant an extra hour each day as an extra precaution.

Celebrate Rather Than Fix

Looking at the title of this chapter, "No Place to Park," I was reminded today that when Jesus was born, there was "no room in the inn"—that is, for Christ too, there was no place to park. The Outpouring was an opportunity of a lifetime. But the opportunity of a lifetime must come during the lifetime of the opportunity—and I think the university did its very best to make the most of the occasion.

As I look back on the experience, we as a city could have done a few things more effectively. The event was unplanned, and it happened on private property. Thus, the city had little control. When the event began to almost overwhelm us with the number of people coming into the area, we as a city—including me, the police department, the fire department, and the emergency personnel—should have started to dialogue earlier. Asbury was doing their part; they had resources, they had volunteers, they had food, and they had a plan. They were meeting regularly, but we were separate and acted more reactively instead of proactively. Maybe we just needed to look at what was happening and celebrate it instead of trying to correct it. That, to me, is the greatest fault that I see from the city: We began to respond with an attitude of "We have to fix something," or "This is overwhelming," or "This is too big." Instead, we needed to recognize that this was a celebration of a lifetime.

Someone else suggested that we needed to consider whether we wanted to be a thermostat or a thermometer. A thermometer simply reflects what is going on—what the temperature is—but a thermostat can regulate the environment. Perhaps the city should have been involved with the seminary and the churches, acting as a bit more of a thermostat.

We also needed to be better at differentiating between those who were asking legitimate questions about what was happening and those who were antagonizing others. Some people were asking excellent questions. Others did not like what was occurring and were trying to stop the event. It is important to recognize the nature of the comments or questions and respond accordingly. A one-size-fits-all approach will not do.

If I were to look back and do this again, we would set up a command center at Wilmore Municipal Building, and we would have probably had a reflection time like the governor did during COVID. Providing updates is important. This was not necessary every day, but updates every couple of days would have been helpful: where do people park, where do visitors go, and what are the resources.

The founding of Asbury College was very closely aligned with the city and the businesses in the city. In the spring of 1890, when John Wesley Hughes came into Wilmore, there were three or four primary businesses in what we would now call downtown. He came here from Carlisle, Kentucky, where the townspeople had rejected the concept of building a Christian school. He asked the businesspeople in Wilmore if they would raise $1,500, and if they did, he would come to Wilmore and build a Christian school. Wilmore's businesspeople embraced the proposal because they wanted their children to receive a Christian education. So going back 133 years, there would not even be an Asbury University or Asbury Theological Seminary if the Wilmore community had not embraced the vision. I feel bad that during this revival there was not more involvement from the city to support the Outpouring or even grow it. As I mentioned earlier, the opportunity of a lifetime must come during the lifetime of the opportunity. We did not know what was coming; we did not see what was coming, and neither did the university. But it had to be nurtured; it had to be cherished.

The Importance of Hospitality

Reactions to the Outpouring included both those who were hostile and those who were hospitable. There was almost no one in the middle. Nonetheless, as I talked to people in the community, very few were hostile; most of our citizens offered open hospitality. The practice of hospitality was an integral part of the life of the early church. Ivan Tan, in his book *Hospitality and Growing the Church*, notes that Hebrews 13:2 instructed the early church not to forget to show hospitality to strangers. The Greek word used here is *philoxenia*, which combines *phileo* (the love of a brother or a sister) and *xenos* (the stranger or the foreigner). So by putting the two words together, hospitality means loving strangers and foreigners as our brothers and sisters. This also includes respecting people. Sometimes we have a fear of "those people coming into town." As I talked to folks in the community during the Outpouring, there was somewhat of a fear of all these strangers coming into town. But most people in Wilmore are hospitable. Hospitality simply involves welcoming guests and making them feel at home. It means accepting with pleasure the presence of our guests.

I am not saying that everybody in Wilmore had to bring guests into their homes, but I am amazed at how many people *did* bring these guests into their homes. I talked to Arvid Metcalf—a longtime Wilmore resident who lives at the top of the hill as one nears Wilmore—and they had people stop at their home to use the restroom, thinking that it was the entrance into Wilmore because of their location. I have heard of people who knew that visitors were sleeping in their cars in the street, and they invited these sojourners into their homes. Others took food to people's cars. Still others took sandwiches to people standing in line that were not going to get into Hughes, even though they had stood there for eight hours on that last Saturday. That is the part I am most proud of: our community's hospitality, the grace of people to accept strangers into their town and then try to feed and accommodate them.

Not everything was perfect. There are some stories that I wish had not happened. Some cars were towed, not by our police department, but by neighborhoods where the cars were probably improperly parked and caused some disruption.

Yet there were no fights, no arrests, no injuries, and no shootings. Think of this: fifty to seventy thousand guests in your town, and nothing really bad happens. That is unheard of in a town of six thousand.

Concluding Management Suggestions

The Outpouring presented unique situations that made it impossible to plan ahead. Nonetheless, we learned many lessons about how to respond to a sudden, overwhelming visitation. As mayor of Wilmore, I recommend the following to those who find themselves in similar situations:

1. *Early conversations are crucial for managing a fluid situation.* Although I became very involved in conversations with the president and vice president of the university, I only began this in the second week. Although

no one could predict the exponential growth of the Outpouring, if I had to do it all over again, I would have joined the conversations earlier.
2. *Daily security briefings help to keep a pulse on the situation.* I was getting briefings from my police command center, but I would have had more frequent briefings so that we could plan more effectively.
3. *Establish a command center that is easily accessible to all concerned parties.* I would have created a command center at a different location off campus that would have been more easily accessible to the fire department, EMTs, and community members. This would not necessarily need to be open twenty-four hours, but long enough each day to allow for responses to the events on campus.
4. *Implement creative parking solutions early.* Providing a place where individuals can park their cars and then board larger shuttles into town helps to limit congestion in front of homes and businesses. Although we eventually implemented the WFMC parking shuttle, we did this too late.
5. *Clear communication is paramount.* Although I communicated with my council regularly, I could have given daily updates. Often we received information through the television news, but we could have provided a more distinct response from the city.

Throughout this outpouring, we encountered unusual circumstances. But the Outpouring was the opportunity of a lifetime. And God was driving that. No one person had a vision for this; rather, God showed up, and God provided for it. Although some people complained about the revival and the issues with parking, we need to keep a greater perspective. If we were in a line of traffic to a ball game in Lexington with sixty-five thousand people, we would still be cheering if our team had won. And God's team won. So we should still be cheering about what took place in our community. It had been fifty-three years since there had been a movement of God such as this. So to God be the glory.

CHAPTER SIXTEEN

SHARING THE OUTPOURING THROUGH WITNESSING TEAMS

Bridgette Campbell

Coordinator of Outreach Ministry Teams, Asbury University

Asbury University has an incredible history of sporadic, spontaneous revivals.[1] In 1950 and 1970, the university experienced revivals similar in scope to the 2023 Outpouring. All three of these were marked by students' lives being transformed in a major and lasting way. The 1970 revival was so life-altering for many students that more than one thousand witness teams from the university and several hundred from Asbury Theological Seminary went out to share what they had seen the Lord do.[2]

Different Needs in a Social Media Age

The 2023 Outpouring unfolded very differently. Because of the much slower pace of communication in 1970, most people did not even know what had happened until weeks, months, or even years after the revival ended. During the 2023 Outpouring, however, people around the world were able to follow it in real time through messaging apps, multiple avenues of social media, FaceTime, and more. Videos going viral on Instagram and TikTok especially minimized the need for witness teams to travel for the purpose of telling people how powerfully God had moved in an obscure college town in Kentucky. Instead, millions of people around the world watched videos and live feeds of people surrendering themselves to the Lord.

1. For a review of these events, see Kevin Anderson's chapter in this volume.
2. Robert J. Kanary, *Spontaneous Revivals: Asbury College 1905–2006, Firsthand Accounts of Lives Transformed* (Las Vegas, NV: CreateSpace, 2017), 110.

Yet many believers yearned for more. The shared glimpses only fueled the desire to understand what had really happened during these phenomenal days and to experience it in whatever way possible. In February and March of 2023, Asbury received over one hundred requests for witness teams to come and share their testimonies about what had transpired. At that time, however, the entire campus was focused on recovering from the beautifully overwhelming season with which they had just been blessed. Initially, there was nobody on the staff assigned to organize witness teams. Most students had fallen behind in their classes during the Outpouring and were trying to catch up, because most classes continued with little interruption during the revival. In addition, many students intentionally focused on processing their own experiences of how God had moved on campus and in their lives. Because of this, even though scores of requests were received, only a few teams of students went out between mid-February and the end of April, when the semester ended.

Meeting the Lingering Hunger

In early May, it became clear that a considerable number of people in the world remained hungry to understand what had happened during the Outpouring. Requests for students to come and share continued to pour in. The university made the commitment to invest in this movement of God by creating a part-time, temporary coordinator position to organize witness teams in response to the continuing requests for testimonies.

God had worked beautifully in my own life before, during, and after the Outpouring. Through incredible God-orchestrated timing, I had begun looking for a part-time job in ministry the day before the coordinator of Outreach Ministry Teams position became available. I had spent many hours at the Outpouring worshiping and volunteering, as well as hosting many pilgrims in our home. My daughter was one of the original nineteen who stayed behind in chapel on February 8, and it was truly an honor and a blessing to begin working at Asbury to coordinate fulfilling the requests for witness teams to go out and share their life-changing stories.

Processing before Speaking

I began working with students several months after the Outpouring. I received a list of approximately fifty students who were interested in traveling and sharing their stories on the witness teams. During the summer, I began sending messages to each of these students and met with them on Zoom or in person. Many were still processing their incredible mountaintop experiences. They were learning how to keep their spiritual fervor alive when they weren't surrounded by thousands of people experiencing the Lord in such a deep way. And mostly, they seemed grateful to have a person dedicated to listening to their testimonies, helping them process the deepest parts of it, all while they learned how to share it with others.

In my time meeting with each student, we dove into their stories and explored scriptural foundations for some of the theological issues with which they were grappling. Sometimes a student needed more practical advice on public speaking. In these cases, I recommended they break their story into before-the-Outpouring, during-the-Outpouring, and after-the-Outpouring sections to give a timeline they could focus on while speaking. With some students who wanted to share from their most vulnerable places, I gave the advice to "share the scar, not the wound." I talked with students about boundaries and priorities as they learned new rhythms of ministering to others. Because I was able to meet with students individually both before and after they traveled, I worked to identify the biggest obstacles they might encounter in sharing their Outpouring testimonies and worked to overcome these challenges in a personal way.

When I asked each student how I could be praying for them, I honestly expected the responses to be more focused on internal concerns, such as the student's own anxiety about speaking or catching up from classes when they returned. Instead, I was both surprised and inspired by the responses I continually received from the students: "Less of me, more of the Lord"; "His words, not mine"; "Please pray that the Holy Spirit would speak through me exactly what the congregation needs to hear." This is a beautiful depiction of how the students were following the example set by the leadership who had modeled radical humility during the Outpouring.

Going Where the Spirit Leads

In responding to the various requests, it didn't matter if the request was big or small, near or far. The goal of the Spiritual Life team was to share the gospel with all those who would listen and could accommodate the students' travel needs. The students shared in a wide variety of venues. Some were as small as a tiny congregation or a Sunday School class with only a few dozen people. Others were on a much larger scale, like at a festival near London, England, where three students and an Asbury staff member shared in front of nine thousand young people.

At the writing of this in the summer of 2024, more than sixty student witness teams have gone out and shared what God did during the Outpouring. Over half of those were at churches around the United States, from Idaho to Texas, from California to North Carolina. Students gave their testimonies at over forty church services and four Sunday schools. They've also shared at fifteen conferences (attended by hundreds, and in some cases, thousands), five colleges and universities, festivals, camps, youth groups, and summits. Additionally, they testified about the healing power of God to those on the margins: at a senior citizen home, a recovery center, and even a maximum-security prison.

But it was not only in the United States that people wanted to hear about what had transpired. All around the world, a hunger remained for people to hear from students about their experiences and how their lives continued being impacted after the move of the Spirit in February. Students shared in the Netherlands, England, Canada, China, Australia, Thailand, South Africa, Germany, and beyond.

In addition to these opportunities, some people requested that an Asbury University worship arts band come and lead worship at festivals, conferences, or other large events. These requests were handled differently, as the focus was on music similar to that of the Outpouring. The university's worship arts professor fielded these requests, which often included the opportunity for students to share their testimonies as well as music. These bands were able to perform to large audiences, sometimes even sharing the stage with well-known Christian music artists.

The witness teams did more than just travel. They also spoke on a TV show, a radio show, YouTube channels, and countless podcasts. At each destination, the students shared their Outpouring stories, how they had felt the Holy Spirit so strongly in February 2023, and how their lives continued to be changed every day since.

Students remained flexible in how they shared their testimonies, responding to the needs in each context. At some venues, the students only shared briefly; at others, they would have the stage for hours for several days in a row. Sometimes the students would be asked to share their prepared, individual stories on stage; sometimes the hosts would request a panel of students, asking them questions that they answered more spontaneously.

To accommodate the varied requests we received, I worked closely with a representative from each venue. Priority was given to ensure they understood we were not trying to replicate the Outpouring, as that blessing was a gift given from the Holy Spirit as he willed, not something that could be re-created on demand. The few times it became apparent that a venue was hoping we would start a revival or that we would offer how-to sessions on how to create one, that request was immediately declined. Most often, though, the requests were simply from people wanting to experience the Outpouring through the stories the students shared. They wanted to see students who were putting their faith into action and have these young people pray with them after they spoke. Seeing Gen Z students voluntarily ministering in this way was an incredible encouragement to many. Ava ('26) described it well: "The easiest thing to notice is that God is just doing a sweet work to gently encourage his body."[3]

Once it was clear that the venue's expectations aligned with what the students could provide, I would ensure that they were able to pay the students' expenses in coming. This involved money for flights or gas, food, and lodging. Most of the churches also provided an honorarium to bless the students who were sacrificing their time to share. This was not required but was left open to each church or nonprofit to do as they felt led and to determine the amount.

When I first started working with the witness teams, I was concerned with the inequality of this, as some churches were extremely generous and others were unable to give beyond the required expenses. But the students' sensitivity to the prompting of the Holy Spirit proved my concerns to be unfounded. Several times, a student would be given far more than they felt they needed. They would ask me to give their surplus anonymously to another witness team student or group who hadn't been compensated for their time. This generosity of spirit was one of many ways I was blessed by the students as they lived into their transformed lives.

God's provision showed up in other ways as well. One example was a witness team trip to a conference in Germany. The organizer had a flight budget for three students, yet there was a group of four students who perfectly fit the needs of the conference, were all available, and wished to travel together. On faith, we committed the four students to go, and God provided the money for the fourth student through several different avenues, to almost the exact dollar of the amount needed.

3. The number following the student's name in the citations that follow indicate the year in which the student is expected to graduate from Asbury University.

Testifying to God's Work

Prayer and discernment were necessary to determine whether to accept requests and which students to send in response. We almost always sent the students in groups of two (same gender) or four (two males and two females). As I worked with the representative from a venue, sometimes it became immediately clear which students would best fit the request. Other times, I would post the request to a large group chat with all the witness team students and work with those who said they were willing and available for a specific trip. Sometimes, given my human limitations, I would wonder about the group that the Holy Spirit brought together for a trip, unsure about the relational dynamics involved or how a certain group would work with a particular venue. Yet without exception, the Lord brought together in beautiful harmony each group of witness team students. The stories of personal growth and camaraderie that the students shared on returning were yet another example of God's perfect wisdom as we all submitted to his will together.

I am often reminded of Isaiah 6:8: "Then I heard the voice of the Lord saying, 'Whom shall I send? And who will go for us?' And I said, 'Here am I. Send me!'" Likewise, the students on the witness teams have raised their hands and asked to be sent out. An entire book could be written on the witness team students themselves. More than fifty-five individual students have shared at least once to an audience requesting their stories. Tens of thousands of people in a variety of settings have heard Outpouring testimonies from the witness teams.

The students on these teams did not offer prepackaged theological systems or lift up any individual as a Christian celebrity. Instead, they focused on testifying to the work of God they had experienced in their lives. Rebecca ('24) declared, "We are not sharing the Outpouring; we are sharing the gospel." This perspective paralleled the heart cry of students going out as witness teams after Asbury's 1970 revival. Student David Perry—who went on a nine-month revival crusade after that event—claimed, "We affirm this is God's revival. He will not allow an individual to take control of it or get glory from it."[4]

One of the insights Gabe ('25) realized through the Outpouring was how task-oriented and works-based he sometimes allowed his faith to be. God

4. Wayne Atcheson, *The Asbury Revival: When God Used Students to Wake a Nation* (Hartselle, AL: Soncoast, 2020), 71.

is showing him how to balance his calling to ministry with the need to be still in the Lord. He continues to rest in the reassurance that his salvation is not works-based. He now has a greater sense of purpose as he lives his days focused on the Caller more than the calling.

Asher ('24) was one of the first students who went out and spoke, even while the Outpouring was still occurring. "I've absolutely loved the opportunities to go and testify/preach about the revival and just what the Lord has done in my heart! I would absolutely love to continue testifying and speaking however and wherever I can. It has been such a life-giving experience and something I truly believe God has called me to do!"

A lot of intentionality was given to ensure that the students had processed through their testimony, not just specifically thinking about what things looked like for them in February but really leaning into how the Lord continually works in their lives today as a result of this experience. When these groups of students returned, I met with them to process their ongoing growth. We want to emphasize that the Outpouring was not a blip in a believer's life but the start of a journey of daily leaning into the Holy Spirit. As witness teams testify to the work of God in a variety of venues and contexts, the following three main themes have arisen.

Spiritual Hunger

The audiences run the full gauntlet in age. Yet while those over the age of twenty-five are very encouraged by the students' testimonies, those in Gen Z express the most hunger to hear how God is moving; they desperately need the hope of the Lord that these students offer. Crowner ('24) shared how a twelve-year-old girl came up to him, hungry to hear how God was moving, and simply said as soon as she met him, "I need you to tell me everything."

Mary ('24) observed this same desire when she went with a group to speak to college students at the Wesley Foundation at the University of Mississippi. "The students listened carefully with a hunger I have not seen in a long time," Mary said. "They were so excited to grow in their personal relationships with the Lord and asked really good questions afterward in conversations. I had a conversation this morning with one of the girls about spiritual warfare! I believe the Lord will bless their hunger for his presence and overflow there in an intimate way." Weeks later when I checked back in with Mary, she was still talking with the girl about spiritual warfare and acting as a mentor to her.

In addition to the evident spiritual hunger in the audiences they spoke to, the teams themselves continued seeking after the Lord and his calling in their lives. Quite a few students on the teams felt called into full-time ministry during their time serving this way after the Outpouring. Kaitrin ('26) shares this passion and calling well:

> After the Outpouring, I had a wonderful opportunity to go and share about it in Costa Rica. There was a youth conference called Resurrection, which is a weekend gathering with different sessions. I was able to see how God moved in them and how he was continuing to meet people and pour out his presence. It was cool to see how even when I did not speak their language, I could still go share and let God impact them through my story. This opportunity, among many others, started opening the door again for God to start calling. I started to feel the call again in late January 2024. This time there was no doubt that it was from God and that I was going to have to choose if I was going to listen or if I was going to ignore this call. It was February 23, 2024, when I changed my major to Christian Ministries and when I truly started to say yes to what God was calling me to do. God is continuing to call and guide me, and I am here to say yes and to obey. I am starting a new chapter of my story that has started with a yes to God.

Healing

Common themes that arise when you talk to Gen Z students are those of anxiety and depression. In fact, a number of students shared that they did not participate in the Outpouring *because* of their anxiety at something so foreign, something they didn't know how to define or handle. These issues were the focus of much prayer and surrender at the altar at the Outpouring. As they worshiped, many students experienced breakthroughs as the chains of addictions, bitterness, depression, and anxiety lost their hold.

This freedom composed much of the testimony of students as they went to different churches. Sarah ('25) shared how Jesus changed her from the inside out. She declares that she was healed from anxiety and depression during the Outpouring, and over a year later, she is still "putting her identity and worth in Jesus, nowhere else."

Crowner ('24) described how God smacked him on the head (like his mom used to), and he experienced a "loud peace." Now when he's in the midst of stress that would've made him anxious in the past, he instead feels the same peace he felt back in February.

Not all healings have been experienced in the same way. Jacklyn ('25) shared about how she went to Memphis right after the Outpouring and spoke about what the Lord did with her mental health, specifically regarding self-harm. She was able to share with teenagers how the Lord had brought her out of that. She saw so many lives changed during the Outpouring, and she thought her chains were forever broken. Eventually, however, she went back to old patterns of behavior. She became angry that she didn't have lasting healing. But she learned from Jeannie Banter (director of Asbury's Christian Life Project) about incremental growth in the spiritual life and how she needed just to continue putting one foot in front of the other.

Lena ('25) summarized the continual struggle of the spiritual life beautifully:

> It's been so cool to see how God has orchestrated healing through the generations. People from older generations have trouble believing anything those of us in Gen Z say, but the revival equalized things. Gen Z is the generation that has experienced 9/11, school shootings, COVID, and so much more. We are a generation who shares what's really going on, and it's beautiful and a new kind of healing to share in the grief. The OP [what she calls the Outpouring] was awesome. Life is still really hard, but we have learned how to deal with it in the aftermath of the revival.

The Empowerment of the Holy Spirit

Another common theme discussed among the students is the movement of the Holy Spirit in their lives. Ellie ('26) describes living a Spirit-filled life well:

> Once you've experienced it, you learn to acknowledge it in the small places in your day. It's a sense of peace that you are compelled to walk into. Freshman year, when one thing went wrong or one overwhelming thought took over, I would spiral and feel like I was losing control. But now, because of the peace of the Holy Spirit that I carry throughout my day, I am learning to live in his presence. I long to dwell in such peace that people are compelled to ask why, not for my own validation, but so I can point people toward the Lord. Even when I went through some really difficult, chaotic things my sophomore year, I felt like I was being held. I feel stable, and my capability to do things is not on my own, not of my own power.

This empowerment of the Spirit often overturned well-laid plans. As students prepared to go out on witness teams, they practiced their timing if their hosts had set specific time limits for the speakers. Yet often the students would get to their destinations with their notes and plans, and then the Holy Spirit would take over. They learned to arrive with a feeling of expectancy, not with expectations.

They are learning to depend on the Lord for strength in their own weakness as speakers. Gabe ('25), after speaking in Iowa, declared, "The Holy Spirit was so prevalent there. The whole experience has been such a blessing!"

Zoe ('25) shared how speaking on these witness teams allowed her to take the relationship she'd developed with the Holy Spirit during the Outpouring and lean into that as she and the others on her witness team were "sweep-kicked by the Holy Spirit. When we get out of the way, it's amazing what God will do."

In the words of Rebecca ('24) after sharing in front of nine thousand young people at the New Day festival near London, England, "I feel an amazing peace that God did and said everything we needed to do while we were there. Everything was said that needed to be said. So many crazy answered prayers left me more awestruck of him."

Another student, Lexie ('23), shared about how when she went to speak at a church in Indiana, she was fully prepared to share one thing. Yet just before she was to speak, God shifted in her what she was to share. Because she was so in tune with the Holy Spirit, he was able to speak directly through her exactly what the audience most needed to hear. As a result, she made an incredible impact on many people.

As I met with the students, they repeatedly referenced Isaiah 43:19: "See, I am doing a new thing! Now it springs up; do you not perceive it?" The students absolutely reveled in the newfound joy they were experiencing as they learned to listen and follow the Spirit's prompting throughout many interactions in their daily lives.

Asbury University was essentially willing to send witness teams to the groups that met these three criteria: desiring to hear about the Outpouring, understanding that we weren't attempting to re-create a revival, and being able to logistically accommodate them. Because we didn't require a venue to adhere to our exact Wesleyan heritage, the students spoke to groups varying widely in their theology. This ranged from Catholic to Methodist to very charismatic. Some venues focused much more on various gifts of the Holy Spirit, and the students would try to redirect their attention to the gift of the Holy Spirit. Oftentimes, the students were challenged with some things they saw, as they varied significantly from what they would typically experience in their home churches. We believed that this was a great way to stretch and strengthen their beliefs. As I processed with students what they had experienced, I would always go back to Scripture as the litmus test by which to examine everything they were experiencing and pray with them for wisdom as they grew in their faith.

Making the Most of Every Opportunity

The students were grateful to be used by the Lord to share his goodness, even when trips did not go exactly as planned. Brenden ('25), for example, found himself stranded at an airport in North Carolina. He had flown there to speak at a conference at the Billy Graham Library. From there he was scheduled to fly to Idaho to meet another witness team member and share at a church there. Once at the Charlotte airport, his flight to Boise was delayed and eventually canceled. Rather than flying to Idaho to speak, he spent the entire day in an airport and eventually had to just fly back home to Kentucky late that night. Although there was naturally some disappointment and frustration in this, he still chose to find ways to share about God's goodness manifested during the Outpouring. He made a video for the church in Boise to share, since he could not make it in person. Then, undeterred, he used the opportunity to talk about the Outpouring and the Lord with multiple people he encountered at the airport.

I had a similar experience on a fall trip to Pennsylvania to share at Messiah University. On the flight home, after several intense days during which the students shared multiple times, I was blessed to overhear one of the witness team students using the flight home to share about the Outpouring with the lady seated next to him on the airplane.

Just as John the Baptist remained fully focused on his calling and seized every opportunity to exalt Jesus and not himself, this is what I saw in these witness team students. They have been God's true servants in the ways in which they sought Jesus's glory, not their own. Their witness reflected that of John 1:7: "He came as a witness to testify concerning that light, so that through him all might believe."

The Continuing Movement of the Spirit

Those who have been blessed to hear the students speak are experiencing the Holy Spirit in their interactions with the students. After a witness team goes out, I follow up with the venue for feedback on the students' sharing, and much of it involves the Holy Spirit becoming more real to the audience.

For example, one of the students on the Messiah University leadership team described their experience: "My biggest takeaway from October 24 was the 'coincidences' with each decision that was made involving the chapel teams and the Asbury students. I could see the Spirit over each decision and even the song selection throughout the day."

Another student leader from Messiah stated,

> The chapels opened my eyes to how active the Holy Spirit really is. I have always believed in the full Trinity, including the Spirit, but it was not until recently that I began to pay close attention to the work the Spirit is doing among us, and the messages given at the chapels as well as my conversations with the students at the Loft only reinforced that the Spirit is indeed moving. I felt God saying to me that he is moving here at Messiah, and that while we should be waiting expectantly for him, it's not anything we do to prepare, but rather God who moves.

At a Kentucky church in the spring of '23, Brother Ken's response to the witness team was similar: "The Spirit was evident in those two girls the whole time they were with us. The congregations responded to that Spirit."

During the autumn after the Outpouring, four students spoke ten times over a long weekend in Pennsylvania. Larry Brown (1980 Asbury alum and chair of the board of trustees) described one of their nights of speaking:

> At Christ Church on Saturday evening, there was a profound presence of the Holy Spirit, and again the students prayed for people and the community having a lasting impact. Large groups, small groups, one-on-one, radio and television, we put them through the paces. In every situation they were solid in their testimony and delivery. I received an email from [Christian broadcaster] John Hall, who said, "Hearing the intimate details of how the Holy Spirit has worked in their young lives has been a balm of peace. We've been producing the show for so many years and have been blessed to speak with thousands about our Lord, and I'll count that brief conversation as one of the most impactful in my life and I hope our listeners do too."[5]

Many people at Asbury prayed over these trips, as they were part of the incredible ripple effect of the Outpouring. Prayers focused on the logistical

5. John Hall is one-half of *The Ride Home*, a daily drive-time radio show at WORD-FM Pittsburgh.

aspects (like safe travel), plus the students representing Asbury, the Outpouring, and the Lord well. Always we wanted to point to the glory of God and share with humility. It was important to take God's love that we had encountered so closely and share it with others.

The witness teams were a way to encourage churches in what they were doing and offer hope for the next generation. After students returned from witnessing, it was clear that the prayers for lasting impact were answered. We received raving responses from the witness team follow-up, including these affirmations:

- "We had a small taste of the Asbury revival: three saved, many came to the altar for healing and prayer. The girls shared with enthusiasm about how the revival impacted them, and the Holy Spirit moved in the life of many at our service" (Graceway Church, Langley, Kentucky).
- "Many said this was the best service they had ever been in. People were encouraged, provoked, and there was an increased hunger. Charlie communicated words from the heart of Jesus. One older gentleman said, 'That was the first time in my fifty-seven years of life that I felt that every word that came out of someone was completely from the Holy Spirit'" (a church in Idaho).
- "The impact was like a bomb in front of people's faces. Seeing the students be so real was a bit of a shock for the congregation. One woman came on Sunday morning and said she didn't sleep at all because she couldn't quit thinking about all that she had heard from the students the night before" (Cornersburg Baptist Church, Kentucky).
- "Attention was very high during the team sharing. You could hear a pin drop in the audience. Many people came forward for prayer for salvation, recommitment, and other needs. We had an extensive team of twenty to twenty-five prayer counselors gathered for this purpose. The prayer time lasted about thirty minutes down in front of the stage. All of the Christians present were greatly encouraged in their faith by hearing the message of Asbury and the stories of the students. They went away challenged that God is real and relevant in the world today. The students were mature and humble beyond their years. I'm very impressed that they are doing this while still studying for classes. This shows a tremendous amount of commitment on their part" (International Crossroads, New York).

Conclusion

At the writing of this chapter, it has been over a year since God graced us with an outpouring of his presence in Wilmore. I have spent the last two days hosting a retreat with some of the students on the witness teams. I have been amazed at several things. One is how the Outpouring comes up so naturally and often because it was such a pivotal moment in these students' lives.

Revival accelerates spiritual growth. Based on the evidence from the lives of these students, I would deem this a revival. The students turn to Scripture more than people of my generation. They flip through their well-marked Bibles with an enthusiasm I have not seen previously, even as a former teacher at a Christian school and with four Gen Z children of my own who love the Lord.

What I have seen in these students since the Outpouring is a new excitement. Like a starving person sitting down to a feast, they revel in it. I have never spent time with people who carry their Bibles with them as often. Although phones have become like a new appendage for us in this digital era, for several of these students, it is their Bible instead. They have experienced such a close encounter with the Lord that they are unwilling to settle for a life not continually infused with the Holy Spirit.

Seeing the fire in these students has made me reevaluate many of my own relationships. Does each part of the Trinity come up as often in my "adult" conversations as it does with these Gen Z students? If not, I am forced to question why as I continue to learn from the generation that I had sometimes been dismissive of in the past.

These witness teams are living out the words of Dr. Kevin Brown: "A fire is brightest when it is tallest and, in that sense, we had a multiweek, spiritual bonfire. But a fire is hottest when it's dying down into smoldering embers."[6] He envisioned the students at Asbury and the fifty thousand people who attended the Outpouring each taking the smoldering embers and becoming torchbearers for all that God has done and continues to do. Each time students from the witness teams share their Outpouring stories, they carry their blazing torches, spreading the light in a desperate world full of darkness.

6. Kevin Brown, "Livestreamed Events from Reunion 2024," https://www.asbury.edu/reunion/livestreams. As of September 2024, the specific video this is from is no longer available online. For similar comments, however, see Kevin Brown's chapter in this volume.

CHAPTER SEVENTEEN

THE ASBURY OUTPOURING

Implications for the Marketplace

Robin Lim

Assistant professor of business and director of Strategic Initiatives and Partnerships, Asbury University

My children love playing in the water, especially by the banks of a river—the joy of wading in the cool waters, the sense of being suspended, floating in the moment. As most parents know, the toughest part is getting them out of the water and back onto land.

Like my children, I was filled with holy elation during the extraordinary days of the Asbury Outpouring, submerged in a river of life that the Spirit of God had poured over Wilmore. The manifest presence of God in Hughes Auditorium was so palpable, so thick, I could empathize with Peter, James, and John, witnesses of the transfiguration of Jesus, who wanted to remain on the high mountain. Yet I could not remain, and acclimating back to the dry banks of ordinary life was—and continues to be—a struggle. I began to ask myself, How do I respond to the themes that God made so apparent, themes of radical humility and holiness? Surely, a profound moment of such life-changing magnitude cannot be redacted from my day-to-day life. And even though much of what God did over those sixteen days was focused on Generation Z, I too was deeply affected—but how does it change what I do? Is the Outpouring relevant beyond the doors of a chapel?

I am a professor in the business school at Asbury University, a former banker who was immersed in the global marketplace. Yet the marketplace and spiritual revivals are rarely associated with one another. Our immediate reflex is to assign marketplaces to secularized spaces, whereas revivals occur in sacred spaces such as churches. This reflects a dualistic worldview, where ordinary workplaces are bereft of extraordinary spiritual influences.

I was reminded of God's intent for the marketplace, however, after speaking to some of my students who were profoundly impacted by the Outpouring and soon to be graduating into a variety of jobs, accounting firms, creative agencies, hospitals, media companies, tech hubs, banks, and small businesses. They were not simply embarking on careers; rather, they felt commissioned into these industries and believed that the marketplace was their parish, a place to live out their Kingdom convictions. Could it be that what God did at Asbury was going to percolate into the secularized marketplace? In 2004, Billy Graham famously declared, "I believe that one of the next great moves of God is going to be through believers in the workplace."[1] With a holy imagination, just maybe the gentle ripples from the Asbury Outpouring, and the many affected by it, will gradually become the swells that break the sacred-spiritual divide and flood into the marketplace.

Why the Marketplace?

Yet, why the marketplace? Today it is not difficult to witness the characteristics of apathetic spiritual neglect. It even has a name—cultural Christianity—which refers to people who value the cultural benefits of Christianity but live an areligious life. These cultural Christians desire a form of Christianity that upholds a culture or tradition they are familiar with, a routine, a guiding moral framework, a community, or even a therapeutic sense of security in a life after death. Yet they have no desire for any form of Christianity that may cost them additional commitment or character change beyond that—this is a faith absent of discipleship. Unfortunately, this slumber is prevalent in the church, manifesting as a Sunday-Monday, faith-work gap among the saints in the secular marketplace as one's own religious convictions are discouraged from being made public. More tragically, when faced with a choice to live as either authentically faithful Christians or to secularize their faith to conform with society, many believers and even the institution of the church have chosen to deprioritize a faithful outwardly expressed witness for Christ. Specifically, in the marketplace, this has led many corporations, organizations, and governments to become breeding grounds for a distorted

1. Billy Graham, quoted in Wong Siew Li, ed., "Marketplace Ministry (LOP 40)," paper presented at the Lausanne Committee for World Evangelization, Pattaya, Thailand, September 29–October 5, 2004, https://www.lausanne.org/content/lop/marketplace-ministry-lop-40.

faith that reduces Christianity to a privatized religious ideal, counter to John Wesley's declaration that "the gospel of Christ knows no religion, but social; no holiness but social holiness."[2] The seduction and influence of the secularized marketplace woos its people to the idols of social acceptance, money, power, comforts, and success. It blunts the witness of Christians and suppresses their gifts, resulting in a spiritual inertia. As Intervarsity Director Pete Hammond said, "This immobilization of 99 percent of God's people is both unbiblical and discriminating, whilst making our task of world evangelization impossible."[3] If there is any place that needs an act of revival, it is the marketplace. Unfortunately, I suspect many would refuse to utter the words of Psalm 85:6—"Will you not *revive us again*, that your people may rejoice in you?" (emphasis added)—since there is little desire to change hearts, let alone rejoice. Rather, they are deceived, bowing to a marketplace that rewards an apathetic faith with earthly success.

The centrality of a revival is the revitalization of people's apathetic hearts toward God, yet there are also broader systemic reasons why the marketplace is ripe for a touch from God. The Second Great Awakening was known for being a revival that was steeped in a revitalization of holiness. One powerful reverberation was its impact on social reform across an entire nation. Garth M. Roswell reflects, "America's mid-nineteenth century religious revivals, reinforced by a passionate quest for personal and corporate holiness, unleashed a veritable flood tide of evangelical social activity—mobilizing tens of thousands of new recruits for the battles against slavery, poverty, and greed."[4] While the centrality of a revival is the manifestation of God's glory and the revitalization of people's hearts, it is evident that the sheer power of God's presence should send holy reverberations across all facets of society. Beyond the reorientation of people's hearts, there is a reorientation across society toward God, reinfusing holy ethics that reveals an inbreaking of the Kingdom of Heaven. From the perspective of the modern marketplace, there have been worrying signs of moral degradation in the name of greed. Following a spate of financial market crises, in 2013 the Vatican labeled the marketplace as a "deified market," a source of "ideologies which defend the absolute autonomy of the marketplace," which "tends

2. John Wesley, *The Works of John Wesley*, 3rd ed., vol. 14 (Peabody, MA: Hendrickson, 1986), 321.
3. Pete Hammond, quoted in Wong, "Marketplace Ministry."
4. Garth M. Roswell, quoted in Timothy L. Smith, *Revivalism and Social Reform* (Eugene, OR: Wipf & Stock, 1957), 3.

to devour everything which stands in the way of increased profits."[5] And while government regulations have attempted to stem the impacts of the idolatry of greed, there is an unfortunate expectancy and regularity of corporate failure fueled by corruption. Could revival among God's people be the answer to a reorientation of the Wall Street golden calf?

While the restoration of the systems and structure of the marketplace may not be the primary objective, historical revivals demonstrate that once the people of God are mobilized, their heightened sense of the *missio Dei* is uncontainable. Thus, revivals have permeated the secular and spiritual divide, compelling Christians to foster incarnational lives within all the spheres of society in which they are positioned.

Ripples of the Outpouring to the Marketplace

The most frequent question I am asked since the Asbury Outpouring is what has happened since. Has the Outpouring had any lasting effect on people, communities, and society? The most immediate pieces of evidence are the well-documented stories of spiritual revival on other college and university campuses across the United States. However, I have also been privy to numerous stories of businesspeople, leaders, and professionals being so impacted by the Outpouring that their disposition has fundamentally changed. Included in this group are the many fresh graduates and current senior students who are preparing for a vocation beyond church walls, careers that are not deemed to be classic vocational ministry roles. While businesspeople may not be ranked on the holiness hierarchy alongside pastors and missionaries, many of them are approaching these "secular" roles with a ministry mindset. The spiritual ripples that God started at Asbury are being brought into the workplace, places typically dry of "spiritualized" traits. While numerous themes eventuated from the Outpouring, I will highlight three that I believe the Spirit has manifested to counter unhealthy marketplace symptoms that are leading to spiritual apathy among individual Christians in the workplace. These themes also confront the questionable practices affecting the marketplace at a macro level.

5. Pope Francis, *Evangelii Gaudium: The Joy of the Gospel* (New York: Image, 2013), 44–45.

The Ripple of Radical Humility

One of the catchphrases of the Outpouring was *radical humility*. Note the superlative "radical," which demonstrates how far our culture has digressed from humility that we need to magnify our watered-down perceptions of humility. There was not a day during the Outpouring where radical humility was not referenced, a counteragent against a pervading culture that has a fetish for pride and celebritization, even within the church. Pride consistently remains in vogue; it is fashionable to boast about our greatest flex, exhibiting our achievement to outrank one another on the status ladder. We revere proud leaders who exhibit power, skills, reputation, and wealth, yearning for their latest secret-to-success manual. Furthermore, it is a culture that discourages us from showing our weaknesses and flaws, so we hide behind filters and altered images to present a picture-perfect view of ourselves to the world. In contrast, radical humility is the modest ability to withhold our self-interests, focusing less on ourselves and more on God and others.

This is not to be confused with a distortion of this theme, false humility. In my home country of Australia, we have a cultural maxim: tall-poppy syndrome. This refers to a belief that success should not be flaunted; rather, those who stand out like tall poppies should be cut down for their bravado. While this may look like humility, it demonstrates an innate pride and often results in a veneer of lowliness that hides a proudful intent. Thus, humility is ornamental, intended for one to look good among others—not too dissimilar to a religious spirit that seeks to appear more devout than others for religious gain.

Those of us at Asbury University who were tasked with stewarding what God had started often referred to radical humility. We were by no means exemplars of humility, and we desperately needed to remind one another not to distort what God had started and to resist cultural patterns that seek to orient things for self-gain. We needed to withhold self-interest, to keep our eyes fixated on Jesus and not get distracted by the global attention. God had commenced something at Asbury without the need for cosmetics. It was unmanufactured, simple, hype-free, and pure—an *unplugged Jesus*. It was free of the bells and whistles that the church had grown accustomed to adding to the cross, empty of the production-grade professional skills that our society is obsessed with, and liberated from the glamorized filters that culture and social media force us to wear to be accepted. What was on display was the raw, potent, and humbling power of the crucified and resurrected Jesus that truly still satisfies, even in our technologically advanced age. And to everyone's surprise, this ancient power drew the masses, capturing the attention of a news-saturated world.

In fact, I believe it was this theme that God used to validate his work. I have testified about the Outpouring to numerous churches and groups and have been surprised by how many people have pointed to the way it was stewarded as a fruit of its authenticity. One moment gets mentioned often—when the president of Asbury University first addressed the crowds without stating his position: "Hi, my name is Kevin, and I work at Asbury." His rationale? He did not want to draw attention away from Jesus. This simple yet symbolic gesture, which I believe set the tone for the Outpouring, served as a reminder to make every effort to deflect all glory to Christ alone. The university took extreme steps to cease all advancement opportunities during the Outpouring and centered its attention on being obedient hosts to what God was doing among us. It was actions such as these, attempted by ordinary people, that I believe God used for his glory.

Does this kind of radical humility have a place in the marketplace? This trait, while appealing at a spiritual level, appears at odds with the realities presented to us in the business and political realms. In 2014, only a few years after a global financial crisis characterized by greed and pride, *Forbes* magazine published an article promoting the art of self-promotion: "Why Being Humble Will Get You Nowhere."[6] Its rationale? Self-promotion facilitates career acceleration to climb the lucrative business-executive ladder. While many Christians may find radical humility attractive in theory, its cost is too high—especially as it pertains to career advancement. Yet at the same time, society recognizes that something is amiss. According to Gallup's "Honesty/Ethics in Professions" poll, business executives rank near the bottom of professions perceived to act ethically, with 85 percent of those surveyed rated at or below average. Disturbingly, 91 percent perceived politicians' ethical standards as being at or below average.[7] At face value, radical humility and the current marketplace are like water and oil—they just do not mix.

6. Cindy Wahler, "Why Being Humble Will Get You Nowhere," *Forbes*, December 31, 2014, https://www.forbes.com/sites/ellevate/2014/12/31/why-being-humble-will-get-you-nowhere/?sh=5bcb29866df4.
7. "Please Tell Me How You Would Rate the Honesty and Ethical Standards of People in These Different Fields—Very High, High, Average, Low or Very Low?" Gallup Poll, November 9–December 2, 2022, https://news.gallup.com/poll/1654/Honesty-Ethics-Professions.aspx.

Yet God did something unique at Asbury. It is well known that the Outpouring caused a bubbling of curiosity within society, effervescing into a mass spiritual pilgrimage that included businesspeople. I regularly served at the prayer altar, ministering to multitudes who were moved by the Spirit. It was there that I met numerous marketplace saints. A middle-aged couple, owners of a large financial services company, confessed how they had forsaken their faith amid marketplace success. I met a café chain owner who repented of careerism. I met the company CEO who confessed to arrogance that had led to sins that had never been uttered upon his lips until now. I prayed over countless college students who sought to consecrate their careers to the Lord, renouncing their own selfish ambitions. I can attest to many more who were convicted to embrace the call to radical humility within the marketplace. These were not soft religious prayers uttered for the sake of convenience; rather, they were deep prayers of lament, desperation for forgiveness, and recognition of an inability to do things apart from Jesus. It demonstrated that the all-too-common aspirations of the marketplace do not quench one's thirst. Since that time, I have heard from some of these businesspeople. They offer testimonies that demonstrate how radical humility has manifested in their business setting. They have shifted their paradigms from self-centeredness to other-oriented, from being profit-driven to purity-driven, from exploiting staff to seeking their flourishing, from identifying solely with their job title to identifying as a child of the living God. Time will tell how effective these changes will be. I believe, however, these gentle ripples of radical humility in the marketplace bear the same power that we witnessed at the Outpouring—a power of revolutionary proportions that could lead to the *restoratio humani*, the restoration of humanity. Harvey Cox states, "The soul of The Market needs to be saved, but the Market cannot save itself. Only the restoratio . . . can do that. The result could be a kind of salvation for a wide range of people."[8] And maybe, just maybe, this gentle ripple of radical humility will restore marketplace peoples.

The Ripple of Perichoretic Relationships

With tens of thousands of spiritual pilgrims descending upon Wilmore, Kentucky, a significant need for volunteers arose. The logistical feat was immense, yet God had already prepared hundreds to steward the Asbury

8. Harvey Cox, *The Market as God* (Cambridge, MA: Harvard University Press, 2016), 278.

Outpouring, woven together by the Holy Spirit on tracks of trust that were laid beforehand. This was captured via a saying that arose during the Outpouring, *Revival runs on the track of relationships*. There were countless times when I had only just met someone and within moments we were working together. During the Outpouring, God's Spirit accelerated the trust between individuals, clarified objectives among teams, and unified a community behind a vision. Undergirding this was radical humility, which prepared the hearts of each volunteer to be selfless and generous in their service. The relationships were genuine, dependable, ripples of authentic relationships. It reminds me of the perichoretic bond between the Triune God—Father, Son, and Holy Spirit. No self-benefit, no suspicious agendas, no fear of being exploited for utilitarian gain; instead, perichoresis involves a reciprocal selfless giving of oneself for the sake of the other.

Perichoretic relationships are alien in the marketplace. I was previously a global banker and can attest to the dog-eat-dog world of banking. Behind the smiles, suits, and groomed hair, bankers are known for their suave personas, yet also their hidden agendas. In my former career as a banker, I recall being labeled a smiling assassin, an image that embodies a charming persona disguising a calculated commercial agenda. In fact, this is a mainstay for much of the corporate world. At the root of this ethos lies a utilitarian view of relationships—a contrived approach to engaging one another, measured by one factor alone: What is in it for me? If I kowtow to the boss, will it further my career? If I take on this client, will it increase my earnings? Corporate culture drilled this transactional relational approach into me, to not waste time on those who cannot help you.

Yet the Spirit has convicted me via the image of the Triune God that such charades are not reflective of who he is. The perichoresis between the Father, Son, and Holy Spirit is not simply theology; it is an example I am to imitate. God's divine and embodied essence can be seen through authentic, intentional relationship. Throughout my career, I have been told that I have a talent for networking. God has reminded me, however, that this is not a mechanical corporate skill but a divine spiritual gift, not for the purposes of self, but for the purposes of authentic relationships in the image of God's perichoresis. As Steve Seamands states, "The Trinity not only reveals that persons are essentially relational, it also discloses characteristics that define healthy interpersonal relationships."[9] Thus, I am to imitate

9. Stephen A. Seamands, *Ministry in the Image of God: The Trinitarian Shape of Christian Service* (Downers Grove, IL: InterVarsity, 2005), 35.

the Triune example of relationships even in the marketplace, moving away from utilitarian networking to a love for others. For "as love grows, it spills over into our immediate situation . . . pointing to the Trinity."[10] Too often, I have limited the expression of my faith in the marketplace to preaching the gospel, yet I am reminded that embracing relationship in a way akin to the Trinity is itself an act of evangelizing.

Since the Outpouring, I have been in awe of God as he has rapidly woven together believers around the world who have been impacted by the Outpouring. This has caused relationships to be fostered between utter strangers as they have talked about what happened at Asbury and immediately bonded over a shared desire to see similar outpourings in their own context, even the marketplace. For example, after the Outpouring, I was invited to a Christian business innovation lab in Asia where I was astounded by how many young professionals not only were impacted by the testimonies from Asbury but were also now contending for outpourings in their own countries, even audaciously praying for their marketplace settings. The Outpouring has birthed hope, hope that revivals are not relegated to history books but that God still acts in our age. There are countless examples such as this, demonstrating an unearthed thirst among a remnant of marketplace saints, with the Outpouring having a catalytic effect of fast-tracking perichoretic relationships with one another. With this assembling of marketplace saints, thirsty for a move of God in their own spheres, I am confident that the Spirit is orchestrating a network of perichoretic relationships among his people for a significant move in the marketplace.

The Ripple of a Consecrated Life

Hidden behind the platform in Hughes Auditorium was a small room that students had established during the Outpouring, the consecration room. This discreet space was one of the most important innovations that Generation Z students birthed during the Outpouring. Its purpose was simple yet profound: to ensure that every person who stepped onto the platform had pure motives and was approaching their role with reverence. The consecration room called people to adopt a posture like Isaiah, who confessed how inadequate he was before God (Isa. 6:5), recognized his dependence

10. Adrian Van Kaam and Susan Muto, *Christian Articulation of the Mystery*, vol. 2 of *Formation Theology* (Pittsburgh, PA: Epiphany Association, 2005), 135.

upon God as his lips were made clean (Isa. 6:6), and only then stood up to be commissioned: "Here am I. Send me!" (Isa. 6:7). From here, ripples of a consecrated life were poured over the masses. I was touched by the number of businesspeople who responded to the call toward a consecrated life. They woke up to the reality that consecration involves the whole of life, not just a tithe, that their role was not simply to be ATM machines for the institutional church but to be disciples of Christ.

When we think of consecration, we often default to religious categories—to consecrate a church, a newly appointed church leader, or the elements during Holy Communion. Rarely if ever do we extend consecration to musicians, volunteers, or those not in vocational ministry roles. This supposition is a product of the sacred-secular divide, a dichotomy that has cemented a dividing wall in the Western mindset. Yet what occurred at the Asbury Outpouring demonstrated a crack in the sacred-secular divide, as many marketplace people knelt at the altar, confessing to living a hypocritical Christian life that compartmentalized their faith to religious settings and thus had little bearing upon the way they lived beyond Sunday. Instead, compelled by the Spirit, they were now desiring to embrace a wholly consecrated life. Furthermore, they were illuminated to the Kingdom-laden opportunities inherent within their marketplace vocations. A prevalent distortion exists that consecration, and therefore a holy vocation, is exclusive to the clergy, pastor, or priest. This misrepresentation was viral in the early sixteenth century, and it was Martin Luther who renounced it with his doctrine of the priesthood of all believers, referring to 1 Peter 2:9a: "But you are a chosen people, a royal priesthood." We are called to exercise the authority that we hold as children of God, not delegate it to higher authorities, for there is none except Jesus Christ. Likewise, church leaders must resist the pleasure that may come with being revered for their position of ministerial authority and instead authorize their congregants to be bold in their faith. As Gordon Preece emphasized, the adherence to the implicit clericalism of the Old Testament is outdated. In that system, "the Spirit came occasionally upon special people like prophets, priests and kings. This leads to our suppressing the New Testament's radical universalizing of the Spirit's presence and empowering for all believers as prophets, priests and kings."[11]

During the apostle Paul's ministry, he too went to the marketplaces, the metropolises, the commercial centers and hubs. He even leveraged his vocation to live incarnationally among the people, not for short periods of

11. Gordon Preece, quoted in Wong, "Marketplace Ministry."

time, but extended stays. It was a "seed of grace" for Paul to be gifted in tentmaking to provide a bridge between the message of life that he held and the people and systems bound by the strongholds of their bustling culture. God's glory is not simply contained within a church building. His power can cut through the fabric of every sphere of society. And it is his people, Christ's body, who have been called to engage in this work. The consecrated marketplace believer's vocation is not simply a job; it is a God-given opportunity to live out this calling via the power of the Holy Spirit to see his Kingdom come and his will be done on earth as it is in heaven, to intercede in the marketplace with spiritual stamina, to be present and incarnational among the peoples, to proclaim the truth with zeal, and to be expectant for a move of God. As Tommy Tenney states, "The anointing and power of God's presence are going to come upon us so strongly that His presence will literally go before us into our offices, plants, prisons, and shopping malls. Because this great revival is based on His glory and presence and not on the works of man, it cannot be contained within the four walls of the churches."[12]

Therefore, we cannot merely sit back in passivity. We are to act. Martin Lloyd Jones states, "There is really no purpose in looking at the present situation and considering the great movements of the Spirit in the past, unless it leads to a determination on our part to act and to do something in the light of the position in which we find ourselves."[13] When we do not act, we reduce the agency of the Holy Spirit within our lives. Instead, we are to act in faith, believing in the "incomparably great power for us who believe" (Eph. 1:19). For those in the marketplace, it means living a consecrated life while performing our vocation among the people and systems within the marketplace. It also means leaning into the full arsenal of spiritual gifts that have been bestowed upon us, not merely out of a desire to see a restoration in the marketplace, but also out of holy responsibility. As Luke 12:48 states, "From everyone who has been given much, much will be demanded; and from the one who has been entrusted with much, much more will be asked." If it is the gift of creativity, we are to reimagine new ways of seeing his Kingdom amplified. If it is the gift of leadership, we are to exercise servant leadership. If it is the gift of administration, we are responsible for maintaining momentum for the move of God. If it is the gift of managing

12. Tommy Tenney, quoted in C. Neal Johnson, *Business as Mission* (Downers Grove, IL: InterVarsity, 2009), 486.

13. Martin Lloyd Jones, *Revival* (Wheaton, IL: Crossway, 1987), 251.

legal affairs, we are to speak truth amid corrupt systems and structures. If it is the gift of medical practice, we are to heal the sick and wounded. In the words of John Wesley, the world really is our parish.

Since the Outpouring, I have heard of more and more churches and groups adopting a call for their members to consecrate their whole lives, even their marketplace vocations, for the Lord. For example, one well-known pastor in Georgia felt compelled to call out his marketplace parishioners to come to the altar of his church as he consecrated them to be agents of God's outpouring in their industries. The ripple of a consecrated life that emanated from the Asbury Outpouring has had a deregulatory effect on what we define as missional. It has restored a proper and potent understanding of the *missio Dei*. While we may never get a whole picture of the impact this ripple has had on inspiring businesspeople to consecrate their whole lives for Christ, we do know that this ripple is resonating with many who hear it.

Conclusion: What Next?

We will never know why God chose to pour out his Spirit at Asbury University, but we do know the community's characteristics. First, Asbury is not a church or a seminary but rather a liberal arts university that teaches business, media communication, science, arts, and more. While this may seem trivial, God chose an institution that intersects the marketplace as its graduates scatter into an assortment of industries and sectors. This is not isolated to Asbury, as the phenomenon is extending to other colleges and university campuses across the United States. Second, the Asbury community is distinctively Christian, rooted in the Wesleyan tradition, accentuating holiness—a word rarely mentioned in our society today, since many associate it with a lackluster moral code. Holiness properly understood, however, provides a framework for flourishing and wholeness, not simply for self but for others. It is the characteristic of God that we are asked to mimic—to be holy as God is holy (1 Pet. 1:16). Not surprisingly, this concept of flourishing is deficient in the marketplaces of today. I won't repeat the symptoms of moral degradation in the business realm or prevalent market failures, yet it is clear that true flourishing is absent. Could it be that God wants to remind his people of the holiness distinctive, the path to flourishing and wholeness? Third, the community of Asbury is expectant, accommodating, and has a holy imagination for more. Asbury is far from perfect, yet this recognition of its limitations is what I believe lays the foundation for the community's thirst, recognizing that only Jesus Christ can satisfy. My friend Christopher

Segre-Lewis, a former professor at Asbury, describes it best: "Asbury is like a riverbed: When water flows, it knows where to go."

While we may marvel at what God did at Asbury, we must recognize that it is not limited to the sixteen days in February 2023, nor is it limited to Wilmore, Kentucky. Rather, the refreshing river of life we experienced is still flowing through a revitalized people on college campuses, in churches, and even in the marketplace. In fact, this single outpouring at Asbury is not the source of this river. This was a river that flowed from the side of a crucified Savior on Calvary two thousand years earlier. We at Asbury are extremely humbled that an outpouring occurred on our campus, but we are under no illusion that we are the beginning or the end of what God is doing. Such thoughts contradict the manifest theme of radical humility. Yet we do recognize that what God did in our midst is special, an extraordinary move of grace. Those who experienced this profound movement of God are not to be infatuated with this phenomenon to the point of spiritual inertia but to be revitalized for the sake of spiritual animation across all spheres of society. The Holy Spirit empowered a vitality with the potency to break the sacred-spiritual divide that for too long has separated holy flourishing from the marketplace. At this very moment, a growing number of marketplace saints are being commissioned by the Spirit of God. Will you join their ranks? Will you contend for the spaces in which God has appointed you? The river is still flowing, ripples of living water flowing through you to all society, even the marketplace.

CHAPTER EIGHTEEN

THE TENSION OF SPIRITUAL OUTPOURINGS *AND* ORDINARY LIFE

Maria Brown
Ministry associate, Asbury University

I had the immense privilege of being present in chapel on February 8. The sense of God's immediate presence—of an opening up and a pouring out of God himself—will be seared forever in my memory. The weight of his glory and the intimacy of his nearness changed my spiritual imagination for what is possible through his Spirit. The experience of the Outpouring has expanded into expectations, prayers, and ways of being that are in some ways even fuller today than in the sixteen days in February. We experienced something that is too sacred for words, even while it fills up endless words—something that has no shortage of descriptions, even while it defies an adequate one.

And those sixteen days were some of the most intense, exhausting, unpredictable days of my life. In the wave of his love and grace, I sometimes felt insecure and unsure—wondering if I was getting it right. While I stood in the miraculous, I also sat with unanswered prayers. And even as I experienced God in a more profound way than ever before, I had never felt my humanity so deeply.

And. With all the things being written and recorded about the Outpouring, I want to write about the *and*. *And* is a "not yet" place, a place of tension and sometimes confusion, an ordinary messy place. But *and* is not a word of negation. It is a word that adds, that brings another layer of understanding. For me, the *and* has become a holy conjunction.

The Complexities of Spiritual Outpourings

Near what would end up being the middle of the Outpouring, as the number of people coming to campus was swelling and more complex lines and crowd control were forming, I was a volunteer assigned to "line duty." I bundled up and spent hours outside among the crowd, helping people to get in the right line, stay in line, stay away from dorm windows, and not blow shofars or fly flags. Already introverted by nature and tired from the previous days, I felt a bit overwhelmed by the number of people and the questions about logistics. I found myself wondering if it looked like a circus and, if it did, if that was OK. I even got so far as to wonder if it should be shut down.

Later in the day, I stepped into Hughes. Standing to the right of the stage, looking out into the crowd, I was captured by what I saw. Here, in uncomfortable wooden seats, with no special lights or video productions or amazing music, I witnessed a crowd of people attentive to the presence of God—leaning forward, listening, digesting a message of God's invitation to a life with him. There were little to no cell phones out as the crowd fully engaged with the message, feeding on the authentic love and truth of God. I remember saying (almost out loud, because it struck me so profoundly), "They are so hungry." I felt for those moments that I had the gift of seeing the crowd, us, myself, as God sees. In the space of hours, the crowd was unwieldy *and* hungry for the living God, a source of stress *and* a window into the heart of God for his children.

The next day I was confronted again with the complexity of the crowds of people, physical exhaustion, and the uncertainty that comes from upended schedules and no predictability. The tension of the *and* was with me as I navigated the tangible sense of God's presence that I was experiencing in some moments *and* the questions I had about what this would or should look like for my own children. I lived this *and* on my way to Hughes early one cold morning as I chided myself for ever signing up for such an early shift, doubting that God was even still there, *and* then I experienced one of the most profound times of prayer I have had in my life. I felt this tension as I was witnessing the miraculous *and* questioning how I should pray for someone in a wheelchair who was desperate to walk and did not. This *and* was there as I watched a student step miraculously into a relationship with God in a moment *and* then disappear into their busy schedule without what they needed to faithfully walk this out. I carried this tension as I prayed for a student I was convinced would say a full yes to God, *and* yet I watched them walk heavily out of Hughes without a visible movement toward him.

This tension appeared in the questions I found myself asking about the ordinary and the complex, as our prayers expanded beyond what I had experienced previously, *and* there were still human details and anxieties. The glory of God seemed smashed against competing emotional, mental, and physical states, our own humanity, and the limits of our ability to stay in this heightened spiritual place, which for some felt like anxiety or fear. Our bodies grew tired, and sometimes our emotions frayed. Decisions about how to manage crowds, how to protect vulnerable individuals experiencing mental disequilibrium, how to discern what was and wasn't from the Holy Spirit, and how to prioritize students while welcoming thousands of people, had to be made. In the midst of these crucial decisions, we did not always have quick and easy agreement about what should be done. Some students were unsettled or even panicked about the number of guests on campus. Not everyone who entered Hughes received what they thought they came for. Not everyone was healed, not everyone "felt" something, not everyone had a miraculous story. Toilets overflowed, sinks needed to be cleaned, kids needed routines, we still had bad breath, and we needed to sleep, eat, and shower.

Embracing the Ongoing Complexities

The *and*—the ordinary and complex—continues to meet us in the days after February 23. Students who met Jesus need to be discipled; miraculous transformations need to become daily walking. Some students feel anxious. Some wonder if they missed God because they didn't have a special experience. Others are processing a difficult relationship or situation that was unfolding during the Outpouring and negatively colored their experience. Some students who experienced God don't yet know how to walk with him well, and their steps are faltering and unsteady. Others are still seeking and searching. One desperate parent who had brought their ill child to be prayed over is still waiting to see healing. Some gave testimony to the work of God in them during the Outpouring and now find themselves in difficult and life-altering situations brought about by choices made before those days in February.

I am disturbed by this tension, this *and*. It brings unsettling questions for me. If we experienced such an abundant outpouring of God's Spirit, why was there tension at all? In the presence of something so dramatic and miraculous, why didn't everything change? Why is there still complexity and unanswered prayer? Why did the ordinary mess of life not disappear? What are we to do with the things that are not yet done? How do these fit into the beautiful Outpouring of God's Spirit? Do complexity and ordinary anxieties and issues take away from God's gracious Outpouring? Why do I feel so very human?

As I press into the *and*, however, I find that embracing this tension and sitting in these questions, rather than taking away from the Outpouring, leads me further into God. I believe that digging into the *and* can bring us into a deeper knowledge of the reality of God-with-us. God is with us in the miraculous *and* in the very human, ordinary, complex spaces. If after deeply spiritual experiences we drop the *and*, then we are left alone in the ordinary places in which most of our lives are lived out. But keeping the tension allows us to experience the hope that comes with the work of the Spirit in our most human places. Here the *and* becomes sacred ground.

The power of God for the complex and ordinary does not diminish either what he did in the sacred moments in Hughes or his power for transformation. But failing to acknowledge the after and the ordinary leaves us with a crippled view of God and his meaning for our daily lives. We need a voice that gives credence to the power of God when things are not powerfully or immediately fixed by him. We need to hear from those who are giving words to a conflicted human experience while not diminishing the miraculous work of God. We need reassurance that God can come and still not fix everything or bowl everyone over into submission. We need to know that what we were experiencing in those sixteen days is not invalidated by what we were not experiencing or by the days ahead that require steady yeses and obedience borne out of the (often) slow work of the Spirit. We need the confidence that comes with seeing that while his in-breaking was indeed miraculous, he did it through very human people and circumstances.

As I read stories and accounts of other revivals, I find that sometimes the stories seem varnished, sanitized just enough to lose some of their grittiness. This is not to say that these stories are untrue, only that in the retelling, the complexity fades. Our narratives tend to be an arc, and arcs drop the jagged lines that don't quite fit. But we experienced the profound glory of God in the midst of ourselves, our space, our time, our people. As humans, we aren't clean arcs, so I don't want to drop the jagged lines. I am convinced that doing so can have a deleterious effect on how we interpret God's work in our lives. If Jesus—God with us—is not present when the gospel is taking on flesh in us, when the hard work of changing habits is ongoing, when the biases and blind spots temporarily keep us from moving forward, when we are anxious and confused—then we are alone in the spaces where we actually live.

Alternatively, we can try to make sense of the complexity of being human by ignoring the transcendent. The jagged lines become the whole story, and there is no room for the holy work of God. Perhaps we think that we might even be giving God an excuse when we do this. If it's not all fixed, that's OK—we should not expect too much from God anyway, he isn't all that interested in these places or capable of entering them. Here we can keep the ordinariness of humanity separate from his divinity. But if God is far from us, not involved and present in the mundane, human, complex tensions of our lives, grittiness is all there is. We are alone in the spaces where we actually live.

We need the *and*.

But remember, *and* is not a word that takes away; this conjunction adds. It links two things together. It's not just that God is miraculous in some very visible ways and holds the rest of the moments together so that we can stand it. It's not just that the miraculous moments are enough to give us hope, to help us endure the *and*. It is that the *and* is just as sacred, just as holy, just as pregnant with God's power—but in ways that are less visible, slower, softer, more complicated. Elizabeth Barrett Browning described this earth as being "crammed with heaven and every common bush afire with God." For those days in February, we were common bushes afire with God. We were moving in ordinary places crammed full of heaven. And those days have opened up the reality that **all** of the common places in our lives are burning with the presence of God.

I remember standing near the stage in Hughes and laughing about how very ordinary we were. Notes were jotted on brown paper sacks, cell phone chargers were trailing off the edge of the platform, caution tape decorated the frayed carpet on the altar, a pile of mints had been dumped out near the stairs. And yet people were meeting God in profound ways here, kneeling on the frayed carpet. Their stories of God's power were being recorded on those brown paper sacks. In another memory, after witnessing the beginning of the Outpouring, a confidant and I were momentarily hiding in a room off Hughes, sharing with tears our insecurities and fears, convinced that we were not the right people to be near this even as we were experiencing what we knew was God's power. Yet I watched my friend speak, pray, and lead, with all their insecurities and fears *and* the undeniable power of the Spirit.

The *and* means that there is hope for the in-between places. It means that I can be insecure and tired *and* entrusted with holding a piece of God's glory. I can pray with someone who is desperate for healing even while I wait for healing in some areas of my own life. Our bodies can have the gift of sensing the presence of God and also be physically exhausted. It is consistently God's story that the most profound and miraculous work is done among the most ordinary and complex human people and circumstances. On a threshing floor in Israel, Ruth, a childless widow and a foreigner, finds refuge in a kinsman redeemer and enters the line of Jesus; Moses, convinced he is inadequate, leads God's people out of slavery; a young unmarried girl gives birth to the Christ in a stable; plain and unknown fishermen become Kingdom disciples; a Samaritan woman at a well shares Jesus with her community. This both shocks and comforts me. One of the most hopeful things about the Outpouring is that it happened to ordinary people on an ordinary day in ordinary times, and it did not make us extraordinary.

The *And* of the Incarnation

This *and* is the truth of the Incarnation, which gives us theology for the miraculous *and* the complexity of our lives. The most surprising thing about the Incarnation is its particularity. Jesus, the God of the universe, came in a particular time, context, space, and culture, with a particular body, language, and family. Here in the specificity of the body and human life of Jesus, we find the indefatigable hope that redemption is housed in the ordinary and walks among the complexity of being human.

The Incarnation shows us that "God's love for us is not some idealized longing for a sanitized, universal idea of humanity. It is real love for real people. . . . It is not just a love for ideas or for souls. It is a love that encompasses bodies as well as souls, a love concrete enough to become incarnate, to extend to fingers and toes: both Jesus's and ours. God's love is big enough to love specifics."[1]

Because "what is not assumed is not healed,"[2] the Incarnation opens up every detail of our lives to the transforming work of God. What Christ took on, he dignified. What he entered, he redeemed. Because Jesus did not turn away from humanity, even in his own body, he does not turn away from us. Because Jesus entered the complexity of daily life and relationships, the complexity of our daily lives and relationships is fully within his

1. Beth Felker Jones, *Practicing Christian Doctrine: An Introduction to Thinking and Living Theologically* (Grand Rapids, MI: Baker Academic, 2014), 137.
2. Maurice Wiles, quoted in Felker Jones, *Practicing Christian Doctrine*, 58.

sphere of love and care. This is what we desperately need—"God with us, not God associated with us"![3]

Oden, building on the work of Tertullian, describes well the complexity and beauty of the Incarnation: "No more complete revelation of emphatic love is possible than this: that God almighty shares our human frame, participates in our human limitations, enters into our human sphere."[4]

That Jesus walked among us, fully aware of our capacities and our frailties, tells us that his coming does not wipe all that away. He knows how we are made, that we are but dust, housed in jars of clay. And yet he himself took on our flesh, not eliminating humanness but elevating it.

Jesus embraced the coming together of humanity and divinity in his own self, but he also embraced the human tension in the world and the people he lived with, walked with, and encountered. The disciples and the crowds that followed Jesus came with myriad problems, life details, personalities, and malformed theologies. He moved in the ordinary spaces of meals, synagogues, homes, fields, roads, boats, and crowds. He did not "fix" everything and everyone. He walked with them, bringing sacredness to the ordinary complexities of their lives.

The Complexities of Discipleship

We find ourselves in good company with the people around Jesus. They also felt tired and hungry, sometimes distracted and confused. Even as Emmanuel walked with them physically, his disciples did not see clearly all the time, nor did they have full understanding or capacity. They even argued among themselves about who would be the greatest, in the very presence of their Creator!

But I resonate with the humanity of the disciples more than ever before. When they encountered a hungry crowd, they advised sending them away to buy food. I will admit, I had the same thought when portable toilets appeared on the front sidewalks. Like the disciples, I falsely separated the messiness and complexity of human needs from Jesus's gospel message. But where did the miraculous occur? Right among the tired and hungry. Jesus meets us in our ordinary human needs. Hughes was sacred space, but so were the lines and the volunteer room. Like the loaves and fish given to

3. Felker Jones, *Practicing Christian Doctrine*, 131.
4. Thomas C. Oden, *The Word of Life*, bk 2, *Classic Christianity* (New York: HarperCollins, 1992), 270.

Jesus, snacks and time and even portable toilets were being multiplied to meet the needs of hungry crowds.

The outpouring of the Holy Spirit on the early church at Pentecost was no small move of God and no small movement of his Spirit. But a quick reading of Paul's letters to the people of the emerging churches tells us that enormous work still needed to be done. The apostles had to settle disputes, teach theology, navigate the complexities of the Gentile response and the Jewish law, answer questions about common things like food, and form leadership structures. Here again, I hear echoes of the messy ways of humanity being crammed full of the holy.

We too are walking in unfinished, in-process places. As one student put it, "I don't recognize myself anymore, and I have to figure out what it looks like to know Jesus like this in my daily life." The student who said yes in a moment and then disappeared? Now they are meeting with a mentor, slowly talking through and walking out what it means to belong to Jesus. The student who walked away with no response? Over the course of several weeks, they came back to someone they trusted with their hesitation and fears, and then in an unexpected place away from the energy of a packed Hughes, they asked to be baptized. These are just a few of the unfinished holy stories that remind me that Jesus is in the ordinary places doing his work. One of the most powerful decisions in my own life since the Outpouring has been a commitment to weekly accountability conversations with a trusted friend. The miracle for us has not occurred in just one glorious moment of transformation, but in week after week of asking and answering hard and vulnerable questions. We have found that the most sacred places of God's work have happened in the quiet space of an office where simple chairs become altars of transformation.

Unlike me, God is not distracted by complexity—he keeps on pointing us to his purposes and encourages us to follow with confidence the one who is faithful (Heb. 10:23). Jesus himself had an unfailing confidence that his Father's will was at work and history was being shaped. The Incarnation brought about the will of God *through* human complexities, not in spite of them.

Conclusion

The theology of the Outpouring is about the in-breaking of God in otherwise unexplainable ways as well as the empowering grace for the complexity, the not yet, and the ordinary. All is transformed—our imagination of what

God can do, our memory of what God has done, and our experience of him in the everyday moments. The pockets of distress, fear, the unknown, and the undone are not out of reach of the Outpouring. Though they may seem to fit awkwardly, without them, the story is only half told. Those complex or confusing moments are not outliers or embarrassing details better left unsaid. They are part of the ongoing work of God, testaments to the God who really does come and dwell among us—yes, even us. This does not make us unique, but rather ordinary, a living praise to the God who is not appalled by our flesh, nor unaware of it, nor hiding his face from it. Just as Jesus pulled together the fully divine and fully human, and filled muscle and tendons with the Godhead, so he pulls together the divine and sacred moments of our lives with the human, mundane, and muddied. He is in all and through all.

When people are cynical about the Outpouring, my heart responds, "I was there. I know what I experienced." And when people varnish the Outpouring or overspiritualize in ways that take away from the reality, my heart responds, "I was there. I know what I experienced." To take away from either end of this spectrum demeans the work of God. We are human, *and* we experienced the power of God. He multiplied the loaves and fishes of our time and efforts, *and* we were tired. Weird things happened, *and* he calmed moments inside Hughes that kept things from getting out of hand. He orchestrated the whole Outpouring, *and* we organized ushers and lines. I was exhausted and high-strung, *and* I experienced the palpable peace and the power of his presence. The volunteer hub was an amazing testament to both the power of community and the power of God to use what we could give him, *and* there was a fair bit of chaos and disagreement. He invited each and every one of us, with our personalities and quirks, our misguided ideas and diverse backgrounds, with our habits and routines, blind spots and disagreements, into this. And he did it through us. He didn't wipe us out; he allowed us to hold a piece, to give what we could. And he is still giving the same invitation in these ordinary days.

We need a voice for the spaces that don't feel fixed and the spaces that are not yet whole. We need a word for the places of tension and the places that feel conflicted and undone. We need a nod to what seems to be the unmiraculous and the routine. We need a light for working out what has been done within. We need hope for the messiness, the blind spots, and the myriad ways that we can miss the gentle leading of the Spirit. We need courage for the days marked more by complexity than power. *And* we have it.

About the Contributors

Carol Anderson serves as adjunct professor of Theatre at Asbury University, where she teaches courses in acting and directing and has directed several plays. She holds an MFA in Acting from UNC-Chapel Hill and a BA in Biblical Studies and American Studies from Barrington College. She also performs and speaks internationally with her husband, Jim Shores, through their theatre ministry called Acts of Renewal.

Kevin Anderson serves as professor of Bible and Theology at Asbury University. He holds a PhD in New Testament from London School of Theology / Brunel University, an MDiv from Nazarene Theological Seminary, and a BA in Biblical Studies and Ministry from Trinity Bible College. He has published articles and books on Hebrews, Acts of the Apostles, and the resurrection of Jesus.

Sarah Baldwin serves as vice president of Student Life and dean of students at Asbury University. She holds a DMin from Portland Seminary, an MDiv from Asbury Theological Seminary, and a BA in Psychology from Asbury University and is an ordained elder in the Free Methodist Church. She has served in Christian higher education as a university pastor, resident director, student affairs administrator, and professor.

Jeannie Banter serves as director of the Christian Life Project and works in Advancement at Asbury University, where she has also worked in Spiritual Life. She holds an MA in Counseling Psychology from Trevecca Nazarene University and a BA in Missions from Asbury University. She has served as a missionary in Uganda and on numerous short-term trips to various countries.

Madeline Black serves as assistant director of the World Gospel Mission Student Center on Asbury University's campus. She has an MA in Christian Ministries from Asbury Theological Seminary and a BA in Intercultural Studies and History from Asbury University. Her passion is to walk with people on the journey of becoming more like Jesus.

Kevin Brown serves as president of Asbury University. He holds a PhD in Theology and Religious Studies from the University of Glasgow, an MLitt in Bible and the Contemporary World from the University of St. Andrews, and both an MBA and a BS from the University of Indianapolis. He has written books and articles on the intersection of economics and theology.

Maria Brown serves as ministry associate at Asbury University. She holds an MA in Marriage and Family Therapy from Indiana Wesleyan University and a BS in Psychology from the University of Indianapolis. She is currently pursuing an MA in Theological Studies with an emphasis in Spiritual Formation at Asbury Theological Seminary.

Julianne Burnett serves as assistant professor of Old Testament at Asbury University. She holds a PhD in Hebrew Bible from the University of Manchester, an MA in Theology from Wesley Biblical Seminary, and both an MA in Biblical Studies and a BA in Theological Studies from the University of Exeter. She has lived in England, Mexico, and the United States and has been involved in theological education in a variety of contexts.

Bridgette Campbell serves as coordinator of Outreach Ministry Teams for Asbury University. She holds a master's degree in Education from the University of Cincinnati and a BS degree in K–12 Education from Campbellsville University. She has passionately worked with students for fifteen years.

Christine Endicott has served as director of Conference Services at Asbury University since 2019. She holds a BS in Communications with minors in Marketing and Psychology from Ball State University. She has worked as an event planner for thirteen years and is the author of a parenting book.

Juan Gonzalez serves as the coordinator of Intercultural Life at Asbury University. He is from Mexico and received his MA in Theology from Wesley Biblical Seminary in Jackson, Mississippi, and his bachelor's degree in Biblical Studies and Theology from Instituto Biblico: La Buena Tierra in Saltillo, Mexico. Juan is an ordained minister with the Church of God (Anderson, IN).

Barbara Hamilton serves as associate professor of Middle and Secondary Education for Asbury University. She holds an EdD in Literacy, Culture, and Language Education from Indiana University and both an MA in Literacy and a BA in Secondary Education English from Asbury University. She taught in both public and private schools for more than a decade before becoming a teacher educator to invest in the next generation of teachers.

Greg Haseloff serves as associate dean of Spiritual Life and University Pastor at Asbury University. He holds both an MDiv and an MA in Counseling from Asbury Theological Seminary and a BS in Animal Business from Texas Tech University. He has served over twenty-seven years in college ministry, loves leading students into cross-cultural experiences, and is an elder in the Global Methodist Church.

Sam Kim serves as assistant professor of Intercultural Studies at Asbury University. She holds a PhD in Intercultural Studies from Asbury Theological Seminary, an MDiv from Seoul Theological Seminary, a ThM in Missiology from Asian Center for Theological Studies, and a BA in Pharmacology from Sungkyunkwan University. Her current research focuses on reconciliation in religions and cultures.

Jessica LaGrone serves as dean of chapel at Asbury Theological Seminary. She holds a DMin from Wesley Seminary (Indiana Wesleyan University), an MDiv from Asbury Theological Seminary, and a BA in Biology from Southwestern University in Georgetown, Texas. She is an elder in the Global Methodist Church and has written numerous books and studies.

Abby Laub serves as director of Strategic Communications for Asbury University. She holds a BA in Journalism from Palm Beach Atlantic University. Prior to working at Asbury, she owned a photography and media business, published a photography book, and worked for magazines, newspapers, and nonprofits.

Robin Lim serves as assistant professor of Business as well as director of Strategic Initiatives for Asbury University. He holds an MDiv from Asbury Theological Seminary and Bachelor of Commerce and Bachelor of Information Technology degrees from The Australian National University. Prior to teaching, he was a global banking executive for one of the world's largest banks across Australia and Asia.

Suzanne Nicholson serves as professor of New Testament at Asbury University. She holds a PhD in New Testament from the University of Durham (England), an MDiv from Asbury Theological Seminary, and a BA in Journalism from the University of Minnesota. She is an elder in the Global Methodist Church and serves as assistant lead editor of *Firebrand* magazine.

Dan Pinkston serves as worship pastor at New Community Church in Spokane, Washington; he previously served as professor of Worship Arts at Asbury University and professor of Music at Simpson University. He holds a doctorate of Musical Arts in Music/Administration and a master's of Music Theory and Composition from Southwestern Baptist Theological Seminary, as well as a BA in Music/Communications from Ouachita Baptist University. His musical compositions have been featured at numerous international festivals.

Harold Rainwater has served as mayor of Wilmore since 1976. He has also previously served as the director of the Equine Program at Asbury University and currently serves as Equine Ambassador. He holds a BA in Physical Education from Asbury College and an MS in Recreation from Eastern Kentucky University.

Craig Saunders serves as adjunct professor of Biblical/Theological Studies and Christian Ministries at Asbury University as well as adjunct professor of New Testament Studies at Bethel University (graduate program). He holds a PhD in New Testament from Middlesex University (London School of Theology), an MDiv from Asbury Theological Seminary, and a BA in Religion and Philosophy from Roberts Wesleyan University. He is ordained in the Free Methodist Church of North America and serves as Pastor of Evangelism at Wilmore Free Methodist Church.

W. Brian Shelton serves as professor of Theology and dean of the School of Christian Studies at Asbury University, where he is also the Wesley Scholar in Residence. He holds a PhD in Historical Theology from Saint Louis University, an MDiv from Covenant Theological Seminary, and a BA in Biology from Asbury University. In addition to publishing multiple books and articles, he also leads study tours to Europe.

Joy Vaughan serves as assistant professor of New Testament at Asbury University. She holds a PhD in Biblical Studies from Asbury Theological Seminary, both an MA in Biblical Literature and an MDiv from Oral Roberts University, and a Bachelor of Music degree from Bowling Green State University. She has recently published a book on biblical and multicultural accounts of spirit possession.